The Elements of Moral Philosophy

FOURTH EDITION

JAMES RACHELS

University of Alabama at Birmingham

Boston   Burr Ridge, IL   Dubuque, IA   Madison, WI   New York
San Francisco   St. Louis   Bangkok   Bogotá   Caracas   Kuala Lumpur
Lisbon   London   Madrid   Mexico City   Milan   Montreal   New Delhi
Santiago   Seoul   Singapore   Sydney   Taipei   Toronto

McGraw-Hill Higher Education

A Division of The **McGraw-Hill** Companies

THE ELEMENTS OF MORAL PHILOSOPHY

Published by McGraw-Hill, a business unit of The McGraw-Hill Companies, Inc., 1221 Avenue of the Americas, New York, NY, 10020. Copyright © 2003, 1999, 1993, 1986 by The McGraw-Hill Companies, Inc. All rights reserved.

This book is printed on acid-free paper.

domestic   5 6 7 8 9 0 DOC/DOC 0 9 8 7 6 5 4
international   1 2 3 4 5 6 7 8 9 0 DOC/DOC 0 9 8 7 6 5 4 3 2

ISBN 0-07-247690-7

Publisher: *Ken King*
Sponsoring editor: *Jon-David Hague*
Marketing manager: *Greg Brueck*
Project manager: *Diane M. Folliard*
Production supervisor: *Carol A. Bielski*
Designer: *Matthew Baldwin*
Typeface: *11/12 Baskerville*
Compositor: *Carlisle Communications, Ltd.*
Printer: *R. R. Donnelley & Sons Company*

Cover art: *RODCHENKO, Aleksandr.*
Non-Objective Painting: *Black on Black, 1918.*
Oil on canvas, 32 1/4 X 31 1/4" (81.9 X 79.4 cm).
The Museum of Modern Art, New York. Gift of the artist, through Jay Leyda.
Photograph ©1998 The Museum of Modern Art, New York.

INTERNATIONAL EDITION ISBN 0-07-119876-8

Library of Congress Cataloging-in-Publication Data

Rachels, James, 1941-
    The elements of moral philosophy / James Rachels.–4th ed.
      p. cm.
    Includes bibliographical references and index.
    ISBN 0-07-247690-7 (alk. paper) –ISBN 0-07-119876-8 (International : alk. paper)
    1. Ethics. I. Title.
BJ1012 .R29 2003
170–dc21   2002018898

www.mhhe.com

*A*bout the Author

JAMES RACHELS is University Professor of Philosophy at the University of Alabama at Birmingham. He is also the author of *The End of Life: Euthanasia and Morality* (1986), *Created from Animals: The Moral Implications of Darwinism* (1990), and *Can Ethics Provide Answers? And Other Essays in Moral Philosophy* (1997).

Contents

Preface

Socrates, one of the first and best moral philosophers, said that the subject deals with "no small matter, but how we ought to live." This book is an introduction to moral philosophy, conceived in this broad sense.

The subject is, of course, too large to be encompassed in one short book, so there must be some way of deciding what to include and what to leave out. I have been guided by the following thought: Suppose there is someone who knows nothing at all about the subject, but who is willing to spend a modest amount of time learning about it. What are the first and most important things he or she needs to learn? This book is my answer to that question. I do not try to cover every topic in the field; I do not even try to say everything that could be said about the topics that are covered. But I do try to discuss the most important ideas that a newcomer should confront.

The chapters have been written so that they may be read independently of one another—they are, in effect, separate essays on a variety of topics. Thus someone who is interested in Ethical Egoism could go directly to the sixth chapter and find there a self-contained introduction to that theory. When read in order, however, they tell a more or less continuous story. The first chapter presents a "minimum conception" of what morality is; the middle chapters cover the most important general ethical theories (with some digressions as seem appropriate); and the final chapter sets out my own view of what a satisfactory moral theory would be like.

The point of the book is not to provide a neat, unified account of "the truth" about the matters under discussion. That would be a poor way to introduce the subject. Philosophy is not like physics. In physics, there is a large body of established truth, which no competent physicist would dispute and which beginners must patiently master. (Physics instructors rarely invite undergraduates to make up their own minds about the laws of thermodynamics.) There are, of course, disagreements among physicists and unresolved controversies, but these generally take place against the background of large and substantial agreements. In philosophy, by contrast, everything is controversial—or almost everything. "Competent" philosophers will disagree even about fundamental matters. A good introduction will not try to hide that somewhat embarrassing fact.

You will find, then, a survey of contending ideas, theories, and arguments. My own views inevitably color the presentation. I have not tried to conceal the fact that I find some of these ideas more appealing than others, and it is obvious that a philosopher making different assessments might present the various ideas differently. But I have tried to present the contending theories fairly, and whenever I have endorsed or rejected one of them, I have tried to give some reason why it should be endorsed or rejected. Philosophy, like morality itself, is first and last an exercise in reason—the ideas that should come out on top are the ones that have the best reasons on their sides. If this book is successful, the reader will learn enough that he or she can begin to assess, for himself or herself, where the weight of reason rests.

A bout the Fourth Edition

Readers familiar with the previous edition of this book may want to know what changes have been made. There are no new chapters, but there are a couple of new sections; and all the chapters have been spruced up to one degree or another, removing infelicities and adding clarifications. Some of the examples had become dated, and those have been updated or replaced. In Chapter 1, there is new information about the Tracy Latimer case; there is also a new section on the recent conjoined-twins case. In several other chapters, illustrative material has been added. New material has been added to the chapter on absolute moral rules. In Chapter 14, there is a new section which further elaborates "what a satisfactory moral theory would be like."

Howard Pospesel made many suggestions that helped me enormously; it is a pleasure to thank him. Thanks also to Monica Eckman of McGraw-Hill, a wonderful editor.

CHAPTER 1

What Is Morality?

We are discussing no small matter, but how we ought to live.
SOCRATES, IN PLATO'S *REPUBLIC* (CA. 390 B.C.)

1.1. The Problem of Definition

Moral philosophy is the attempt to achieve a systematic understanding of the nature of morality and what it requires of us—
in Socrates's words, of "how we ought to live," and why. It would
be helpful if we could begin with a simple, uncontroversial definition of what morality is, but that turns out to be impossible.
There are many rival theories, each expounding a different conception of what it means to live morally, and any definition that
goes beyond Socrates's simple formulation is bound to offend
one or another of them.

This should make us cautious, but it need not paralyze us.
In this chapter I will describe the "minimum conception" of
morality. As the name suggests, the minimum conception is a
core that every moral theory should accept, at least as a starting
point. We will begin by examining some recent moral controversies, all having to do with handicapped children. The features of the minimum conception will emerge from our consideration of these examples.

1.2. First Example: Baby Theresa

Theresa Ann Campo Pearson, an anencephalic infant known
to the public as "Baby Theresa," was born in Florida in 1992.
Anencephaly is among the worst congenital disorders. Anencephalic infants are sometimes referred to as "babies without
brains," and this gives roughly the right picture, but it is not
quite accurate. Important parts of the brain—the cerebrum

1

and cerebellum—are missing, as well as the top of the skull. There is, however, a brain-stem, and so autonomic functions such as breathing and heartbeat are possible. In the United States, most cases of anencephaly are detected during pregnancy and aborted. Of those not aborted, half are stillborn. About 300 each year are born alive, and they usually die within a few days.

Baby Theresa's story would not be remarkable except for an unusual request made by her parents. Knowing that their baby could not live long and that, even if she could survive, she would never have a conscious life, Baby Theresa's parents volunteered her organs for transplant. They thought her kidneys, liver, heart, lungs, and eyes should go to other children who could benefit from them. The physicians agreed that this was a good idea. At least 2,000 infants need transplants each year, and there are never enough organs available. But the organs were not taken, because Florida law does not allow the removal of organs until the donor is dead. By the time Baby Theresa died, nine days later, it was too late for the other children—her organs could not be transplanted because they had deteriorated too much.

The newspaper stories about Baby Theresa prompted a great deal of public discussion. Would it have been right to remove the infant's organs, thereby causing her immediate death, to help other children? A number of professional "ethicists"— people employed by universities, hospitals, and law schools, whose job it is to think about such matters—were called on by the press to comment. Surprisingly few of them agreed with the parents and physicians. Instead they appealed to time-honored philosophical principles to oppose taking the organs. "It just seems too horrifying to use people as means to other people's ends," said one such expert. Another explained, "It is unethical to kill in order to save. It's unethical to kill person A to save person B." And a third added: "What the parents are really asking for is: Kill this dying baby so that its organs may be used for someone else. Well, that's really a horrendous proposition."

Was it really horrendous? Opinions were divided. These ethicists thought so, while the parents and doctors did not. But we are interested in more than what people happen to think. We want to know the truth of the matter. In fact, were the parents right or wrong to volunteer the baby's organs for transplant? If we want to discover the truth, we have to ask what reasons, or arguments, can be given for each side. What can be said to justify the parents' request, or to justify thinking the request was wrong?

The Benefits Argument. The parents' suggestion was based on the idea that, because Theresa was going to die soon anyway, her organs were doing her no good. The other children, however, could benefit from them. Thus, their reasoning seems to have been: *If we can benefit someone, without harming anyone else, we ought to do so. Transplanting the organs would benefit the other children without harming Baby Theresa. Therefore, we ought to transplant the organs.*

Is this correct? Not every argument is sound; and in addition to knowing what arguments can be given for a view, we also want to know whether those arguments are any good. Generally speaking, an argument is sound if its premises are true and the conclusion follows logically from them. In this case, we might wonder about the assertion that Teresa wouldn't be harmed. After all, she would die, and isn't that bad for her? But on reflection, it seems clear that, in these tragic circumstances, the parents were right—being alive was doing her no good. Being alive is a benefit only if it enables you to carry on activities and have thoughts, feelings, and relations with other people—in other words, if it enables you to *have a life.* In the absence of such things, mere biological existence is worthless. Therefore, even though Theresa might remain alive for a few more days, it would do her no good. (We might imagine circumstances in which other people would gain from keeping her alive, but that is not the same as her benefiting.)

The Benefits Argument, therefore, provides a powerful reason for transplanting the organs. What are the arguments on the other side?

The Argument That We Should Not Use People as Means. The ethicists who opposed the transplants offered two arguments. The first was based on the idea that *it is wrong to use people as means to other people's ends.* Taking Theresa's organs would be using her to benefit the other children; therefore, it should not be done.

Is this a sound argument? The idea that we should not "use" people is obviously appealing, but this is a vague notion that needs to be sharpened. What, exactly, does it mean? "Using people" typically involves violating their autonomy—their ability to decide for themselves how to live their own lives, according to their own desires and values. A person's autonomy may be violated through manipulation, trickery, or deceit. For example, I may pretend to be your friend, when I am only interested in meeting your sister; or I may lie to you in order to get a loan; or I may try to convince you that you will enjoy attending a concert in another city, when I only want you to take me. In each case, I am manipulating you in order to get something for myself. Autonomy is also violated when people are forced to do things against their will. This explains why "using people" is wrong; it is wrong because deception, trickery, and coercion are wrong.

Taking Theresa's organs would not involve deceit, trickery, or coercion. Would it be "using her" in any other morally significant sense? We would, of course, be making use of her organs for someone else's benefit. But we do that every time we perform a transplant. In this case, however, we would be doing it without her permission. Would that make it wrong? If we were doing it *against* her wishes, that might be reason for objecting; it would be a violation of her autonomy. But Baby Theresa is not an autonomous being: she has no wishes and is unable to make any decisions for herself.

When people are unable to make decisions for themselves, and others must do it for them, there are two reasonable guidelines that might be adopted. First, we might ask *what would be in their own best interests?* If we apply this standard to Baby Theresa, there would seem to be no objection to taking her organs, for, as we have already seen, her interests will not be affected one way or the other. She is going to die soon no matter what.

The second guideline appeals to the person's own preferences: we may ask, *if she could tell us what she wants, what would she say?* This sort of thought is often helpful when we are dealing with people who are known to have preferences but are unable to express them (for example, a comatose patient who has signed a Living Will). But, sadly, Baby Teresa has no preferences about anything, and never will have. So we can get no guidance from her, even in our imaginations. The upshot is that we are left to do what we think is best.

The Argument from the Wrongness of Killing. The ethicists also appealed to the principle that *it is wrong to kill one person to save another.* Taking Theresa's organs would be killing her to save others, they said; so taking the organs would be wrong.

Is this argument sound? The prohibition on killing is certainly among the most important moral rules. Nevertheless, few people believe it is always wrong to kill—most people believe that exceptions are sometimes justified. The question, then, is whether taking Baby Theresa's organs should be regarded as an exception to the rule. There are many reasons in favor of this, the most important being that she is going to die soon anyway, no matter what is done, while taking her organs would at least do some good for the other babies. Anyone who accepts this will regard the main premise of the argument as false. Usually it is wrong to kill one person to save another, but not always.

But there is another possibility. Perhaps the best way of understanding the whole situation would be to regard Baby Theresa as already dead. If this sounds crazy, remember that "brain death" is now widely accepted as a criterion for pronouncing people legally dead. When the brain-death standard was first proposed, it was resisted on the grounds that someone can be brain dead while a lot is still going on inside them—with mechanical assistance, their heart can continue to beat, they can breathe, and so on. But eventually brain death was accepted, and people became accustomed to regarding it as "real" death. This was reasonable because when the brain ceases to function there is no longer any hope for conscious life.

Anencephalics do not meet the technical requirements for brain death as it is currently defined; but perhaps the definition should be rewritten to include them. After all, they also lack any hope for conscious life, for the profound reason that they have no cerebrum or cerebellum. If the definition of brain death were reformulated to include anencephalics, we would become accustomed to the idea that these unfortunate infants are born dead, and so we would not regard taking their organs as killing them. The Argument from the Wrongness of Killing would then be moot.

On the whole, then, it looks like the argument in favor of transplanting Baby Theresa's organs is stronger than these arguments against it.

1.3. Second Example: Jodie and Mary

In August 2000, a young woman from Gozo, an island near Malta, discovered that she was carrying conjoined twins. Knowing that health-care facilities on Gozo were inadequate to deal with the complications of such a birth, she and her husband came to St. Mary's Hospital in Manchester, England to have the babies delivered. The infants, known as Mary and Jodie, were joined at the lower abdomen. Their spines were fused, and they had one heart and one set of lungs between them. Jodie, the stronger, was providing blood for her sister.

No one knows how many sets of conjoined twins are born each year. They are rare, although the recent birth of three sets in Oregon led to speculation that the number is on the rise. ("The United States has very good health care and very poor record keeping," commented one doctor.) The causes of the phenomenon are largely unknown, but we do know that conjoined twins are a variant of identical twins. When the cell-cluster (the "pre-embryo") splits three to eight days after fertilization, identical twins are created; when the split is delayed a few days longer, the division may be incomplete and the twins may be conjoined.

Some sets of conjoined twins do well. They grow to adulthood and sometimes marry and have children themselves. But the outlook for Mary and Jodie was grim. The doctors said that, without intervention, they would die within six months. The only hope was an operation to separate them. This would save Jodie, but Mary would die immediately.

The parents, who are devout Catholics, refused permission for the operation on the grounds that it would hasten Mary's death. "We believe that nature should take its course," said the parents. "If it's God's will that both our children should not survive then so be it." The hospital, believing it was obliged to do what it could to save at least one of the infants, asked the courts for permission to separate them despite the parents' wishes. The courts granted permission, and on November 6 the operation was performed. As expected, Jodie lived and Mary died.

In thinking about this case, we should separate the question of *who should make the decision* from the question of *what the decision should be.* You might think, for example, that the decision should be left to the parents, in which case you will object to the court's intrusion. But there remains the separate question of what would be the wisest choice for the parents (or anyone else) to make. We will focus on the latter question: Would it be right or wrong, in these circumstances, to separate the twins?

The Argument That We Should Save as Many as We Can. The obvious argument for separating the twins is that we have a choice between saving one infant or letting both die. Isn't it plainly better to save one? This argument is so appealing that many people will conclude, without further ado, that this settles the matter. At the height of the controversy over this case, when the newspapers were full of stories about Jodie and Mary, the *Ladies Home Journal* commissioned a poll to discover what Americans thought. The poll showed that 78% approved of the operation. People were obviously persuaded by the idea that we should save as many as we can. Jodie and Mary's parents, however, believed there is an even stronger argument on the other side.

The Argument from the Sanctity of Human Life. The parents loved both their children, and they thought it would be wrong to sacrifice one of them even to save the other. Of course, they were not alone in taking this view. The idea that all human life is precious, regardless of age, race, social class, or handicap, is at the core of the Western moral tradition. It is especially emphasized in religious writings. In traditional ethics, the prohibition upon killing innocent humans is said to be absolute. It does not matter if the killing would serve a very good purpose; it simply cannot be done. Mary is an innocent human being, and so she may not be killed.

Is this a sound argument? The judges who heard the case in court did not think so, for a surprising reason. They denied that the traditional principle applies in this case. Lord Justice Robert Walker said that, in performing the operation, Mary would not be killed. She would merely be separated from her sister, and then "She would die, not because she was intentionally killed, but because her own body cannot sustain her life." In other words, the cause of her death would not be the operation but her own weakness. The physicians also seem to have taken this view. When the operation finally was performed, they went through the motions of trying to keep Mary alive—"giving her every chance"—even though they knew it was futile.

The judge's point may seem a bit sophistical. Surely, you might think, it doesn't matter whether we say that Mary's death is caused by the operation or by her own body's weakness. Either way, she will be dead, and her death will have come sooner than if she had not been separated from her sister.

There is, however, a more natural objection to the Argument from the Sanctity of Life, that does not rely on such a strained point. One might reply that it is *not* always wrong to kill innocent human beings. In rare situations, it may be right. In particular, if (a) the innocent human has no future because she is going to die soon no matter what; (b) the innocent human has no wish to go on living, perhaps because she is so mentally undeveloped as to have no wishes at all; and (c) killing the innocent human will save the lives of others, who can then go on to have good full lives—in these rare circumstances, the killing of the innocent might be justified. Of course, many moralists, especially religious thinkers, will not be convinced. Nevertheless, this is a line of thought that many people may find persuasive.

1.4. Third Example: Tracy Latimer

Tracy Latimer, a 12-year-old victim of cerebral palsy, was killed by her father in 1993. Tracy lived with her family on a prairie farm in Saskatchewan, Canada. On a Sunday morning while his wife and other children were at church, Robert Latimer put Tracy in the cab of his pickup truck and piped in exhaust fumes until she died. At the time of her death, Tracy weighed less than 40 pounds; she was described as "functioning at the mental level of a three-month-old baby." Mrs. Latimer said that she was relieved to find Tracy dead when she arrived home and added that she "didn't have the courage" to do it herself.

Mr. Latimer was tried for murder, but the judge and jury did not want to treat him harshly. The jury found him guilty of only second-degree murder and they recommended that the judge ignore the mandatory 25-year sentence. The judge agreed and sentenced him to one year in prison, to be followed by a one-year confinement to his farm. However, the Supreme Court of Canada stepped in and ruled that the mandatory sentence must be imposed. Robert Latimer is now in prison, serving the 25-year term.

Legal questions aside, did Mr. Latimer do anything wrong? This case involves many of the issues that we have already seen in the other cases. One argument against Mr. Latimer is that Tracy's life was morally precious, and so he had no right to kill her. In his defense, it may be replied that Tracy's condition was so catastrophic that she had no prospects of a "life" in any but a biological sense. Her existence had been reduced to nothing but pointless suffering, so that killing her was an act of mercy. Considering those arguments, it appears that Mr. Latimer may have acted defensibly. There were, however, other points made by his critics.

The Argument from the Wrongness of Discriminating against the Handicapped. When Robert Latimer was given a lenient sentence by the trial court, many handicapped people took it as an insult. The president of the Saskatoon Voice of People with Disabilities, who has multiple sclerosis, said: "Nobody has the right to decide my life is worth less than yours. That's the bottom line." Tracy was killed because she was handicapped, he said, and that is unconscionable. Handicapped people should be given the same respect and the same rights as everyone else.

What are we to make of this? Discrimination against any group is, of course, a serious matter. It is objectionable because it involves treating some people differently than others, when there are no relevant differences between them that would justify it. Common examples involve such matters as discrimination in employment. Suppose a blind person is refused a job simply because the employer doesn't like the idea of employing someone who can't see. This is no better than refusing to employ people because they are black or Jewish. To point up the offensiveness of this, we may ask why this person is being treated differently. Is he less able to do the job? Is he more stupid or less industrious? Does he somehow deserve the job less? Is he less able to benefit from employment? If there is no good reason for excluding him, then it is simply arbitrary to treat him in this way.

At the same time, there are *some* circumstances in which treating the handicapped differently may be justified. For example, no one would argue seriously that a blind person should be employed as an air traffic controller. Because we can easily explain why this is not desirable, the "discrimination" is not arbitrary, and it is not a violation of the handicapped person's rights.

Should we think of the death of Tracy Latimer as a case of discrimination against the handicapped? Mr. Latimer argued that Tracy's cerebral palsy was not the issue. "People are saying this is a handicap issue," he said, "but they're wrong. This is a torture issue. It was about mutilation and torture for Tracy." Just before her death, Tracy had undergone major surgery on her back, hips, and legs, and more surgery was planned. "With the combination of a feeding tube, rods in her back, the leg cut and flopping around and bedsores," said her father, "how can people say she was a happy little girl?" At the trial, three of Tracy's physicians testified about the difficulty of controlling her pain. Thus, Mr. Latimer denied that she was killed because of the cerebral palsy; she was killed because of the pain and because there was no hope for her.

The Slippery Slope Argument. This leads naturally to one further argument. When the Canadian Supreme Court upheld Robert Latimer's sentence, Tracy Walters, director of the Canadian Association of Independent Living Centres, said that she was "pleasantly surprised" to hear of the decision. "It would have really been the slippery slope, and opening the doors to other people to decide who should live and who should die," she said.

Other disability advocates echoed this idea. We may feel sympathy for Robert Latimer, it was said; we may even be tempted to think that Tracy is better off dead. However, it is dangerous to engage in this kind of thinking. If we accept any sort of mercy killing, we will have stepped onto a "slippery slope" down which we will inevitably slide, and in the end all life will be held cheap. Where will we draw the line? If Tracy Latimer's life is not worth protecting, what about other disabled people? What about the elderly, the infirm, and other "useless" members of society? In this connection, the Nazis, who sought to "purify the race," are often mentioned, and the implication is that if we do not want to end up like them, we had better not take the first dangerous steps.

Similar "slippery slope arguments" have been used in connection with all sorts of other issues. Abortion, in vitro fertilization (IVF), and most recently cloning have all been opposed because of what they might lead to. Because such arguments involve speculations about the future, they are notoriously hard to evaluate. Sometimes, in hindsight, it is possible to see that the worries were unfounded. This has happened with IVF. When Louise Brown, the first "test-tube baby," was born in 1978, there were dire predictions about what might be in store for her, her family, and society as a whole. But nothing bad happened and IVF became a routine procedure that has been used to help thousands of couples to have children.

When the future is unknown, however, it can be difficult to determine whether such an argument is sound. Otherwise reasonable people might disagree about what would likely happen if mercy killing in cases like Tracy Latimer's was accepted. This makes possible a frustrating sort of impasse: Disagreements about the merits of the argument may depend simply on the prior dispositions of the disputants—those inclined to defend Mr. Latimer may think the predictions are unrealistic, while those predisposed to condemn him insist the predictions are sensible.

It is worth noting, however, that this kind of argument is easy to abuse. If you are opposed to something, but you have no good arguments against it, you can always make up a prediction about what it might lead to; and no matter how implausible your prediction is, no one can prove you wrong. This method can be used to oppose almost anything. That is why such arguments should be approached with caution.

1.5. Reason and Impartiality

What can we learn from all this about the nature of morality? As a start, we may note two main points: first, that moral judgments must be backed by good reasons; and second, that morality requires the impartial consideration of each individual's interests.

Moral Reasoning. The cases of Baby Theresa, Jodie and Mary, and Tracy Latimer, like many others to be discussed in this book, are liable to arouse strong feelings. Such feelings are often a sign of moral seriousness and so may be admired. But they can also be an impediment to discovering the truth: When we feel strongly about an issue, it is tempting to assume that we just *know* what the truth must be, without even having to consider the arguments on the other side. Unfortunately, however, we cannot rely on our feelings, no matter how powerful they may be. Our feelings may be irrational: they may be nothing but the products of prejudice, selfishness, or cultural conditioning. (At one time, for example, people's feelings told them that members of other races were inferior and that slavery was God's own plan.) Moreover, different people's feelings often tell them opposite things: In the case of Tracy Latimer, some people feel very strongly that her father should have been given a long prison term, whereas others feel equally strongly that he should never have been prosecuted. But both these feelings cannot be correct.

Thus, if we want to discover the truth, we must try to let our feelings be guided as much as possible by the arguments that can be given for the opposing views. Morality is, first and foremost, a matter of consulting reason. The morally right thing to do, in any circumstance, is whatever there are the best reasons for doing.

This is not a narrow point about a small range of moral views; it is a general requirement of logic that must be accepted by everyone regardless of their position on any particular moral issue. The fundamental point may be stated simply. Suppose someone says that you ought to do thus-and-so (or that doing thus-and-so would be wrong). You may legitimately ask why you should do it (or why it would be wrong), and if no good reason can be given, you may reject the advice as arbitrary or unfounded.

In this way, moral judgments are different from expressions of personal taste. If someone says "I like coffee," he does not need to have a reason—he is merely stating a fact about himself, and nothing more. There is no such thing as "rationally defending" one's like or dislike of coffee, and so there is no arguing about it. So long as he is accurately reporting his tastes, what he says must be true. Moreover, there is no implication that anyone else should feel the same way; if everyone else in the world hates coffee, it doesn't matter. On the other hand, if someone says that something is morally wrong, he does need reasons, and if his reasons are sound, other people must acknowledge their force. By the same logic, if he has no good reason for what he says, he is just making noise and we need pay him no attention.

Of course, not every reason that may be advanced is a good reason. There are bad arguments as well as good ones, and much of the skill of moral thinking consists in discerning the difference. But how does one tell the difference? How are we to go about assessing arguments? The examples we have considered illustrate some of the pertinent points.

The first thing is to get one's facts straight. Often this is not as easy as it sounds. One source of difficulty is that the "facts" are sometimes hard to ascertain—matters may be so complex and difficult that not even the experts can agree. Another problem is human prejudice. Often we will *want* to believe some version of the facts because it supports our preconceptions. Those who disapprove of Robert Latimer's action, for example, will want to believe the predictions in the Slippery Slope Argument; those who are sympathetic to him will not want to believe those predictions. It is easy to think of other examples of the same sort: people who do not want to give money to charity often say that charitable organizations are wasteful, even when they have no very good evidence for this; and people who dislike homosexuals say that gay people include a disproportionate number of child molesters, despite evidence to the contrary. But the facts exist independently of our wishes, and responsible moral thinking begins when we try to see things as they are.

After the facts have been established as well as they can be, moral principles are brought into play. In our three examples, a number of principles were involved: that we should not "use" people; that we should not kill one person to save another; that we should do what will benefit the people affected by our actions; that every life is sacred; and that it is wrong to discriminate against the handicapped. Most moral arguments consist of principles being applied to the facts of particular cases, and so the obvious questions to be asked are whether the principles are sound and whether they are being intelligently applied.

It would be nice if there were a simple recipe for constructing good arguments and avoiding bad ones. Unfortunately, there is no easy method. Arguments can go wrong in an indefinite number of ways, as is evident from the various arguments about the handicapped babies; and one must always be alert to the possibility of new complications and new kinds of error. But that is not surprising. The rote application of routine methods is never a satisfactory substitute for critical intelligence, in any area. Moral thinking is no exception.

The Requirement of Impartiality. Almost every important theory of morality includes the idea of impartiality. The basic idea is that each individual's interests are equally important; from within the moral point of view, there are no privileged persons. Therefore, each of us must acknowledge that other people's welfare is just as important as our own. At the same time, the requirement of impartiality rules out any scheme that treats the members of particular *groups* as somehow morally inferior, as blacks, Jews, and others have sometimes been treated.

The requirement of impartiality is closely connected with the point that moral judgments must be backed by good reasons. Consider the position of a white racist, for example, who holds that it is right for the best jobs in society to be reserved for white people. He is happy with a situation in which the major corporation executives, government officials, and so on are white, while blacks are limited mostly to menial jobs; and he supports the social arrangements by which this situation is maintained. Now we can ask for reasons; we can ask why this is thought to be right. Is there something about white people that makes them better fitted for the highest-paying and most prestigious positions? Are they inherently brighter or more industrious? Do they care more about themselves and their families? Are they capable of benefiting more from the availability of such positions? In each case, the answer seems to be no; and if there is no good reason for treating people differently, discrimination is unacceptably arbitrary.

The requirement of impartiality, then, is at bottom nothing more than a proscription against arbitrariness in dealing with people. It is a rule that forbids us from treating one person differently from another *when there is no good reason to do so.* But if this explains what is wrong with racism, it also explains why, in some special kinds of cases, it is not racist to treat people differently. Suppose a film director was making a movie about the life of Martin Luther King, Jr. He would have a perfectly good reason for ruling out Tom Cruise for the starring role. Obviously, such casting would make no sense. Because there would be a good reason for it, the director's "discrimination" would not be arbitrary and so would not be open to criticism.

1.6. The Minimum Conception of Morality

The minimum conception may now be stated very briefly: Morality is, at the very least, the effort to guide one's conduct by reason—that is, to do what there are the best reasons for doing—while giving equal weight to the interests of each individual who will be affected by what one does.

This gives us, among other things, a picture of what it means to be a conscientious moral agent. The conscientious moral agent is someone who is concerned impartially with the interests of everyone affected by what he or she does; who carefully sifts facts and examines their implications; who accepts principles of conduct only after scrutinizing them to make sure they are sound; who is willing to "listen to reason" even when it means that earlier convictions may have to be revised; and who, finally, is willing to act on the results of this deliberation.

Of course, as one might expect, not every ethical theory accepts this "minimum." As we shall see, this picture of the moral agent has been disputed in various ways. However, theories that reject the minimum conception encounter serious difficulties. Most philosophers have realized this, and so most theories of morality incorporate the minimum conception, in one form or another. They disagree not about the minimum but about how it should be expanded, or perhaps modified, in order to achieve a fully satisfying account.

CHAPTER 2

The Challenge of Cultural Relativism

> Morality differs in every society, and is a convenient term for socially approved habits.
>
> RUTH BENEDICT, *PATTERNS OF CULTURE* (1934)

2.1. How Different Cultures Have Different Moral Codes

Darius, a king of ancient Persia, was intrigued by the variety of cultures he encountered in his travels. He had found, for example, that the Callatians (a tribe of Indians) customarily ate the bodies of their dead fathers. The Greeks, of course, did not do that—the Greeks practiced cremation and regarded the funeral pyre as the natural and fitting way to dispose of the dead. Darius thought that a sophisticated understanding of the world must include an appreciation of such differences between cultures. One day, to teach this lesson, he summoned some Greeks who happened to be present at his court and asked them what they would take to eat the bodies of their dead fathers. They were shocked, as Darius knew they would be, and replied that no amount of money could persuade them to do such a thing. Then Darius called in some Callatians, and while the Greeks listened asked them what they would take to burn their dead fathers' bodies. The Callatians were horrified and told Darius not even to mention such a dreadful thing.

This story, recounted by Herodotus in his *History*, illustrates a recurring theme in the literature of social science: Different cultures have different moral codes. What is thought right within one group may be utterly abhorrent to the members of another group, and vice versa. Should we eat the bodies

16

of the dead or burn them? If you were a Greek, one answer would seem obviously correct; but if you were a Callatian, the opposite would seem equally certain.

It is easy to give additional examples of the same kind. Consider the Eskimos(of which the largest group is the Inuit). They are a remote and inaccessible people. Numbering only about 25,000, they live in small, isolated settlements scattered mostly along the northern fringes of North America and Greenland. Until the beginning of the 20th century, the outside world knew little about them. Then explorers began to bring back strange tales.

Eskimo customs turned out to be very different from our own. The men often had more than one wife, and they would share their wives with guests, lending them for the night as a sign of hospitality. Moreover, within a community a dominant male might demand and get regular sexual access to other men's wives. The women however, were free to break these arrangements simply by leaving their husbands and taking up with new partners—free, that is, so long as their former husbands chose not to make trouble. All in all, the Eskimo practice was a volatile scheme that bore little resemblance to what we call marriage.

But it was not only their marriage and sexual practices that were different. The Eskimos also seemed to have less regard for human life. Infanticide, for example, was common. Knud Rasmussen, one of the most famous early explorers, reported that he met one woman who had borne 20 children but had killed 10 of them at birth. Female babies, he found, were especially liable to be destroyed, and this was permitted simply at the parents' discretion, with no social stigma attached to it. Old people also, when they became too feeble to contribute to the family, were left out in the snow to die. So there seemed to be, in this society, remarkably little respect for life.

To the general public, these were disturbing revelations. Our own way of living seems so natural and right that for many of us it is hard to conceive of others living so differently. And when we do hear of such things, we tend immediately to categorize the other peoples as "backward" or "primitive." But to anthropologists, there was nothing particularly surprising about the Eskimos. Since the time of Herodotus, enlightened observers have been accustomed to the idea that conceptions of right and wrong differ from culture to culture. If we assume that our ethical ideas will be shared by all peoples at all times, we are merely naive.

2.2. Cultural Relativism

To many thinkers, this observation—"Different cultures have different moral codes"—has seemed to be the key to understanding morality. The idea of universal truth in ethics, they say, is a myth. The customs of different societies are all that exist. These customs cannot be said to be "correct" or "incorrect," for that implies we have an independent standard of right and wrong by which they may be judged. But there is no such independent standard; every standard is culture-bound. The great pioneering sociologist William Graham Sumner, writing in 1906, put it like this:

> The "right" way is the way which the ancestors used and which has been handed down. The tradition is its own warrant. It is not held subject to verification by experience. The notion of right is in the folkways. It is not outside of them, of independent origin, and brought to test them. In the folkways, whatever is, is right. This is because they are traditional, and therefore contain in themselves the authority of the ancestral ghosts. When we come to the folkways we are at the end of our analysis.

This line of thought has probably persuaded more people to be skeptical about ethics than any other single thing. Cultural Relativism, as it has been called, challenges our ordinary belief in the objectivity and universality of moral truth. It says, in effect, that there is no such thing as universal truth in ethics; there are only the various cultural codes, and nothing more. Moreover, our own code has no special status; it is merely one among many. As we shall see, this basic idea is really a compound of several different thoughts. It is important to separate the various elements of the theory because, on analysis, some parts turn out to be correct, while others seem to be mistaken. As a beginning, we may distinguish the following claims, all of which have been made by cultural relativists:

1. Different societies have different moral codes.
2. The moral code of a society determines what is right within that society; that is, if the moral code of a society

says that a certain action is right, then that action *is* right, at least within that society.
3. There is no objective standard that can be used to judge one society's code better than another's.
4. The moral code of our own society has no special status; it is merely one among many.
5. There is no "universal truth" in ethics; that is, there are no moral truths that hold for all peoples at all times.
6. It is mere arrogance for us to try to judge the conduct of other peoples. We should adopt an attitude of tolerance toward the practices of other cultures.

Although it may seem that these six propositions go naturally together, they are independent of one another, in the sense that some of them might be false even if others are true. In what follows, we will try to identify what is correct in Cultural Relativism, but we will also be concerned to expose what is mistaken about it.

2.3. The Cultural Differences Argument

Cultural Relativism is a theory about the nature of morality. At first blush it seems quite plausible. However, like all such theories, it may be evaluated by subjecting it to rational analysis; and when we analyze Cultural Relativism, we find that it is not so plausible as it first appears to be.

The first thing we need to notice is that at the heart of Cultural Relativism there is a certain *form of argument*. The strategy used by cultural relativists is to argue from facts about the differences between cultural outlooks to a conclusion about the status of morality. Thus we are invited to accept this reasoning:

(1) The Greeks believed it was wrong to eat the dead, whereas the Callatians believed it was right to eat the dead.

(2) Therefore, eating the dead is neither objectively right nor objectively wrong. It is merely a matter of opinion that varies from culture to culture.

Or, alternatively:

(1) The Eskimos see nothing wrong with infanticide, whereas Americans believe infanticide is immoral.

(2) Therefore, infanticide is neither objectively right nor objectively wrong. It is merely a matter of opinion, which varies from culture to culture.

Clearly, these arguments are variations of one fundamental idea. They are both special cases of a more general argument, which says:

(1) Different cultures have different moral codes.

(2) Therefore, there is no objective "truth" in morality. Right and wrong are only matters of opinion, and opinions vary from culture to culture.

We may call this the Cultural Differences Argument. To many people, it is persuasive. But from a logical point of view, is it sound?

It is not sound. The trouble is that the conclusion does not follow from the premise—that is, even if the premise is true, the conclusion still might be false. The premise concerns what people *believe*—in some societies, people believe one thing; in other societies, people believe differently. The conclusion, however, concerns what *really is the case*. The trouble is that this sort of conclusion does not follow logically from this sort of premise.

Consider again the example of the Greeks and Callatians. The Greeks believed it was wrong to eat the dead; the Callatians believed it was right. Does it follow, *from the mere fact that they disagreed,* that there is no objective truth in the matter? No, it does not follow; for it could be that the practice was objectively right (or wrong) and that one or the other of them was simply mistaken.

To make the point clearer, consider a different matter. In some societies, people believe the earth is flat. In other societies, such as our own, people believe the earth is (roughly) spherical. Does it follow, from the mere fact that people disagree, that there is no "objective truth" in geography? Of course not; we would never draw such a conclusion because we realize that, in their beliefs about the world, the members of some societies might simply be wrong. There is no reason to think that if the world is round everyone must know it. Similarly, there is no reason to think that if there is moral truth everyone must know it. The fundamental mistake in the Cultural Differences Argument is that it attempts to derive a substantive conclusion about a subject from the mere fact that people disagree about it.

This is a simple point of logic, and it is important not to misunderstand it. We are not saying (not yet, anyway) that the conclusion of the argument is false. That is still an open question. The logical point is just that the conclusion does not *follow from* the premise. This is important, because in order to determine whether the conclusion is true, we need arguments in its support. Cultural Relativism proposes this argument, but unfortunately the argument turns out to be fallacious. So it proves nothing.

2.4. The Consequences of Taking Cultural Relativism Seriously

Even if the Cultural Differences Argument is invalid, Cultural Relativism might still be true. What would it be like if it were true?

In the passage quoted above, William Graham Sumner summarizes the essence of Cultural Relativism. He says that there is no measure of right and wrong other than the standards of one's society: "The notion of right is in the folkways. It is not outside of them, of independent origin, and brought to test them. In the folkways, whatever is, is right." Suppose we took this seriously. What would be some of the consequences?

1. *We could no longer say that the customs of other societies are morally inferior to our own.* This, of course, is one of the main points stressed by Cultural Relativism. We would have to stop condemning other societies merely because they are "different." So long as we concentrate on certain examples, such as the funerary practices of the Greeks and Callatians, this may seem to be a sophisticated, enlightened attitude.

However, we would also be stopped from criticizing other, less benign practices. Suppose a society waged war on its neighbors for the purpose of taking slaves. Or suppose a society was violently anti-Semitic and its leaders set out to destroy the Jews. Cultural Relativism would preclude us from saying that either of these practices was wrong. (We would not even be able to say that a society tolerant of Jews is *better* than the anti-Semitic society, for that would imply some sort of transcultural standard of comparison.) The failure to condemn *these* practices does not seem enlightened; on the contrary, slavery and anti-Semitism seem wrong wherever they occur. Nevertheless, if we took Cultural Relativism seriously, we would have to regard these social practices as immune from criticism.

2. *We could decide whether actions are right or wrong just by consulting the standards of our society.* Cultural Relativism suggests a simple test for determining what is right and what is wrong: All one need do is ask whether the action is in accordance with the code of one's society. Suppose in 1975 a resident of South Africa was wondering whether his country's policy of apartheid—a rigidly racist system—was morally correct. All he has to do is ask whether this policy conformed to his society's moral code. If it did, there would have been nothing to worry about, at least from a moral point of view.

This implication of Cultural Relativism is disturbing because few of us think that our society's code is perfect—we can think of all sorts of ways in which it might be improved. Yet Cultural Relativism not only forbids us from criticizing the codes of *other* societies; it also stops us from criticizing our own. After all, if right and wrong are relative to culture, this must be true for our own culture just as much as for other cultures.

3. *The idea of moral progress is called into doubt.* Usually, we think that at least some social changes are for the better. (Although, of course, other changes may be for the worse.) Throughout most of Western history the place of women in society was narrowly circumscribed. They could not own property; they could not vote or hold political office; and generally they were under the almost absolute control of their husbands. Recently much of this has changed, and most people think of it as progress.

But if Cultural Relativism is correct, can we legitimately think of this as progress? Progress means replacing a way of doing things with a better way. But by what standard do we judge the new ways as better? If the old ways were in accordance with the social standards of their time, then Cultural Relativism would say it is a mistake to judge them by the standards of a different time. Eighteenth-century society was a different society from the one we have now. To say that we have made progress implies a judgment that present-day society is better, and that is just the sort of transcultural judgment that, according to Cultural Relativism, is impossible.

Our idea of social *reform* will also have to be reconsidered. Reformers such as Martin Luther King, Jr., have sought to change their societies for the better. Within the constraints imposed by Cultural Relativism, there is one way this might be done. If a society is not living up to its own ideals, the reformer may be regarded as acting for the best; the ideals of the society are the standard by which we judge his or her proposals as worthwhile. But no one may challenge the ideals themselves, for those ideals are by definition correct. According to Cultural Relativism, then, the idea of social reform makes sense only in this limited way.

These three consequences of Cultural Relativism have led many thinkers to reject it as implausible on its face. It does make sense, they say, to condemn some practices, such as slavery and anti-Semitism, wherever they occur. It makes sense to think that our own society has made some moral progress, while admitting that it is still imperfect and in need of reform. Because Cultural Relativism implies that these judgments make no sense, the argument goes, it cannot be right.

2.5. Why There Is Less Disagreement Than It Seems

The original impetus for Cultural Relativism comes from the observation that cultures differ dramatically in their views of right and wrong. But just how much do they differ? It is true that there are differences. However, it is easy to overestimate the extent of those differences. Often, when we examine what seems to be a dramatic difference, we find that the cultures do not differ nearly as much as it appears.

Consider a culture in which people believe it is wrong to eat cows. This may even be a poor culture, in which there is not enough food; still, the cows are not to be touched. Such a society would appear to have values very different from our own. But does it? We have not yet asked *why* these people will not eat cows. Suppose it is because they believe that after death the souls of humans inhabit the bodies of animals, especially cows, so that a cow may be someone's grandmother. Now shall we say that their values are different from ours? No; the difference lies elsewhere. The difference is in our belief systems, not in our values. We agree that we shouldn't eat Grandma; we simply disagree about whether the cow is (or could be) Grandma.

The point is that many factors work together to produce the customs of a society. The society's values are only one of them. Other matters, such as the religious and factual beliefs held by its members, and the physical circumstances in which they must live, are also important. We cannot conclude, then, merely because customs differ, that there is a disagreement about values. The difference in customs may be attributable to some other aspect of social life. Thus there may be less disagreement about values than there appears to be.

Consider again the Eskimos, who often kill perfectly normal infants, especially girls. We do not approve of such things; in our society, a parent who killed a baby would be locked up. Thus there appears to be a great difference in the values of our two cultures. But suppose we ask why the Eskimos do this. The explanation is not that they have less affection for their children or less respect for human life. An Eskimo family will always protect its babies if conditions permit. But they live in a harsh environment, where food is in short supply. A fundamental postulate of Eskimo thought is: "Life is hard, and the margin of safety small." A family may want to nourish its babies but be unable to do so.

As in many "primitive" societies, Eskimo mothers will nurse their infants over a much longer period of time than mothers in our culture. The child will take nourishment from its mother's breast for four years, perhaps even longer. So even in the best of times there are limits to the number of infants that one mother can sustain. Moreover, the Eskimos are a nomadic people—unable to farm, they must move about in search of food. Infants must be carried, and a mother can carry only one baby in her parka as she travels and goes about her outdoor work. Other family members help however they can.

Infant girls are more readily disposed of because, first, in this society the males are the primary food providers—they are the hunters, following the traditional division of labor—and it is obviously important to maintain a sufficient number of food providers. But there is an important second reason as well. Because the hunters suffer a high casualty rate, the adult men who die prematurely far outnumber the women who die early. Thus if male and female infants survived in equal numbers, the female adult population would greatly outnumber the male adult population. Examining the available statistics, one writer concluded that "were it not for female infanticide . . . there would be approximately one-and-a-half times as many females in the average Eskimo local group as there are food-producing males."

So among the Eskimos, infanticide does not signal a fundamentally different attitude toward children. Instead, it is a recognition that drastic measures are sometimes needed to ensure the family's survival. Even then, however, killing the baby is not the first option considered. Adoption is common; childless couples are especially happy to take a more fertile couple's "surplus." Killing is only the last resort. I emphasize this in order to show that the raw data of the anthropologists can be misleading; it can make the differences in values between cultures appear greater than they are. The Eskimos' values are not all that different from our values. It is only that life forces upon them choices that we do not have to make.

2.6. How All Cultures Have Some Values in Common

It should not be surprising that, despite appearances, the Eskimos are protective of their children. How could it be otherwise? How could a group survive that did not value its young? It is easy to see that, in fact, all cultural groups must protect their infants. Babies are helpless and cannot survive if they are not given extensive care for a period of years. Therefore, if a group did not care for its young, the young would not survive, and the older members of the group would not be replaced. After a while the group would die out. This means that any cultural group that continues to exist must care for its young. Infants that are not cared for must be the exception rather than the rule.

Similar reasoning shows that other values must be more or less universal. Imagine what it would be like for a society to place no value at all on truth telling. When one person spoke to another, there would be no presumption that she was telling the truth, for she could just as easily be speaking falsely. Within that society, there would be no reason to pay attention to what anyone says. (I ask you what time it is, and you say "Four o'clock." But there is no presumption that you are speaking truly; you could just as easily have said the first thing that came into your head. So I have no reason to pay attention to your answer. In fact, there was no point in my asking you in the first place.) Communication would then be extremely difficult, if not impossible. And because complex societies cannot exist without communication among their members, society would become impossible. It follows that in any complex society there must be a presumption in favor of truthfulness. There may of course be exceptions to this rule: There may be situations in which it is thought to be permissible to lie. Nevertheless, these will be exceptions to a rule that *is* in force in the society.

Here is one further example of the same type. Could a society exist in which there was no prohibition on murder? What would this be like? Suppose people were free to kill other people at will, and no one thought there was anything wrong with it. In such a "society," no one could feel safe. Everyone would have to be constantly on guard. People who wanted to survive would have to avoid other people as much as possible. This would inevitably result in individuals trying to become as self-sufficient as possible—after all, associating with others would be dangerous. Society on any large scale would collapse. Of course, people might band together in smaller groups with others that they could trust not to harm them. But notice what this means: They would be forming smaller societies that did acknowledge a rule against murder. The prohibition of murder, then, is a necessary feature of all societies.

There is a general theoretical point here, namely, that *there are some moral rules that all societies must have in common, because those rules are necessary for society to exist.* The rules against lying and murder are two examples. And in fact, we do find these rules in force in all viable cultures. Cultures may differ in what they regard as legitimate exceptions to the rules, but this disagreement exists against a background of agreement on the larger issues. Therefore, it is a mistake to overestimate the amount of difference between cultures. Not every moral rule can vary from society to society.

2.7. Judging a Cultural Practice to Be Undesirable

In 1996, a 17-year-old girl named Fauziya Kassindja arrived at Newark International Airport and asked for asylum. She had fled her native country of Togo, a small west African nation, to escape what people there call "excision." Excision is a permanently disfiguring procedure that is sometimes called "female circumcision," although it bears little resemblance to the Jewish practice. More commonly, at least in Western newspapers, it is referred to as "female genital mutilation."

According to the World Health Organization, the practice is widespread in 26 African nations, and two million girls each year are "excised." In some instances, excision is part of an elaborate tribal ritual, performed in small traditional villages, and girls look forward to it because it signals their acceptance into the adult world. In other instances, the practice is carried out by families living in cities on young women who desperately resist. Fauziya Kassindja was the youngest of five daughters in a devoutly Muslim family. Her father, who owned a successful trucking business, was opposed to excision, and he was able to defy the tradition because of his wealth. His first four daughters were married without being mutilated. But when Fauziya was 16, he suddenly died. Fauziya then came under the authority of his father, who arranged a marriage for her and prepared to have her excised. Fauziya was terrified, and her mother and oldest sister helped her to escape. Her mother, left without resources, eventually had to formally apologize and submit to the authority of the patriarch she had offended.

Meanwhile, in America, Fauziya was imprisoned for two years while the authorities decided what to do with her. She was finally granted asylum, but not before she became the center of a controversy about how we should regard the cultural practices of other peoples. A series of articles in the *New York Times* encouraged the idea that excision is a barbaric practice that should be condemned. Other observers were reluctant to be so judgmental—live and let live, they said; after all, our culture probably seems just as strange to them.

Suppose we are inclined to say that excision is bad. Would we merely be imposing the standards of our own culture? If Cultural Relativism is correct, that is all we can do, for there is no culture-neutral moral standard to which we may appeal. But is that true?

Is There a Culture-Neutral Standard of Right and Wrong? There is, of course, a lot that can be said against excision. Excision is painful and it results in the permanent loss of sexual pleasure. Its short-term effects include hemorrhage, tetanus, and septicemia. Sometimes the woman dies. Long-term effects include chronic infection, scars that hinder walking, and continuing pain.

Why, then, has it become a widespread social practice? It is not easy to say. Excision has no apparent social benefits. Unlike

Eskimo infanticide, it is not necessary for the group's survival. Nor is it a matter of religion. Excision is practiced by groups with various religions, including Islam and Christianity, neither of which commend it.

Nevertheless, a number of reasons are given in its defense. Women who are incapable of sexual pleasure are said to be less likely to be promiscuous; thus there will be fewer unwanted pregnancies in unmarried women. Moreover, wives for whom sex is only a duty are less likely to be unfaithful to their husbands; and because they will not be thinking about sex, they will be more attentive to the needs of their husbands and children. Husbands, for their part, are said to enjoy sex more with wives who have been excised. (The women's own lack of enjoyment is said to be unimportant.) Men will not want unexcised women, as they are unclean and immature. And above all, it has been done since antiquity, and we may not change the ancient ways.

It would be easy, and perhaps a bit arrogant, to ridicule these arguments. But we may notice an important feature of this whole line of reasoning: It attempts to justify excision by showing that excision is beneficial—men, women, and their families are said to be better off when women are excised. Thus we might approach this reasoning, and excision itself, by asking whether this is true: Is excision, on the whole, helpful or harmful?

In fact, this is a standard that might reasonably be used in thinking about any social practice whatever: We may ask *whether the practice promotes or hinders the welfare of the people whose lives are affected by it.* And, as a corollary, we may ask if there is an alternative set of social arrangements that would do a better job of promoting their welfare. If so, we may conclude that the existing practice is deficient.

But this looks like just the sort of independent moral standard that Cultural Relativism says cannot exist. It is a single standard that may be brought to bear in judging the practices of any culture, at any time, including our own. Of course, people will not usually see this principle as being "brought in from the outside" to judge them, because, like the rules against lying and homicide, the welfare of its members is a value internal to all viable cultures.

Why, Despite All This, Thoughtful People May Nevertheless Be Reluctant to Criticize Other Cultures. Although they are personally horrified by excision, many thoughtful people are reluctant to say it is wrong, for at least three reasons.

First, there is an understandable nervousness about "interfering in the social customs of other peoples." Europeans and their cultural descendents in America have a shabby history of destroying native cultures in the name of Christianity and Enlightenment. Recoiling from this record, some people refuse to make any negative judgments about other cultures, especially cultures that resemble those that have been wronged in the past. We should notice, however, that there is a difference between (a) judging a cultural practice to be deficient, and (b) thinking that we should announce the fact, conduct a campaign, apply diplomatic pressure, or send in the army. The first is just a matter of trying to see the world clearly, from a moral point of view. The second is another matter altogether. Sometimes it may be right to "do something about it," but often it will not be.

People also feel, rightly enough, that they should be tolerant of other cultures. Tolerance is, no doubt, a virtue—a tolerant person is willing to live in peaceful cooperation with those who see things differently. But there is nothing in the nature of tolerance that requires you to say that all beliefs, all religions, and all social practices are equally admirable. On the contrary, if you did not think that some were better than others, there would be nothing for you to tolerate.

Finally, people may be reluctant to judge because they do not want to express contempt for the society being criticized. But again, this is misguided: To condemn a particular practice is not to say that the culture is on the whole contemptible or that it is generally inferior to any other culture, including one's own. It could have many admirable features. In fact, we should expect this to be true of most human societies—they are mixes of good and bad practices. Excision happens to be one of the bad ones.

2.8. What Can Be Learned from Cultural Relativism

At the outset, I said that we were going to identify both what is right and what is wrong in Cultural Relativism.   But I have dwelled on its mistakes: I have said that it rests on an invalid argument, that it has consequences that make it implausible on its face, and that the extent of moral disagreement is far less than it implies. This all adds up to a pretty thorough repudiation of the theory. Nevertheless, it is still a very appealing idea, and the reader may have the feeling that all this is a little unfair. The theory must have something going for it, or else why has it been so influential? In fact, I think there is something right about Cultural Relativism, and now I want to say what that is. There are two lessons we should learn from the theory, even if we ultimately reject it.

First, Cultural Relativism warns us, quite rightly, about the danger of assuming that all our preferences are based on some absolute rational standard. They are not. Many (but not all) of our practices are merely peculiar to our society, and it is easy to lose sight of that fact. In reminding us of it, the theory does a service.

Funerary practices are one example. The Callatians, according to Herodotus, were "men who eat their fathers"—a shocking idea, to us at least. But eating the flesh of the dead could be understood as a sign of respect. It could be taken as a symbolic act that says: we wish this person's spirit to dwell within us. Perhaps this was the understanding of the Callatians. On such a way of thinking, burying the dead could be seen as an act of rejection, and burning the corpse as positively scornful. If this is hard to imagine, then we may need to have our imaginations stretched. Of course we may feel a visceral repugnance at the idea of eating human flesh in any circumstances. But what of it? This repugnance may be, as the relativists say, only a matter of what is customary in our particular society.

There are many other matters that we tend to think of in terms of objective right and wrong that are really nothing more than social conventions. We could make a long list. Should women cover their breasts? A publicly exposed breast is scandalous in our society, whereas in other cultures it is unremarkable. Objectively speaking, it is neither right nor wrong—there is no objective reason why either custom is better. Cultural Relativism begins with the valuable insight that many of our practices are like this; they are only cultural products. Then it goes wrong by inferring that, because some practices are like this, all must be.

The second lesson has to do with keeping an open mind. In the course of growing up, each of us has acquired some strong feelings: We have learned to think of some types of conduct as acceptable, and others we have learned to reject. Occasionally, we may find those feelings challenged. For example, we may have been taught that homosexuality is immoral, and we may feel quite uncomfortable around gay people and see them as alien and "different." Now someone suggests that this may be a mere prejudice; that there is nothing evil about homosexuality; that gay people are just people, like anyone else, who happen, through no choice of their own, to be attracted to others of the same sex. But because we feel so strongly about the matter, we may find it hard to take this seriously. Even after we listen to the arguments, we may still have the unshakable feeling that homosexuals must, somehow, be an unsavory lot.

Cultural Relativism, by stressing that our moral views can reflect the prejudices of our society, provides an antidote for this kind of dogmatism. When he tells the story of the Greeks and Callatians, Herodotus adds:

> For if anyone, no matter who, were given the opportunity of choosing from amongst all the nations of the world the set of beliefs which he thought best, he would inevitably, after careful consideration of their relative merits, choose that of his own country. Everyone without exception believes his own native customs, and the religion he was brought up in, to be the best.

Realizing this can result in our having more open minds. We can come to understand that our feelings are not necessarily perceptions of the truth—they may be nothing more than the result of cultural conditioning. Thus when we hear it suggested that some element of our social code is *not* really the best, and we find ourselves instinctively resisting the suggestion, we might stop and remember this. Then we may be more open to discovering the truth, whatever that might be.

We can understand the appeal of Cultural Relativism, then, even though the theory has serious shortcomings. It is an attractive theory because it is based on a genuine insight, that many of the practices and attitudes we think so natural are really only cultural products. Moreover, keeping this thought firmly in view is important if we want to avoid arrogance and have open minds. These are important points, not to be taken lightly. But we can accept these points without going on to accept the whole theory.

CHAPTER 3

Subjectivism in Ethics

Take any action allow'd to be vicious: Wilful murder, for instance.
Examine it in all lights, and see if you can find that matter of fact, or
real existence, which you call vice . . . You can never find it, till you
turn your reflexion into your own breast, and find a sentiment of
disapprobation, which arises in you, toward this action. Here is a
matter of fact; but 'tis the object of feeling, not reason.

DAVID HUME, *A TREATISE OF HUMAN NATURE* (1740)

3.1. The Basic Idea of Ethical Subjectivism

In 2001 there was a mayoral election in New York, and when it
came time for the city's annual Gay Pride Day parade, every single Democratic and Republican candidate showed up to march.
"There is not a single candidate who can be described as not
good on our issues," said Matt Foreman, executive director of
the Empire State Pride Agenda, a gay rights organization. He
added that "In other parts of the country, the positions taken
here would be extremely unpopular, if not deadly at the polls."
The national Republican Party apparently agrees; at the urging
of religious conservatives, it has made opposition to gay rights a
part of its national stance.

What do people around the country actually think? The
Gallup Poll has been asking Americans "Do you feel that homosexuality should be considered an acceptable alternative
lifestyle or not?" since 1982, when 34% responded affirmatively.
The number has been rising, however, and in 2000, a majority—
52%—said that they think homosexuality should be considered
acceptable. This means, of course, that almost as many think
otherwise. People on both sides have strong feelings. The Rev-
erend Jerry Falwell spoke for many when he said in a television
interview, "Homosexuality is immoral. The so-called 'gay rights'

are not rights at all, because immorality is not right." Falwell is a Baptist. The Catholic view is more nuanced, but it agrees that gay sex is impermissible. Gays and lesbians, according to the *Catechism of the Catholic Church,* "do not choose their homosexual condition," and "They must be accepted with respect, compassion, and sensitivity. Every sign of unjust discrimination in their regard should be avoided." Nonetheless, "homosexual acts are intrinsically disordered" and "Under no circumstances can they be approved." Therefore, to lead virtuous lives, homosexual persons must be chaste.

What attitude should we take? We might say that homosexuality is immoral, or we might say it is all right. But there is a third alternative. We might say something like this:

> People have different opinions, but where morality is concerned, there are no "facts," and no one is "right." People just feel differently, and that's the end of it.

This is the basic thought behind Ethical Subjectivism. Ethical Subjectivism is the idea that our moral opinions are based on our feelings and nothing more. On this view, there is no such thing as "objective" right or wrong. It is a fact that some people are homosexual and some are heterosexual; but it is not a fact that one is good and the other bad. So when someone such as Falwell says that homosexuality is wrong, he is not stating a fact about homosexuality. Instead, he is merely saying something about his feelings toward it.

Of course, Ethical Subjectivism is not just an idea about the evaluation of homosexuality. It applies to all moral matters. To take a different example, it is a fact that the Nazis exterminated millions of innocent people; but according to Ethical Subjectivism, it is not a fact that what they did was evil. When we say their actions were evil, we are only saying that we have negative feelings toward them. The same applies to any moral judgment whatever.

3.2. The Evolution of the Theory

Often the development of a philosophical idea will go through several stages. At first the idea will be put forward in a crude, simple form, and many people will find it attractive for one reason or another. But then the idea will be subjected to critical analysis, and it will be found to have defects. Arguments will be made against it. At this point some people may be so impressed with the objections that they abandon the idea altogether, concluding that it cannot be right. Others, however, may continue to have confidence in the basic idea, and so they will try to refine it, giving it a new, improved formulation that will not be vulnerable to the objections. For a time it may appear that the theory has been saved. But then new arguments may be found that cast doubt on the new version of the theory. Once again the new objections may cause some to abandon the idea, while others keep the faith and try to salvage the theory by formulating still another "improved" version. The whole process of revision and criticism will then start over again.

The theory of Ethical Subjectivism has developed in just this way. It began as a simple idea—in the words of David Hume, that morality is a matter of sentiment rather than fact. But as objections were raised to the theory, and as its defenders tried to answer the objections, the theory evolved into something much more sophisticated.

3.3 The First Stage: Simple Subjectivism

The simplest version of the theory, which states the main idea but does not attempt to refine it very much, is this: When a person says that something is morally good or bad, this means that he or she approves of that thing, or disapproves of it, and nothing more. In other words:

> "X is morally acceptable"
> "X is right"   all mean: "I (the speaker)
> "X is good"   approve of X"
> "X ought to be done"

And similarly:

> "X is morally unacceptable"
> "X is wrong"   all mean: "I (the speaker)
> "X is bad"   disapprove of X"
> "X ought not to be done"

We may call this version of the theory Simple Subjectivism. It expresses the basic idea of Ethical Subjectivism in a plain, uncomplicated form, and many people have found it attractive. However, Simple Subjectivism is open to several objections, because it has implications that are contrary to what we know (or at least, contrary to what we think we know) about the nature of moral evaluation. Here are two of the most prominent objections.

Simple Subjectivism Cannot Account for Our Fallibility. None of us is infallible. We are sometimes wrong in our evaluations, and when we discover that we are mistaken, we may want to correct our judgments. But if Simple Subjectivism were correct, this would be impossible, because Simple Subjectivism implies that each of us is infallible.

Consider Falwell again, who says homosexuality is immoral. According to Simple Subjectivism, he is merely saying that he, Falwell, disapproves of homosexuality. Now, of course, it is possible that he is not speaking sincerely—it is possible that he really does not disapprove of homosexuality, but is merely playing to his conservative audience. However, if we assume he is speaking sincerely—if we assume he really does disapprove of it—then it follows that what he says is true. So long as he is honestly representing his own feelings, he cannot be mistaken.

But this contradicts the plain fact that none of us is infallible. We are sometimes wrong. Therefore, Simple Subjectivism cannot be correct.

Simple Subjectivism Cannot Account for Disagreement. The second argument against Simple Subjectivism is based on the idea that this theory cannot account for the fact of disagreement in ethics. Matt Foremen does not believe that homosexuality is immoral. So, on the face of it, it appears that he and Falwell disagree. But consider what Simple Subjectivism implies about this situation.

According to Simple Subjectivism, when Foreman says that homosexuality is not immoral, he is merely making a statement about his attitude—he is saying that he, Foreman, does not disapprove of homosexuality. Would Falwell disagree with that? No, Falwell would agree that Foreman does not disapprove of homosexuality. At the same time, when Falwell says that homosexuality is immoral, he is only saying that he, Falwell, disapproves of it. And how could anyone disagree with that? Thus, according to Simple Subjectivism, there is no disagreement between them; each should acknowledge the truth of what the other is saying. Surely, though, there is something wrong here, for Falwell and Foreman *do* disagree about whether homosexuality is immoral.

There is a kind of eternal frustration implied by Simple Subjectivism: Falwell and Foreman are deeply opposed to one another; yet they cannot even state their positions in a way that joins the issue. Foreman may try to deny what Falwell says, but according to Simple Subjectivism he succeeds only in changing the subject.

The argument may be summarized like this. When one person says "X is morally acceptable" and someone else says "X is morally unacceptable," they are disagreeing. However, if Simple Subjectivism were correct, there would be no disagreement between them. Therefore, Simple Subjectivism cannot be correct.

These arguments, and others like them, show that Simple Subjectivism is a flawed theory. It cannot be maintained, at least not in such a crude form. In the face of such arguments, some thinkers have chosen to reject the whole idea of Ethical Subjectivism. Others, however, have worked to produce a better version of the theory that would not be vulnerable to such objections.

3.4. The Second Stage: Emotivism

The improved version was a theory that came to be known as Emotivism. Developed chiefly by the American philosopher Charles L. Stevenson (1908–1979), Emotivism was one of the most influential theories of ethics in the 20th century. It is far more subtle and sophisticated than Simple Subjectivism.

Emotivism begins with the observation that language is used in a variety of ways. One of its principal uses is in stating facts, or at least in stating what we believe to be facts. Thus we may say:

> "Abraham Lincoln was president of the United States."
>
> "I have an appointment at four o'clock."
>
> "Gasoline costs $1.39 per gallon."
>
> "Shakespeare is the author of Hamlet."

In each case, we are saying something that is either true or false, and the purpose of our utterance is, typically, to convey information to the listener.

However, there are other purposes for which language may be used. Suppose I say "Close the door!" This utterance is neither true nor false. It is not a statement of any kind; it is a command, which is something different. Its purpose is not to convey information; rather, its purpose is to get you to do something. I am not trying to alter your beliefs; I am trying to influence your conduct.

Or consider utterances such as these, which are neither statements of fact nor commands:

"Hurrah for Abraham Lincoln!"

"Alas!"

"Would that gasoline did not cost so much!"

"Damn Hamlet."

These are familiar types of sentences that we understand easily enough. But none of them is "true" or "false." (It makes no sense to say, "It is true that hurrah for Abraham Lincoln" or "It is false that alas.") Again, these sentences are not used to state facts. Instead, they are used to express the speaker's attitudes.

We need to note clearly the difference between *reporting* an attitude and *expressing* the same attitude. If I say "I like Abraham Lincoln," I am reporting the fact that I have a positive attitude toward him. This is a statement of fact, which is either true or false. On the other hand, if I shout "Hurrah for Lincoln!" I am not stating any sort of fact, not even a fact about my attitudes. I am expressing an attitude, but I am not reporting that I have it.

Now, with these points in mind, let us turn our attention to moral language. According to Emotivism, moral language is not fact-stating language; it is not typically used to convey information. Its purpose is different. It is used, first, as a means of influencing people's behavior: If someone says "You ought not to do that," he is trying *to stop you from doing it.* Thus the utterance is more like a command than a statement of fact; it is as though he had said, "Don't do that!" Second, moral language is used to express (not report) one's attitude. Saying "Lincoln was a good man" is not like saying "I like Lincoln," but it is like saying "Hurrah for Lincoln!"

The difference between Emotivism and Simple Subjectivism should now be obvious. Simple Subjectivism interpreted ethical sentences as statements of fact, of a special kind—namely, as reports of the speaker's attitude. According to Simple Subjectivism, when Falwell says, "Homosexuality is immoral," this means the same as "I (Falwell) disapprove of homosexuality"—a statement of fact about Falwell's attitude. Emotivism, on the other hand, denies that his utterance states any fact at all, even a fact about himself. Instead, Emotivism interprets his utterance as equivalent to something like "Homosexuality—yecch!" or "Do not engage in homosexual acts!" or "Would that there was no homosexuality."

Now this may seem to be a trivial, nit-picking difference that isn't worth bothering with. But from a theoretical point of view, it is actually a very big and important difference. One way to see this is to consider again the arguments against Simple Subjectivism. While those arguments were severely embarrassing to Simple Subjectivism, they do not affect Emotivism at all.

1. The first argument was that if Simple Subjectivism is correct, then we are all infallible in our moral judgments; but we certainly are not infallible; therefore, Simple Subjectivism cannot be correct.

This argument is effective only because Simple Subjectivism interprets moral judgments as statements that can be true or false. "Infallible" means that one's judgments are always true; and Simple Subjectivism assigns moral judgments a meaning that *will* always be true, so long as the speaker is sincere. That is why, on that theory, people turn out to be infallible. Emotivism, on the other hand, does not interpret moral judgments as statements that are true-or-false; and so the same argument will not work against it. Because commands and expressions of attitude are not true-or-false, people cannot be "infallible" with respect to them.

2. The second argument had to do with moral disagreement. If Simple Subjectivism is correct, then when one person says "X is morally acceptable" and someone else says "X is morally unacceptable," they are not really disagreeing. They are, in fact, talking about entirely different things—each is making a statement about his or her own attitude with which the other can readily agree. But, the argument goes, people who say such things really are disagreeing with one another, and so Simple Subjectivism cannot be correct.

Emotivism emphasizes that there is more than one way in which people may disagree. Compare these two kinds of disagreement:

First: I believe that Lee Harvey Oswald acted alone in the assassination of John Kennedy, and you believe there was a conspiracy. This is a disagreement about the facts—I believe something to be true that you believe to be false.

Second: I favor gun-control legislation and you are opposed to it. Here, it is not our beliefs that are in conflict but our desires—I want something to happen that you do not want to happen. (You and I may agree about all the facts surrounding the gun-control controversy and still take different sides concerning what we want to see happen.)

In the first kind of disagreement, we believe different things, both of which cannot be true. In the second, we want different things, both of which cannot happen. Stevenson calls the latter kind of disagreement *disagreement in attitude,* and he contrasts it with disagreement *about* attitudes. You and I may agree in all our judgments about our attitudes: We agree that you are opposed to gun control, and we agree that I am for it. But we still disagree *in* our attitudes. Moral disagreements, says Stevenson, are like this: They are disagreements in attitude. Simple Subjectivism could not explain moral disagreement because, once it interpreted moral judgments as statements *about* attitudes, the disagreement vanished.

Simple Subjectivism was an attempt to capture the basic idea of Ethical Subjectivism and express it in an acceptable form. It ran into trouble because it assumed that moral judgments are statements about attitudes. Emotivism was better because it jettisoned the troublesome assumption and replaced it with a more sophisticated view of how moral language works. But as we shall see, Emotivism also had its difficulties. One of its main problems was that it could not account for the place of reason in ethics.

3.5. Are There Any Moral Facts?

A moral judgment—or for that matter, any kind of value judgment—must be supported by good reasons. If someone tells you that a certain action would be wrong, you may ask why it would be wrong, and if there is no satisfactory answer, you may reject that advice as unfounded. In this way, moral judgments are different from mere expressions of personal preference. If someone says "I like coffee," she does not need to have a reason; she may be making a statement about her personal taste and nothing more. But moral judgments require backing by reasons, and in the absence of such reasons, they are merely arbitrary.

Any adequate theory of the nature of moral judgment should, therefore, be able to give some account of the connection between moral judgments and the reasons that support them. It is at just this point that Emotivism foundered.

What did Emotivism imply about reasons? Remember that for the emotivist, a moral judgment is like a command—it is primarily a verbal means of trying to influence people's attitudes and conduct. The view of reasons that naturally goes with this basic idea is that reasons are any considerations that will have the desired effect, that will influence attitudes and conduct in the desired way. But consider what this means. Suppose I am trying to convince you that Goldbloom is a bad man (I am trying to influence your attitude toward him) and you are resisting. Knowing you are a bigot, I say: "Goldbloom, you know, is Jewish." That does the trick; your attitude toward him changes, and you agree that he is a scoundrel. It would seem that for the emotivist, then, the fact that Goldbloom is Jewish is, at least in some contexts, a reason in support of the judgment that he is a bad man. In fact, Stevenson takes exactly this view. In his classic work *Ethics and Language* (1944), he says: "*Any* statement about *any* fact which *any* speaker considers likely to alter attitudes may be adduced as a reason for or against an ethical judgment."

Obviously, something had gone wrong. Not just any fact can count as a reason in support of just any judgment. For one thing, the fact must be relevant to the judgment, and psychological influence does not necessarily bring relevance with it. (Jewishness is irrelevant to viciousness, regardless of the psychological connections in anyone's mind.) There is a small lesson and a larger lesson to be learned from this. The small lesson is that a particular moral theory, Emotivism, seems to be flawed, and with it, the whole idea of Ethical Subjectivism is brought into doubt. The larger lesson has to do with the importance of reason in ethics.

Hume emphasized that if we examine wicked actions— "wilful murder, for instance"—we will find no "matter of fact" corresponding to the wickedness. The universe, apart from our attitudes, contains no such facts. This realization has often been taken as cause for despair, because people assume this must mean that values have no "objective" status. But why should Hume's observation come as a surprise? Values are not the kinds of things that could exist in the way that stars and planets exist. (What would a "value," thus conceived, be like?) A fundamental mistake, which many people fall into when they think about this subject, is to assume just two possibilities:

1. There are moral facts, in the same way that there are facts about stars and planets; or
2. Our values are nothing more than the expression of our subjective feelings.

This is a mistake because it overlooks a crucial third possibility. People have not only feelings but reason, and that makes a big difference. It may be that:

3. Moral truths are truths of reason; that is, a moral judgment is true if it is backed by better reasons than the alternatives.

Thus, if we want to understand the nature of ethics, we must focus on reasons. A truth of ethics is a conclusion that is backed by reasons: The correct answer to a moral question is simply the answer that has the weight of reason on its side. Such truths are objective in the sense that they are true independently of what we might want or think. We cannot make something good or bad just by wishing it to be so, because we cannot merely will that the weight of reason be on its side or against it. And this also explains our fallibility: We can be wrong about what is good or bad because we can be wrong about what reason commends. Reason says what it says, regardless of our opinions or desires.

3.6. Are There Proofs in Ethics?

If Ethical Subjectivism is not true, why are so many people attracted to it? One reason is that science provides our paradigm of objectivity, and when we compare ethics to science, ethics seems to lack the features that make science so compelling. For example, it seems a great deficiency that there are no proofs in ethics. We can prove that the world is round, that there is no largest prime number, and that dinosaurs lived before human beings. But can we prove that abortion is right or wrong?

The general idea that moral judgments can't be proved sounds appealing. Anyone who has ever argued about a matter like abortion knows how frustrating it can be to try to "prove" that one's point of view is correct. However, if we inspect this idea more closely, it turns out to be dubious.

Suppose we consider a matter that is much simpler than abortion. A student says that a test given by a teacher was unfair. This is clearly a moral judgment—fairness is a basic moral value. Can this judgment be proved? The student might point out that the test covered in detail matters that were quite trivial, while ignoring matters the teacher had stressed as important. The test also included questions about some matters that were not covered in either the readings or the class discussions. Moreover, the test was so long that not even the best students could complete it in the time allowed (and it was to be graded on the assumption that it should be completed).

Suppose all this is true. And further suppose that the teacher, when asked to explain, has no defense to offer. In fact, the teacher, who is rather inexperienced, seems muddled about the whole thing and doesn't seem to have had any very clear idea of what he was doing. Now, hasn't the student proved the test was unfair? What more in the way of proof could we want? It is easy to think of other examples that make the same point:

Jones is a bad man. Jones is a habitual liar; he manipulates people; he cheats when he thinks he can get away with it; he is cruel to other people; and so on.

Dr. Smith is irresponsible. He bases his diagnoses on superficial considerations; he drinks before performing delicate surgery; he refuses to listen to other doctors' advice; and so on.

A certain used-car dealer is unethical. She conceals defects in her cars; she takes advantage of poor people by pressuring them into paying exorbitant prices for cars she knows to be defective; she runs misleading advertisements in any newspaper that will carry them; and so on.

The process of giving reasons might even be taken a step further. If one of our reasons for saying that Jones is a bad man is that he is a habitual liar, we can go on to explain why lying is bad. Lying is bad, first, because it harms people. If I give you false information, and you rely on it, things may go wrong for you in all sorts of ways. Second, lying is bad because it is a violation of trust. Trusting another person means leaving oneself vulnerable and unprotected. When I trust you, I simply believe what you say, without taking precautions; and when you lie, you take advantage of my trust. That is why being given the lie is such an intimate and personal offense. And finally, the rule requiring truthfulness is necessary for society to exist—if we could not assume that other people will speak truthfully, communication would be impossible, and if communication were impossible, society would be impossible.

So we can support our judgments with good reasons, and we can provide explanations of why those reasons matter. If we can do all this, and for an encore show that no comparable case can be made on the other side, what more in the way of "proof" could anyone want? It is nonsense to say, in the face of all this, that ethical judgments can be nothing more than "mere opinions."

Nevertheless, the impression that moral judgments are "unprovable" is remarkably persistent. Why do people believe this? Three points might be mentioned.

First, when proof is demanded, people often have in mind an inappropriate standard. They are thinking about observations and experiments in science; and when there are no comparable observations and experiments in ethics, they conclude that there is no proof. But in ethics, rational thinking consists in giving reasons, analyzing arguments, setting out and justifying principles, and the like. The fact that ethical reasoning differs from reasoning in science does not make it deficient.

Second, when we think of "proving our ethical opinions to be correct," we tend to think automatically of the most difficult issues. The question of abortion, for example, is enormously complicated and difficult. If we think only of questions like this, it is easy to believe that "proof" in ethics is impossible. But the same could be said of the sciences. There are complicated matters that physicists cannot agree on; and if we focused entirely on them, we might conclude that there are no proofs in physics. But of course, there are many simpler matters about which all competent physicists agree. Similarly, in ethics there are many simpler matters about which all reasonable people agree.

Finally, it is easy to conflate two matters that are really very different:

1. Proving an opinion to be correct.
2. Persuading someone to accept your proof.

You may have an impeccable argument that someone refuses to accept. But that does not mean that there must be something wrong with the argument or that "proof " is somehow unattainable. It may mean only that someone is being stubborn. When this happens, it should not be surprising. In ethics, we should expect people sometimes to refuse to listen to reason. After all, ethics may require us to do things we don't want to do, so it is only to be expected that we will try to avoid hearing its demands.

3.7. The Question of Homosexuality

We may conclude by returning to the dispute about homosexuality. If we consider the relevant reasons, what do we find? The most pertinent fact is that homosexuals are pursuing the only way of life that affords them a chance of happiness. Sex is a particularly strong urge—it isn't hard to understand why—and few people are able to fashion a happy life without satisfying their sexual needs. We should not, however, focus simply on sex. More than one gay writer has said that homosexuality is not about who you have sex with; it's about who you fall in love with. A good life, for gays and lesbians as well as for everyone else, may mean uniting with someone you love, with all that this involves. Moreover, individuals do not choose their sexual orientations; both homosexuals and heterosexuals find themselves to be what they are without having exercised any option in the matter. Thus to say that people should not express their homosexuality is, more often than not, to condemn them to unhappy lives.

If it could be shown that gays and lesbians pose some sort of threat to the rest of society, that would be a powerful argument for the other side. And in fact, people who share Falwell's view have often claimed as much. But when examined dispassionately, those claims have always turned out to have no factual basis. Apart from the nature of their sexual relationships, there is no difference between homosexuals and heterosexuals in their moral characters or in their contributions to society. The idea that homosexuals are somehow sinister characters proves to be a myth similar to the myth that black people are lazy or that Jews are avaricious.

The case against homosexuality thus reduces to the familiar claim that it is "unnatural," or to the claim often made by religious conservatives that it is a threat to "family values." As for the first argument, it is hard to know what to make of it because the notion of "unnaturalness" is so vague. What exactly does it mean? There are at least three possible meanings.

First, "unnatural" might be taken as a statistical notion. In this sense, a human quality is unnatural if it is not shared by most people. Homosexuality would be unnatural in this sense, but so would left-handedness. Clearly, this is no reason to judge it bad. On the contrary, rare qualities are often good.

Second, the meaning of "unnatural" might be connected with the idea of a thing's *purpose*. The parts of our bodies seem to serve particular purposes. The purpose of the eyes is to see, and the purpose of the heart is to pump blood. Similarly, the purpose of our genitals is procreation: Sex is for making babies. It may be argued, then, that gay sex is unnatural because it is sexual activity that is divorced from its natural purpose.

This seems to express what many people have in mind when they object to homosexuality as unnatural. However, if gay sex were condemned for this reason, a host of other sexual practices would also have to be condemned: masturbation, oral sex, and even sex by women after menopause. They would be just as "unnatural" (and, presumably, just as bad) as gay sex. But there is no reason to accept these conclusions, because this whole line of reasoning is faulty. It rests on the assumption that *it is wrong to use parts of one's body for anything other than their natural purposes,* and this is surely false. The "purpose" of the eyes is to see; is it therefore wrong to use one's eyes for flirting or for giving a signal? Again, the "purpose" of the fingers may be grasping and poking; is it therefore wrong to snap one's fingers to keep time with music? Other examples come easily to mind. The idea that it is wrong to use things for any purpose other than their "natural" ones cannot reasonably be maintained, and so this version of the argument fails.

Third, because the word *unnatural* has a sinister sound, it might be understood simply as a term of evaluation. Perhaps it means something like "contrary to what a person ought to be." But if that is what "unnatural" means, then to say that something is wrong because it is unnatural would be vacuous. It would be like saying thus-and-so is wrong because it is wrong.

This sort of empty remark, of course, provides no reason for condemning anything.

The idea that homosexuality is unnatural, and that there is something wrong with this, has great intuitive appeal for many people. Nevertheless, it appears that this is an unsound argument. If no better understanding of "unnatural" can be found, this whole way of thinking will have to be rejected.

But what of the claim, often heard from religious fundamentalists, that homosexuality is contrary to "family values"? Falwell and others like him often say that their condemnation of homosexuality is part of their general support of "the family," as is their condemnation of divorce, abortion, pornography, and adultery. But how, exactly, is homosexuality opposed to family values? The campaign for gay rights involves a whole host of proposals designed to make it easier for gays and lesbians to form families—there are demands for social recognition of same-sex marriages, for the right to adopt children, and so on. Gay and lesbian activists find it ironic that the proponents of family values wish to deny them precisely these rights.

There is one other, specifically religious argument that must be mentioned, namely that homosexuality is condemned in the Bible. Leviticus 18:22 says "You may not lie with a man as with a woman; it is an abomination." Some commentators have said that, contrary to appearances, the Bible is really not so harsh about homosexuality; and they explain how each relevant passage (there seem to be nine of them) should be understood. But suppose we concede that the Bible really does teach that homosexuality is an abomination. What may we infer from this? Sacred books have an honored place in religious life, of course, but there are two problems with relying on the literal text for guidance. One problem is practical and one is theoretical.

The practical problem is that sacred texts, especially ones composed a very long time ago, give us more than we bargain for. Not many people have actually read Leviticus, but if they did, they would find that in addition to prohibiting homosexuality, it gives lengthy instructions for treating leprosy, detailed requirements concerning burnt offerings, and an elaborate routine for dealing with women who are menstruating. There is a surprising number of rules about the daughters of priests, including the notation that if a priest's daughter "plays the whore," she shall be burned alive (21:9). Leviticus forbids eating fat (7:23), letting a woman into church until 42 days after giving birth (12:4-5), and seeing your uncle naked. The latter, incidentally, is also called an abomination (18: 14, 26). It says that a beard must have square corners (19:27) and that we may purchase slaves from neighboring states (25:44). There is much more, but this is enough to give the idea.

The problem is that you cannot conclude that homosexuality is an abomination simply because it says so in Leviticus unless you are willing to conclude, also, that these other instructions are moral requirements; and in the 21st century anyone who tried to live according to all those rules would go crazy. One might, of course, concede that the rules about menstruation, and so on, were peculiar to an ancient culture and that they are not binding on us today. That would be sensible. But if we say that, the door is open for saying the same thing about the rule against homosexuality.

In any case, nothing can be morally right or wrong *simply* because an authority says so. If the precepts in a sacred text are not arbitrary, there must be some reason for them—we should be able to ask *why* the Bible condemns homosexuality, and expect an answer. That answer will then give the real explanation of why it is wrong. This is the "theoretical" problem that I mentioned: In the logic of moral reasoning, the reference to the text drops out, and the reason behind the pronouncement (if any) takes its place.

But the main point here is not about homosexuality. The main point concerns the nature of moral thinking. Moral thinking and moral conduct are a matter of weighing reasons and being guided by them. But being guided by reason is very different from following one's feelings. When we have strong feelings, we may be tempted to ignore reason and go with the feelings. But in doing so, we would be opting out of moral thinking altogether. That is why, in focusing on attitudes and feelings, Ethical Subjectivism seems to be going in the wrong direction.

CHAPTER 4

*D*oes Morality Depend on Religion?

The Good consists in always doing what God wills at any particular moment.

        EMIL BRUNNER, *THE DIVINE IMPERATIVE* (1947)

I respect deities. I do not rely upon them.

        MUSASHI MIYAMOTO, AT ICHIJOJI TEMPLE (CA. 1608)

4.1. The Presumed Connection between Morality and Religion

In 1984 Governor Mario Cuomo of New York announced that he would appoint a special panel to advise him on ethical issues. The governor pointed out that "Like it or not, we are increasingly involved in life-and-death matters." As examples, he mentioned abortion, the problem of handicapped babies, the right to die, and assisted reproduction. The purpose of the panel would be to provide the governor with "expert assistance" in thinking about the moral dimensions of these and other matters.

But who, exactly, would sit on such a panel? The answer tells us a lot about who, in this country, is thought to speak for morality. The answer is: representatives of organized religion. According to the *New York Times*, "Mr. Cuomo, in an appearance at St. Francis College in Brooklyn, said he had invited Roman Catholic, Protestant and Jewish leaders to join the group."

Few people, at least in the United States, would find this remarkable. Among western democracies, the U.S. is an unusually religious country. Nine out of ten Americans say they believe in a personal God; in Denmark and Sweden, the figure is only one in five. It is not unusual for priests and ministers to be treated as moral experts. Most hospitals, for example, have ethics committees, and these committees usually include three types of members: healthcare professionals to advise about technical matters, lawyers to handle legal issues, and religious representatives to address the moral questions. When newspapers want comments about the ethical dimensions of a story, they call upon the clergy, and the clergy are happy to oblige. Priests and ministers are assumed to be wise counselors who will give sound moral advice when it is needed.

Why are clergymen regarded in this way? The reason is not that they have proven to be better or wiser than other people— as a group, they seem to be neither better nor worse than the rest of us. There is a deeper reason why they are regarded as having special moral insight. In popular thinking, morality and religion are inseparable: People commonly believe that morality can be understood only in the context of religion. So because clergymen are the spokesmen for religion, it is assumed that they must be spokesmen for morality as well.

It is not hard to see why people think this. When viewed from a nonreligious perspective, the universe seems to be a cold, meaningless place, devoid of value and purpose. In his essay "A Free Man's Worship," written in 1902, Bertrand Russell expressed what he called the "scientific" view of the world:

> That Man is the product of causes which had no prevision of the end they were achieving; that his origin, his growth, his hopes and fears, his loves and his beliefs, are but the outcome of accidental collocations of atoms; that no fire, no heroism, no intensity of thought and feeling, can preserve an individual life beyond the grave; that all the labours of the ages, all the devotion, all the inspiration, all the noonday brightness of human genius, are destined to extinction in the vast death of the solar system, and that the whole temple of Man's achievement must inevitably be buried beneath the debris of a universe in ruins—all these things, if not quite beyond dispute, are yet so nearly certain, that no philosophy which rejects them can hope to stand. Only within the scaffolding of these truths, only on the firm foundation of unyielding despair, can the soul's habitation henceforth be safely built.

From a religious perspective, however, things look very different. Judaism and Christianity teach that the world was created by a loving, all-powerful God to provide a home for us. We, in turn, were created in his image, to be his children. Thus the world is not devoid of meaning and purpose. It is, instead, the arena in which God's plans and purposes are realized. What could be more natural, then, than to think that "morality" is a part of the religious view of the world, whereas the atheist's world has no place for values?

4.2. The Divine Command Theory

In the major theistic traditions, including Judaism, Christianity, and Islam, God is conceived as a lawgiver who has laid down rules that we are to obey. He does not compel us to obey them. We were created as free agents, so we may choose to accept or to reject his commandments. But if we are to live as we should live, we must follow God's laws. This conception has been elaborated by some theologians into a theory about the nature of right and wrong known as the Divine Command Theory. Essentially, this theory says that "morally right" means "commanded by God" and "morally wrong" means "forbidden by God."

This theory has a number of attractive features. It immediately solves the old problem about the objectivity of ethics. Ethics is not merely a matter of personal feeling or social custom. Whether something is right or wrong is perfectly objective: It is right if God commands it, wrong if God forbids it. Moreover, the Divine Command Theory suggests an answer to the perennial question of why anyone should bother with morality. Why not forget about "ethics" and just look out for oneself? If immorality is the violation of God's commandments, there is an easy answer: On the day of final reckoning, you will be held accountable.

There are, however, serious problems for the theory. Of course, atheists would not accept it, because they do not believe that God exists. But there are difficulties even for believers. The main problem was first noted by Plato, the Greek philosopher who lived 400 years before the birth of Jesus.

Plato's writings were in the form of dialogues, usually between Socrates and one or more interlocutors. In one of these dialogues, the *Euthyphro*, there is a discussion concerning whether "right" can be defined as "that which the gods command." Socrates is skeptical and asks: Is conduct right because the gods command it, or do the gods command it because it is right? This is one of the most famous questions in the history of philosophy. The British philosopher Antony Flew suggests that "one good test of a person's aptitude for philosophy is to discover whether he can grasp its force and point."

The point is that if we accept the theological conception of right and wrong, we are caught in a dilemma. Socrates's question asks us to clarify what we mean. There are two things we might mean, and both lead to trouble.

1. First, we might mean that *right conduct is right because God commands it.* For example, according to Exodus 20:16, God commands us to be truthful. On this option, the reason we should be truthful is simply that God requires it. Apart from the divine command, truth telling is neither good nor bad. It is God's command that *makes* truthfulness right.

But this leads to trouble, for it represents God's commands as arbitrary. It means that God could have given different commands just as easily. He could have commanded us to be liars, and then lying, and not truthfulness, would be right. (You may be tempted to reply: "But God would never command us to lie." But why not? If he did endorse lying, God would not be commanding us to do wrong, because his command would make it right.) Remember that on this view, honesty was not right before God commanded it. Therefore, he could have had no more reason to command it than its opposite; and so, from a moral point of view, his command is arbitrary.

Another problem is that, on this view, the doctrine of the goodness of God is reduced to nonsense. It is important to religious believers that God is not only all-powerful and all-knowing, but that he is also good; yet if we accept the idea that good and bad are defined by reference to God's will, this notion is deprived of any meaning. What could it mean to say that God's commands are good? If "X is good" means "X is commanded by God," then "God's commands are good" would mean only "God's commands are commanded by God," an empty truism. In 1686, Leibniz observed in his *Discourse on Metaphysics:*

> So in saying that things are not good by any rule of goodness, but sheerly by the will of God, it seems to me that one destroys, without realizing it, all the love of God and all his

glory. For why praise him for what he has done if he would be equally praiseworthy in doing exactly the contrary?

Thus if we choose the first of Socrates's two options, we seem to be stuck with consequences that even the most religious people would find unacceptable.

2. There is a way to avoid these troublesome consequences. We can take the second of Socrates's options. We need not say that right conduct is right because God commands it. Instead, we may say that God commands us to do certain things *because they are right*. God, who is infinitely wise, realizes that truthfulness is better than deceitfulness, and so he commands us to be truthful; he sees that killing is wrong, and so he commands us not to kill; and so on for all the moral rules.

If we take this option, we avoid the troublesome consequences that spoiled the first alternative. God's commands are not arbitrary; they are the result of his wisdom in knowing what is best. And the doctrine of the goodness of God is preserved: To say that his commands are good means that he commands only what, in perfect wisdom, he sees to be best.

Unfortunately, however, this second option leads to a different problem, which is equally troublesome. In taking this option, we have abandoned the theological conception of right and wrong—when we say that God commands us to be truthful because truthfulness is right, we are acknowledging a standard of right and wrong that is independent of God's will. The rightness exists prior to and independent of God's command, and it is the reason for the command. Thus, if we want to know why we should be truthful, the reply "Because God commands it" does not really tell us, for we may still ask "But why does God command it?" and the answer to *that* question will provide the underlying reason why truthfulness is a good thing.

All this may be summarized in the following argument:

(1) Suppose God commands us to do what is right. Then either (a) the right actions are right because he commands them or (b) he commands them because they are right.

(2) If we take option (a), then God's commands are, from a moral point of view, arbitrary; moreover, the doctrine of the goodness of God is rendered meaningless.

(3) If we take option (b), then we will have acknowledged a standard of right and wrong that is independent of God's will. We will have, in effect, given up the theological conception of right and wrong.

(4) Therefore, we must either regard God's commands as arbitrary, and give up the doctrine of the goodness of God, or admit that there is a standard of right and wrong that is independent of his will, and give up the theological conception of right and wrong.

(5) From a religious point of view, it is unacceptable to regard God's commands as arbitrary or to give up the doctrine of the goodness of God.

(6) Therefore, even from a religious point of view, a standard of right and wrong that is independent of God's will must be accepted.

Many religious people believe that they must accept a theological conception of right and wrong because it would be impious not to do so. They feel, somehow, that if they believe in God, they should say that right and wrong are to be defined in terms of his will. But this argument suggests otherwise: It suggests that, on the contrary, the Divine Command Theory itself leads to impious results, so that a devout person should not accept it. And in fact, some of the greatest theologians, such as St. Thomas Aquinas (1225–1274), rejected the theory for just this reason. Thinkers such as Aquinas connect morality with religion in a different way.

4.3. The Theory of Natural Law

In the history of Christian thought, the dominant theory of ethics is not the Divine Command Theory. That honor goes to the Theory of Natural Law. This theory has three main parts.

1. The Theory of Natural Law rests upon a certain view of what the world is like. On this view, the world is a rational order with values and purposes built into its very nature. This conception derives from the Greeks, whose way of understanding the world dominated Western thinking for over 1,700 years. A central feature of this conception was the idea that *everything in nature has a purpose.*

Aristotle incorporated this idea into his system of thought around 350 B.C. when he said that, in order to understand any thing, four questions must be asked: What is it? What is it made of? How did it come to exist? And what is it for? (The answers might be: This is a knife, it is made of metal, it was made by a craftsman, and it is used for cutting.) Aristotle assumed that the last question—what is it for?—could sensibly be asked of anything whatever. "Nature," he said, "belongs to the class of causes which act for the sake of something."

It seems obvious that artifacts such as knives have purposes, because craftsmen have a purpose in mind when they make them. But what about natural objects that we do not make? Aristotle believed that they have purposes too. One of his examples was that we have teeth so that we can chew. Such biological examples are quite persuasive; each part of our bodies does seem, intuitively, to have a special purpose—eyes are for seeing, the heart is for pumping blood, and so on. But Aristotle's claim was not limited to organic beings. According to him, *everything* has a purpose. He thought, to take a different sort of example, that rain falls so that plants can grow. As odd as it may seem to a modern reader, Aristotle was perfectly serious about this. He considered other alternatives, such as that the rain falls "of necessity" and that this helps the plants only by "coincidence," and rejected them.

The world, therefore, is an orderly, rational system, with each thing having its own proper place and serving its own special purpose. There is a neat hierarchy: The rain exists for the sake of the plants, the plants exist for the sake of the animals, and the animals exist—of course—for the sake of people, whose well-being is the point of the whole arrangement.

> [W]e must believe, first that plants exist for the sake of animals, second that all other animals exist for the sake of man, tame animals for the use he can make of them as well as for the food they provide; and as for wild animals, most though not all of these can be used for food or are useful in other ways; clothing and instruments can be made out of them. If then we are right in believing that nature makes nothing without some end in view, nothing to no purpose, it must be that nature has made all things specifically for the sake of man.

This seems stunningly anthropocentric. Aristotle may be forgiven, however, when we consider that virtually every important thinker in our history has entertained some such thought. Humans are a remarkably vain species.

The Christian thinkers who came later found this view of the world to be perfectly congenial. Only one thing was missing: God was needed to make the picture complete. (Aristotle had denied that God was a necessary part of the picture. For him, the worldview we have outlined was not religious; it was simply a description of how things are.) Thus the Christian thinkers said that the rain falls to help the plants *because that is what the Creator intended,* and the animals are for human use because *that is what God made them for.* Values and purposes were, therefore, conceived to be a fundamental part of the nature of things, because the world was believed to have been created according to a divine plan.

2. A corollary of this way of thinking is that "the laws of nature" not only describe how things *are,* they specify how things *ought to be* as well. Things are as they ought to be when they are serving their natural purposes. When they do not, or cannot, serve those purposes, things have gone wrong. Eyes that cannot see are defective, and drought is a natural evil; the badness of both is explained by reference to natural law. But there are also implications for human conduct. Moral rules are now viewed as deriving from the laws of nature. Some ways of behaving are said to be "natural," while others are "unnatural"; and "unnatural" acts are said to be morally wrong.

Consider, for example, the duty of beneficence. We are morally required to be concerned for our neighbor's welfare as well as for our own. Why? According to the Theory of Natural Law, beneficence is natural for us, considering the kind of creatures we are. We are by our nature social creatures who want and need the company of other people. It is also part of our natural makeup that we care about others. Someone who does not care at all for others—who really does not care, through and through—is seen as deranged, in the terms of modern psychology, as a sociopath. A malicious personality is defective, just as eyes are defective if they cannot see. And, it may be added, this is true because we were created by God, with a specific "human" nature, as part of his overall plan for the world.

The endorsement of beneficence is relatively uncontroversial. Natural law theory has also been used, however, to support moral views that are more contentious. Religious thinkers have traditionally condemned "deviant" sexual practices, and the theoretical justification of their opposition has come more often than not from theory of natural law. If everything has a purpose, what is the purpose of sex? The obvious answer is procreation. Sexual activity that is not connected with making babies can therefore be viewed as "unnatural," and so such practices as masturbation and oral sex—not to mention gay sex—can be condemned for this reason. This way of thinking about sex dates back at least to St. Augustine in the fourth century, and it is explicit in the writings of St. Thomas Aquinas. (For a critical discussion of this argument about sex, see section 3.7 in this book.) The moral theology of the Catholic Church is based on natural law theory. This line of thought lies behind its whole sexual ethic.

Outside the Catholic Church, the Theory of Natural Law has few advocates today. It is generally rejected for two reasons. First, it seems to involve a confusion of "is" and "ought." In the 18th century David Hume pointed out that *what is the case* and *what ought to be the case* are logically different notions, and no conclusion about one follows from the other. We can say that people are naturally disposed to be beneficent, but it does not follow that they should be beneficent. Similarly, it may be that sex does produce babies, but it does not follow that sex ought or ought not to be engaged in only for that purpose. Facts are one thing; values are another. The Theory of Natural Law seems to conflate them.

Second, the Theory of Natural Law has gone out of fashion (although that does not, of course, prove it is false) because the view of the world on which it rests is out of keeping with modern science. The world as described by Galileo, Newton, and Darwin has no place for "facts" about right and wrong. Their explanations of natural phenomena make no reference to values or purposes. What happens just happens, fortuitously, in consequence of the laws of cause and effect. If the rain benefits the plants, it is only because the plants have evolved by the laws of natural selection in a rainy climate.

Thus modern science gives us a picture of the world as a realm of facts, where the only "natural laws" are the laws of physics, chemistry, and biology, working blindly and without purpose. Whatever values may be, they are not part of the natural order. As for the idea that "nature has made all things specifically for the sake of man," that is only human vanity. To the extent that one accepts the worldview of modern science, then, one will be skeptical of the Theory of Natural Law. It is no accident that the theory was a product, not of modern thought, but of the Middle Ages.

3. The third part of the theory addresses the question of moral knowledge. How are we to go about determining what is right and what is wrong? The Divine Command Theory says that we must consult God's commandments. The Theory of Natural Law gives a different answer. The "natural laws" that specify what we should do are laws of reason, which we are able to grasp because God, the author of the natural order, has made us rational beings with the power to understand that order. Therefore, the Theory of Natural Law endorses the familiar idea that the right thing to do is whatever course of conduct has the best reasons on its side. To use the traditional terminology, moral judgments are "dictates of reason." St. Thomas Aquinas, the greatest of the natural-law theorists, wrote in his masterpiece the *Summa Theologica* that "To disparage the dictate of reason is equivalent to condemning the command of God."

This means that the religious believer has no special access to moral truth. The believer and the nonbeliever are in the same position. God has given both the same powers of reasoning; and so believer and nonbeliever alike may listen to reason and follow its directives. They function as moral agents in the same way, even though the nonbelievers' lack of faith prevents them from realizing that God is the author of the rational order in which they participate and which their moral judgments express.

In an important sense, this leaves morality independent of religion. Religious belief does not affect the calculation of what is best, and the results of moral inquiry are religiously "neutral." In this way, even though they may disagree about religion, believers and nonbelievers inhabit the same moral universe.

4.4. Religion and Particular Moral Issues

Some religious people will find the preceding discussion unsatisfying. It will seem too abstract to have any bearing on their actual moral lives. For them, the connection between morality and religion is an immediate, practical matter that centers on particular moral issues. It doesn't matter whether right and wrong are "defined" in terms of God's will or whether moral laws are laws of nature: Whatever the merits of such theories, there are still the moral teachings of one's religion about particular issues. The teachings of the Scriptures and the church are regarded as authoritative, determining the moral positions one must take. To mention only one example, many Christians think that they have no choice but to oppose abortion because it is condemned both by the church and (they assume) by the Scriptures.

Are there, in fact, distinctively religious positions on major moral issues, which believers are bound to accept? If so, are those positions different from the views that other people might reach simply by trying to reason out the best thing to do? The rhetoric of the pulpit suggests that the answer to both questions is yes. But there are several reasons to think otherwise.

In the first place, it is often difficult to find specific moral guidance in the Scriptures. Our problems are not the same as the problems faced by the Jews and the early Christians many centuries ago; thus, it is not surprising that the Scriptures might be silent about moral issues that seem urgent to us. The Bible contains a number of general precepts, such as the injunctions to love one's neighbor and to treat others as one would wish to be treated oneself, that might be thought relevant to a variety of issues. But worthy as those precepts are, they do not yield definite answers about exactly what position one should take concerning the rights of workers, the extinction of species, the funding of medical research, and so on.

Another problem is that in many instances the Scriptures and church tradition are ambiguous. Authorities disagree, leaving the believer in the awkward position of having to choose which element of the tradition to accept and which authority to believe. Read plainly, for example, the New Testament condemns being rich, and there is a long tradition of self-denial and charitable giving that affirms this teaching. But there is also an obscure Old Testament figure named Jabez who asked God to "enlarge my territories" (I Chronicles 4:10), and God did. A recent book urging Christians to adopt Jabez as their model became a best-seller.

Thus when people say that their moral views are derived from their religious commitments, they are often mistaken. In reality, something very different is going on. They are making up their minds about the moral issues first and then interpreting the Scriptures, or church tradition, in such a way as to support the moral conclusion they have already reached. Of course this does not happen in every case, but it seems fair to say that it happens often. The question of riches is one example; abortion is another. In the debate over abortion, religious issues are never far from the center of discussion. Religious conservatives hold that the fetus is a human being from the moment of conception, and so they say killing it is really a form of murder. They do not believe it should be the mother's choice whether to have an abortion, because that would be like saying she is free to commit murder.

The key premise in the conservative argument is that the fetus is a human being from the moment of conception. The fertilized ovum is not merely a potential human being but an actual human being with a full-fledged right to life. Liberals, of course, deny this—they say that, at least during the early weeks of pregnancy, the embryo is something less than a full human being.

The debate over the humanity of the fetus is enormously complicated, but here we are concerned with just one small part of it. Conservative Christians sometimes say that, regardless of how secular thought might view the fetus, the Christian view is that the fetus is a human being from its very beginning. But is this view mandatory for Christians? What evidence might be offered to show this? One might appeal to the Scriptures or to church tradition.

The Scriptures. It is difficult to derive a prohibition of abortion from either the Jewish or the Christian Scriptures. The Bible does not speak plainly on the matter. There are certain passages, however, that are often quoted by conservatives because they seem to suggest that fetuses have full human status. One of the most frequently cited passages is from the first chapter of Jeremiah, in which God is quoted as saying: "Before I formed you in the womb I knew you, and before you were born I consecrated you." These words are presented as though they were God's endorsement of the conservative position: They are taken to mean that the unborn, as well as the born, are "consecrated" to God.

In context, however, these words obviously mean something quite different. Suppose we read the whole passage in which they occur:

> Now the word of the Lord came to me saying, "Before I formed you in the womb I knew you, and before you were

born I consecrated you; I appointed you a prophet to the
nations."
Then I said, "Ah, Lord God! Behold, I do not know
how to speak, for I am only a youth." But the Lord said
to me,
"Do not say, 'I am only a youth' for to all to whom I
send you you shall go, and whatever I command you you
shall speak. Be not afraid of them, for I am with you to de-
liver you," says the Lord.

Neither abortion, the sanctity of fetal life, nor anything else of
the kind is being discussed in this passage. Instead, Jeremiah is
asserting his authority as a prophet. He is saying, in effect, "God
authorized me to speak for him; even though I resisted, he commanded me to speak." But Jeremiah puts the point more poet-
ically; he has God saying that God had intended him to be a
prophet even before Jeremiah was born.

This often happens when the Scriptures are cited in connection with controversial moral issues. A few words are lifted from a
passage that is concerned with something entirely different from
the issue at hand, and those words are then construed in a way that
supports a favored moral position. When this happens, is it accurate to say that the person is "following the moral teachings of the
Bible"? Or is it more accurate to say that he or she is searching the
Scriptures for support of a moral view he or she already happens
to think is right, and reading the desired conclusion into the
Scriptures? If the latter, it suggests an especially impious attitude—
an attitude that assumes God himself must share one's own moral
opinions. In the case of the passage from Jeremiah, it is hard to see
how an impartial reader could think the words have anything to
do with abortion, even by implication.

The scriptural passage that comes closest to making a specific judgment about the moral status of fetuses occurs in the
21st chapter of Exodus. This chapter is part of a detailed description of the law of the ancient Israelites. Here the penalty
for murder is said to be death; however, it is also said that if a
pregnant woman is caused to have a miscarriage, the penalty is
only a fine, to be paid to her husband. Murder was not a category that included fetuses. The Law of Israel apparently regarded fetuses as something less than full human beings.

Church Tradition. Even if there is little scriptural basis for it,
the contemporary church's stand is strongly antiabortion. The

typical churchgoer will hear ministers, priests, and bishops denouncing abortion in the strongest terms. It is no wonder, then, that many people feel that their religious commitment binds them to oppose abortion.

But it is worth noting that the church has not always taken this view. In fact, the idea that the fetus is a human being "from the moment of conception" is a relatively new idea, even within the Christian church. St. Thomas Aquinas held that an embryo does not have a soul until several weeks into the pregnancy. Aquinas accepted Aristotle's view that the soul is the "substantial form" of man. We need not go into this somewhat technical notion, except to note that one implication is that one cannot have a human soul until one's body has a recognizably human shape. Aquinas knew that a human embryo does not have a human shape "from the moment of conception," and he drew the indicated conclusion. Aquinas's view of the matter was officially accepted by the church at the Council of Vienne in 1312, and to this day it has never been officially repudiated.

However, in the 17th century, a curious view of fetal development came to be accepted, and this had unexpected consequences for the church's view of abortion. Peering through primitive microscopes at fertilized ova, some scientists imagined that they saw tiny, perfectly formed people. They called the little person a "homunculus," and the idea took hold that from the very beginning the human embryo is a fully formed creature that needs only to get bigger and bigger until it is ready to be born.

If the embryo has a human shape from the moment of conception, then it follows, according to Aristotle's and Aquinas's philosophy, that it can have a human soul from the moment of conception. The church drew this conclusion and embraced the conservative view of abortion. The "homunculus," it said, is clearly a human being, and so it is wrong to kill it.

However, as our understanding of human biology progressed, scientists began to realize that this view of fetal development was wrong. There is no homunculus; that was a mistake. Today we know that Aquinas's original thought was right—embryos start out as a cluster of cells; "human form" comes later. But when the biological error was corrected, the church's moral view did not revert to the older position. Having adopted the theory that the fetus is a human being "from the moment of conception," the church did not let it go and held fast to the conservative view of abortion. The Council of Vienne notwithstanding, it has held that view to this day.

Because the church did not traditionally regard abortion as a serious moral issue, Western law (which developed under the church's influence) did not traditionally treat abortion as a crime. Under the English common law, abortion was tolerated even if performed late in the pregnancy. In the United States, there were no laws prohibiting it until well into the 19th century. Thus when the U.S. Supreme Court declared the absolute prohibition of abortion to be unconstitutional in 1973, the Court was not overturning a long tradition of moral and legal opinion. It was only restoring a legal situation that had always existed until quite recently.

The purpose of reviewing this history is not to suggest that the contemporary church's position is wrong. For all that has been said here, its view may be right. I only want to make a point about the relation between religious authority and moral judgment. Church tradition, like Scripture, is reinterpreted by every generation to support its favored moral views. Abortion is just an example of this. We could just as easily have used shifting moral and religious views about slavery, or the status of women, or capital punishment, as our example. In each instance, people's moral convictions are not so much derived from their religion as superimposed on it.

The various arguments in this chapter point to a common conclusion. Right and wrong are not to be defined in terms of God's will; morality is a matter of reason and conscience, not religious faith; and in any case, religious considerations do not provide definitive solutions to the specific moral problems that confront us. Morality and religion are, in a word, different. Because this conclusion is contrary to conventional wisdom, it may strike some readers as antireligious. Therefore, it should be emphasized that this conclusion has not been reached by questioning the validity of religion. The arguments we have considered do not assume that Christianity or any other theological system is false; these arguments merely show that even if such a system is true, morality remains an independent matter.

CHAPTER 5

Psychological Egoism

> But the age of chivalry is gone. That of sophisters, economists, and calculators, has succeeded.
> EDMUND BURKE, *REFLECTIONS ON THE REVOLUTION IN FRANCE* (1790)

5.1. Is Unselfishness Possible?

Raoul Wallenberg, a Swedish businessman who could have stayed safely at home, spent the closing days of World War II in Budapest. Wallenberg had volunteered to be sent there as part of Sweden's diplomatic mission after he heard reports about Hitler's "final solution to the Jewish problem." Once there, he successfully pressured the Hungarian government to stop the deportations to the concentration camps. When the Hungarian government was replaced by a Nazi puppet regime, and the deportations resumed, Wallenberg issued "Swedish Protective Passes" to thousands of Jews, insisting that they all had connections with Sweden and were under the protection of his government. He helped many individuals find places to hide. When they were rounded up, Wallenberg would stand between them and the Nazis, telling the Germans that they would have to shoot him first. At the very end of the war, when everything was chaos and the other diplomats were fleeing, Wallenberg stayed behind. He is credited with saving as many as 120,000 lives. When the war was over, he disappeared, and for a long time no one knew what had happened to him. Now it is believed that he was killed, not by the Germans but by the Soviet occupation forces. Wallenberg's story is more dramatic than most, but it is by no means unique. The Israeli government has documented 6,000 instances of Gentiles protecting their Jewish neighbors during the Holocaust, and there are no doubt thousands more.

Morality demands that we be unselfish. *How* unselfish is a hard question. (Moral theories have been criticized both for requiring too much and for requiring too little.) Perhaps we are not required to be as heroic as Raoul Wallenberg, but still, we are expected to be attentive to other people's needs at least to some degree.

And people do help one another, in ways big and small. People do favors for one another. They build homeless shelters. They volunteer in hospitals. They donate organs and give blood. Mothers sacrifice for their children. Firefighters risk death to rescue people. Nuns spend their lives working among the poor. The list could go on and on. Many people give money to support worthy causes, when they could keep it for themselves. Peter Singer writes that one day

> my mail brought me the newsletter of the Australian Conservation Foundation, Australia's leading conservation lobby group. It included an article by the Foundation's fund-raising co-ordinator, in which he reported on a trip to thank a donor who had regularly sent donations of $1,000 or more. When he reached the address he thought something must be wrong; he was in front of a very modest suburban home. But there was no mistake: David Allsop, an employee of the state department of public works, donates 50 percent of his income to environmental causes.

These are remarkable stories, but should they be taken at face value? Are these people really as unselfish as they seem? In this chapter we will examine some arguments which say that, in fact, no one is ever really unselfish. This may seem absurd, considering the examples we have just listed. Nonetheless, there is a theory of human nature, once widely held among philosophers, psychologists, and economists, and still held by many ordinary people, that says we are not capable of being unselfish. According to this theory, known as Psychological Egoism, *every human action is motivated by self-interest*. We may believe ourselves to be noble and self-sacrificing, but that is only an illusion. In reality, we care only for ourselves.

Could Psychological Egoism possibly be true? Why have so many people believed it, in the face of so much evidence to the contrary?

5.2. The Strategy of Reinterpreting Motives

Everyone knows that people sometimes seem to act altruistically; but perhaps the "altruistic" explanations of behavior are too superficial—it may *seem* that people are unselfish, but if we look deeper we may find that something else is going on. Usually it is not hard to discover that the "unselfish" behavior is actually connected with some benefit for the person who does it.

According to some of Raoul Wallenberg's friends, before going to Hungary he was depressed and unhappy that his life didn't seem to be amounting to much. So he undertook deeds that would make him a heroic figure. His quest for a more significant life was spectacularly successful—here we are, more than a half-century after his death, talking about him. Mother Theresa, the nun who spent her life working among the poor in Calcutta, is often cited as a perfect example of unselfishness—but of course, Mother Theresa believed that she would be handsomely rewarded in heaven. (In fact, she did not have to wait that long for her reward; she was given the Nobel Peace Prize in 1979.) As for David Allsop, who gives 50 percent of his income to support environmental causes, Singer notes that "David had previously worked as a campaigner himself, and said he found it deeply satisfying now to be able to provide the financial support for others to campaign."

So, "altruistic" behavior is in reality connected with such things as the desire to have a more significant life, the desire for public recognition, feelings of personal satisfaction, and the hope of heavenly reward. For any act of apparent altruism, we may be able to find a way to explain away the altruism and replace it with an explanation in terms of more self-centered motives. This technique of reinterpreting motives is perfectly general and may be repeated again and again.

Thomas Hobbes (1588–1679) thought that Psychological Egoism was probably true, but he was not satisfied with such a piecemeal approach. It is not theoretically elegant to deal with each example separately, worrying first about Raoul Wallenberg, then Mother Theresa, then David Allsop, and on and on. If Psychological Egoism is true, we should be able to give a more comprehensive account of human motives, which would establish the theory once and for all. This is what Hobbes attempted to do. His method was to list general types of motives, concentrating especially on the "altruistic" ones, and show how each could be understood in egoistic terms. Once this project was completed, he would have systematically eliminated altruism from our understanding of human nature. Here are two examples of Hobbes at work.

1. *Charity.* This is the most general motive that we ascribe to people when we think they are acting from a concern for others. The *Oxford English Dictionary* devotes almost four columns to "charity." It is defined variously as "The Christian love of our fellowman" and "Benevolence to one's neighbors." But if such neighborly love does not really exist, charitable behavior must be understood in a radically different way. In his essay "On Human Nature," Hobbes describes it like this:

> There can be no greater argument to a man, of his own power, than to find himself able not only to accomplish his own desires, but also to assist other men in theirs: and this is that conception wherein consisteth charity.

Thus charity is a delight one takes in the demonstration of one's powers. The charitable man is demonstrating to himself, and to the world, that he is more resourceful than others: he cannot only take care of himself, he has enough left over for others who are not as capable as he is. In other words, he is just showing off his own superiority.

Of course Hobbes was aware that the charitable man may not *believe* he is doing this. But we are not the best judges of our own motivations. It is only natural that we would interpret our actions in a way that is flattering to us (that is no more than a psychological egoist would expect), and it is flattering to think that we are "unselfish." Hobbes's account aims to provide the *real* explanation of why we act as we do, not the superficial flattery that we naturally want to believe.

2. *Pity.* What is it to pity other people? We might think it is to sympathize with them, to feel unhappy about their misfortunes. And acting from this sympathy, we might try to help them. Hobbes thinks this is all right, as far as it goes, but it does not go far enough. The reason we are disturbed by other people's misfortunes is that we are reminded that the same thing might happen to *us.* "Pity," he says, "is imagination or fiction of future calamity to ourselves, proceeding from the sense of another man's calamity."

This account of pity turns out to be more powerful, from a theoretical point of view, than it first appears. It can explain very neatly some peculiar facts about the phenomenon. It can explain, for example, why we feel greater pity when a good person suffers than when an evil person suffers. Pity, in Hobbes's account, requires a sense of identification with the person suffering—I pity you when I imagine myself in your place. But because each of us thinks of himself or herself as a good person, we do not identify with those we think bad. Therefore, we do not pity the wicked in the same way we pity the good. Our feelings of pity vary directly with the virtue of the person suffering because our sense of identification varies in that way.

The strategy of reinterpreting motives is a persuasive method of reasoning; it has made a great many people feel that Psychological Egoism might be true. It especially appeals to a certain cynicism in us, a suspicion that people are not nearly as noble as they seem. But it is not a conclusive method of reasoning, for it cannot prove that Psychological Egoism is correct. The trouble is, it only shows that it is *possible* to interpret motives egoistically; it does nothing to show that the egoistic motives are deeper or truer than the altruistic explanations they are intended to replace. At most, the strategy shows that Psychological Egoism is possible. We still need arguments to show it is true.

5.3. Two Arguments in Favor of Psychological Egoism

Two general arguments have often been advanced in favor of Psychological Egoism. They are "general" arguments in the sense that each seeks to establish at a single stroke that all actions, and not merely some limited class of actions, are motivated by self-interest. As we will see, neither argument stands up very well under scrutiny.

The Argument That We Always Do What We Most Want to Do. If we describe one person's action as selfish and another person's action as unselfish, we are overlooking the crucial fact that in both cases, assuming the action is done voluntarily, *the person is merely doing what he most wants to do.* If Raoul Wallenberg chose to go to Budapest, and no one was coercing him, that only shows that he wanted to go there more than he wanted to remain in

Sweden—and why should he be praised for "unselfishness" when he was only doing what he most wanted to do? His action was dictated by his own desires, his own sense of what he most wanted. Thus he was not acting unselfishly. And since exactly the same may be said about any alleged act of altruism, we can conclude that Psychological Egoism must be true.

This argument has two primary flaws. First, it depends on the idea that people never voluntarily do anything except what they want to do. But this is plainly false. Sometimes we do things that we do not want to do, because they are a necessary means to an end that we want to achieve—for example, we don't want to go to the dentist, but we go anyway to avoid a toothache. This sort of case may, however, be regarded as consistent with the spirit of the argument, because the ends (such as avoiding the toothache) are wanted.

But there are also things that we do, not because we want to, or even because they are means to an end we want to achieve, but because we feel that we *ought* to do them. For example, someone may do something because she has promised to do it, and thus feels obligated, even though she does not want to do it. It is sometimes suggested that in such cases we do the action because, after all, we want to keep our promises. However, that is not true. If I have promised to do something but I do not want to do it, then it is simply false to say that I want to keep my promise. In such cases we feel a conflict precisely because we do *not* want to do what we feel obligated to do.

If our desires and our sense of obligation were always in harmony, it would be a happy world. Unfortunately, we enjoy no such good fortune. It is an all-too-common experience to be pulled in different directions by desire and obligation. For all we know, Wallenberg may have been like this: Perhaps he wanted to stay in Sweden, but he felt that he had to go to Budapest. In any case, it does not follow from the fact that he chose to go that he wanted to go.

The argument also has a second flaw. Suppose we were to concede, for the sake of argument, that we always act on our strongest desires. Even if this were granted, it would not follow that Wallenberg was acting selfishly or from self-interest. For if he wanted to help other people, even at great risk to himself, that is precisely what makes him *un*selfish. What else could unselfishness be, if not wanting to help others, even at some cost to oneself? Another way to put the point is to say that the *object* of a desire determines whether it is selfish or not. The mere fact that you act on your own desires does not mean that you are acting selfishly; it depends on *what it is* that you desire. If you care only about your own welfare and give no thought for others, then you are selfish; but if you also want other people to be happy, and you act on *that* desire, then you are not selfish.

Therefore, this argument goes wrong in just about every way that an argument can go wrong: The premises are not true, and even if they were true, the conclusion would not follow from them.

The Argument That We Do What Makes Us Feel Good. The second general argument for Psychological Egoism appeals to the fact that so-called unselfish actions produce a sense of self-satisfaction in the person who does them. Acting "unselfishly" makes people feel good about themselves, and that is the real point of it.

According to a 19th-century newspaper, this argument was once advanced by Abraham Lincoln. The Springfield, Illinois *Monitor* reported that

> Mr. Lincoln once remarked to a fellow-passenger on an old-time mud coach that all men were prompted by selfishness in doing good. His fellow-passenger was antagonizing this position when they were passing over a corduroy bridge that spanned a slough. As they crossed this bridge they espied an old razor-backed sow on the bank making a terrible noise because her pigs had got into the slough and were in danger of drowning. As the old coach began to climb the hill, Mr. Lincoln called out, "Driver, can't you stop just a moment?" Then Mr. Lincoln jumped out, ran back, and lifted the little pigs out of the mud and water and placed them on the bank. When he returned, his companion remarked: "Now, Abe, where does selfishness come in on this little episode?" "Why, bless your soul, Ed, that was the very essence of selfishness. I should have had no peace of mind all day had I gone on and left that suffering old sow worrying over those pigs. I did it to get peace of mind, don't you see?"

Lincoln was a great man but, on this occasion at least, he was not a very good philosopher. His argument is vulnerable to the same sorts of objections as the previous one. Why should we think, merely because someone derives satisfaction from help-ing others, that this makes him selfish? Isn't the unselfish per-son precisely the one who *does* derive satisfaction from helping others, whereas the selfish person does not? If Lincoln "got peace of mind" from rescuing the piglets, does this show him to be selfish or, on the contrary, doesn't it show him to be com-passionate and good-hearted? (If a person was truly selfish, why should it bother him that others suffer, much less pigs?) Simi-larly, it is nothing more than sophistry to say that, because some-one finds satisfaction in helping others, they are selfish. If we say this rapidly, while thinking about something else, perhaps it will sound all right; but if we speak slowly and pay attention to what we are saying, it sounds plain silly.

Moreover, suppose we ask *why* someone might derive satis-faction from helping others. Why should it make you feel good to contribute money to support a homeless shelter, when you could spend it on yourself instead? The answer must be, at least in part, that *you are the kind of person who cares about what happens to other people.* If you do not care what happens to them, then giv-ing the money will seem like a waste, not a source of satisfaction. You'll feel more like a sucker than a saint.

There is a general lesson to be learned here, having to do with the nature of desire and its objects. We desire all sorts of things—money, a new car, to play chess, to get married, and so on—and because we desire these things, we may derive satisfac-tion from getting them. But the object of our desire is not the satisfaction—that is not what we are after. What we are after is simply the money, the car, the chess, or the marriage. It is the same with helping others. We must first want to help them be-fore we can get any satisfaction out of it. The good feelings are a by-product; they are not what we are after. Thus, having those feelings is not a mark of selfishness.

5.4. Clearing Away Some Confusions

One of the most powerful theoretical motives is a desire for sim-plicity. When we set out to explain something, we would like to find as simple an explanation as possible. This is certainly true in the sciences—the simpler a scientific theory, the greater its appeal. Consider phenomena as diverse as planetary motion, the tides, and the way objects fall when released from a height.

These appear, at first, to be very different; and it would seem that we would need several different principles to explain them. Who would suspect that they could all be explained by a single simple principle? Yet the theory of gravity does just that. The theory's ability to bring diverse phenomena together under a single explanatory principle is one of its great virtues. It makes order out of chaos.

In the same way, when we think about human conduct, we would like to find one principle that explains everything. We want a single simple formula, if we can find one, that would unite the diverse phenomena of human behavior, in the way that simple formulas in physics bring together apparently diverse phenomena. Since it is obvious that self-regard is an overwhelmingly important factor in motivation, it is only natural to wonder whether all motivation might not be explained in terms of it. And so the idea of Psychological Egoism takes hold.

But the fundamental idea behind Psychological Egoism cannot even be expressed without falling into confusion; and once these confusions have been cleared away, the theory no longer seems plausible.

First, people tend to confuse *selfishness* with *self-interest*. When we think about it, these two are clearly not the same. If I see a physician when I am feeling poorly, I am acting in my own self-interest, but no one would think of calling me "selfish" on account of it. Similarly, brushing my teeth, working hard at my job, and obeying the law are all in my own interest, but none of these are examples of selfish conduct. Selfish behavior is behavior that ignores the interests of others, in circumstances in which their interests ought not to be ignored. Thus, eating a normal meal in normal circumstances is not selfish (although it is definitely in your self-interest); but you would be selfish if you hoarded food while others were starving.

A second confusion is between self-interested behavior and the pursuit of pleasure. We do lots of things because we enjoy them, but that does not mean we are acting from self-interest. The man who continues to smoke cigarettes even after learning about the connection between smoking and cancer is surely not acting from self-interest, not even by his own standards—self-interest would dictate that he quit smoking—and he is not acting altruistically either. He is, no doubt, smoking for the pleasure of it, but this only shows that undisciplined pleasure seeking and acting from self-interest are different. Reflecting on this, Joseph Butler, the leading 18th-century critic of egoism, remarked: "The thing to be lamented is, not that men have so great regard to their own good or interest in the present world, for they have not enough."

Taken together, the last two paragraphs show that (a) it is false that all actions are selfish and (b) it is false that all actions are done from self-interest. When we brush our teeth, at least in normal circumstances, we are not acting selfishly; therefore, not all actions are selfish. And when we smoke cigarettes, we are not acting out of self-interest; therefore, not all actions are done from self-interest. It is worth noting that these two points do not depend on examples of altruism; even if there were no such thing as altruistic behavior, Psychological Egoism would still be false.

A third confusion is the common but false assumption that a concern for one's own welfare is incompatible with any genuine concern for others. Since it is obvious that everyone (or very nearly everyone) desires his or her own well-being, it might be thought that no one can really be concerned for the well-being of others. But this is a false dichotomy. There is no inconsistency in desiring that everyone, including oneself *and* others, be happy. To be sure, our interests may sometimes come into conflict with other people's interests, and then we may have to make hard choices. But even in these cases we sometimes opt for the interests of others, especially when the others are our friends and family. More importantly, however, life is not always like this. Sometimes we are able to help others at little or no cost to ourselves. In those circumstances, not even the strongest self-regard need prevent us from acting generously.

Once these confusions are cleared away, there seems little reason to think Psychological Egoism is a plausible theory. On the contrary, it seems decidedly implausible. If we observe people's behavior with an open mind, we find that much of it is motivated by self-regard, but by no means all of it. There may indeed be one simple formula, as yet undiscovered, that would explain all of human behavior, but Psychological Egoism is not it.

5.5. The Deepest Error in Psychological Egoism

The preceding discussion may seem relentlessly negative. If Psychological Egoism is so obviously confused, you may ask, and if there are no plausible arguments for it, why have so many intelligent people been attracted to it? It is a fair question. Part of the answer is the almost irresistible urge toward theoretical simplicity. Another part is the attraction of what appears to be a hardheaded, deflationary attitude toward human pretensions. But there is a deeper reason: Psychological Egoism has been accepted by many people because they see it as *irrefutable*. And in a certain sense, they are right. Yet in another sense, the theory's immunity from refutation is its deepest flaw.

To explain, let me tell a (true) story that might appear to be far from our subject. A few years ago a group of investigators led by Dr. David Rosenham, a professor of psychology and law at Stanford University, had themselves admitted as patients to various mental hospitals. The hospital staffs did not know there was anything special about them; they thought the investigators were ordinary patients. The investigators wanted to see how they would be treated.

The investigators were perfectly normal, whatever that means, but their very presence in the hospitals created the assumption that they were mentally disturbed. Although they behaved normally—they did nothing to feign illness—they soon discovered that everything they did was interpreted as a sign of whatever mental problem was listed on their admission forms. When some of them were found to be taking notes, entries were made in their records such as "patient engages in writing behavior." During one interview, one "patient" confessed that although he was closer to his mother as a small child, he became more attached to his father as he grew older—a normal turn of events. But this was taken as evidence of "unstable relationships in childhood." Even their protestations of normalcy were turned against them. One of the real patients warned them: "Never tell a doctor that you're well. He won't believe you. That's called a 'flight into health.' Tell him you're still sick, but you're feeling a lot better. That's called insight."

No one on the hospital staffs caught on to the hoax. The real patients, however, saw through it. One of them told an investigator, "You're not crazy. You're checking up on the hospital." And so he was.

Why did the doctors not catch on? The experiment revealed something about the power of a controlling assumption: *Once a hypothesis is accepted, everything can be interpreted to support it.*

Once it became the controlling assumption that the fake patients were mentally disturbed, it did not matter how they behaved. Whatever they did would be construed to fit the assumption. But the "success" of this technique did not prove the hypothesis was true. If anything, it was a sign that something had gone wrong.

The hypothesis that the fake patients were mentally disturbed was faulty because it was *untestable*. If a hypothesis purports to say something factual about the world, then there must be some imaginable conditions that could verify it and some that could conceivably refute it. Otherwise, it is meaningless. If the hypothesis is that all swans are white, for example, we may look at swans to see if any are green or blue or some other color. And although we do not find any green or blue swans, we know *what it would be like* to find some. Our conclusion should rest on the results of these observations. (In fact, there are some black swans, so this hypothesis is false.) Again, suppose someone says "Shaquille O'Neal can't get into my Volkswagen." We know what this means, because we can imagine the circumstances that would make it true and the circumstances that would make it false. To test the statement, we take the car to Mr. O'Neal, invite him to step inside, and see what happens. If it turns out one way, the statement is true; if it turns out the other way, the statement is false.

It should have been possible for the doctors to examine the fake patients, look at the results, and say: "Wait a minute, there's nothing wrong with these people." (Remember, the fake patients behaved normally; they did not fake any psychiatric symptoms.) But the doctors were not operating in that way. For them, *nothing was allowed to count against the hypothesis that the "patients" were ill.*

Psychological Egoism is involved in the same error. Once it becomes the controlling assumption that all behavior is self-interested, everything that happens can be interpreted to fit this assumption. But so what? If there is no conceivable pattern of action or motivation that would count against the theory—if we cannot even imagine what an unselfish act would be like—then the theory is empty.

There is, of course, a way around this problem, both for the doctors and for Psychological Egoism. The doctors could have identified some reasonable way of distinguishing between mentally healthy people and mentally ill people; then they could have observed the fake patients to see which category they belonged in. Similarly, anyone who is tempted to believe Psychological Egoism is true could identify some reasonable way to distinguish self-regarding behavior from nonself-regarding behavior and then look at how people actually behave and see what categories their actions fall into. Of course, anyone who did this would see that people are motivated in all sorts of ways. People act from greed, anger, lust, love, and hate. They do things because they are frightened, jealous, curious, happy, worried, and inspired. They are sometimes selfish and sometimes generous. Sometimes, like Raoul Wallenberg, they are even heroic. In the face of all this, the thought that there is but a single motive cannot be sustained. If Psychological Egoism is held in a form that is testable, the results of the test will be that the theory is false.

CHAPTER **6**

*E*thical Egoism

The achievement of his own happiness is man's highest moral purpose.

AYN RAND, *THE VIRTUE OF SELFISHNESS* (1961)

6.1. Is There a Duty to Help Starving People?

Each year millions of people die of malnutrition and related health problems. A common pattern among children in poor countries is death from dehydration caused by diarrhea brought on by malnutrition. The executive director of the United Nations Children's Fund (UNICEF) has estimated that about 15,000 children die in this way every day. That comes to 5,475,000 children annually. If we add those who die from other preventable causes, the number goes over 10 million. Even if this estimate is too high, the number that die is staggering.

For those of us in the affluent countries, this poses an acute problem. We spend money on ourselves, not only for the necessities of life but for countless luxuries—for fine automobiles, fancy clothes, stereos, sports, movies, and so on. In our country, even people with modest incomes enjoy such things. The problem is that we could forgo our luxuries and give the money for famine relief instead. The fact that we don't suggests that we regard our luxuries as more important than their lives.

Why do we allow people to starve when we could save them? Few of us actually believe our luxuries are that important. Most of us, if asked the question directly, would probably be a bit embarrassed, and we would say that we probably should do more to help. The explanation of why we do not is, at least in part, that we hardly ever think of the problem. Living our own comfortable lives, we are insulated from it. The starving people are dying at some distance from us; we do not see them and we

76

can avoid even thinking of them. When we do think of them, it is only abstractly, as statistics. Unfortunately for the hungry, statistics do not have much power to move us.

We respond differently when there is a "crisis," when a great mass of people in one place are starving, as in Ethiopia in 1984 or Somalia in 1992. Then, it is front-page news and relief efforts are mobilized. But when the needy are scattered, the situation does not seem so pressing. The 5,475,000 children are unfortunate that they are not all gathered in, say, Chicago.

But leaving aside the question of why we behave as we do, what is our duty? What *should* we do? We might think of this as the "commonsense" view of the matter: Morality requires that we balance our own interests against the interests of others. It is understandable, of course, that we look out for our own interests, and no one can be faulted for attending to their own basic needs. But at the same time the needs of others are also important, and when we can help others—especially at little cost to ourselves—we should do so. So, if you have an extra 10 dollars, and giving it to a famine-relief agency would help to save the life of a child, then commonsense morality would say that you should give the money.

This way of thinking involves a general assumption about our moral duties: It is assumed that we have moral duties to other people, and not merely duties that we create, such as by making a promise or incurring a debt. We have "natural" duties to others *simply because they are people who could be helped or harmed by what we do.* If a certain action would benefit (or harm) other people, then that is a reason why we should (or should not) do that action. The commonsense assumption is that other people's interests *count*, for their own sakes, from a moral point of view.

But one person's common sense is another person's naive platitude. Some thinkers have maintained that, in fact, we have no "natural" duties to other people. Ethical Egoism is the idea that each person ought to pursue his or her own self-interest exclusively. It is different from Psychological Egoism, which is a theory of human nature concerned with how people *do* behave. Psychological Egoism says that people do in fact always pursue their own interests. Ethical Egoism, by contrast, is a normative theory—that is, a theory about how we *ought* to behave. Regardless of how we do behave, Ethical Egoism says that our only duty is to do what is best for ourselves.

It is a challenging theory. It contradicts some of our deepest moral beliefs—beliefs held by most of us, at any rate—and it is not easy to refute. We will examine the most important arguments for and against it. If it turns out to be true, then of course that is immensely important. But even if it turns out to be false, there is still much to be learned from examining it, for we may gain some insight into the reasons why we *do* have obligations to other people.

But before looking at the arguments, we should be a little clearer about exactly what this theory says and what it does not say. In the first place, Ethical Egoism does not say that one should promote one's own interests *as well as* the interests of others. That would be an ordinary, commonsensical view. Ethical Egoism is the radical view that one's *only* duty is to promote one's own interests. According to Ethical Egoism, there is only one ultimate principle of conduct, the principle of self-interest, and this principle sums up all of one's natural duties and obligations.

However, Ethical Egoism does not say that you should *avoid* actions that help others. It may happen in many instances that your interests coincide with the interests of others, so that in helping yourself you will be helping them willy-nilly. Or it may happen that aiding others is an effective means for creating some benefit for yourself. Ethical Egoism does not forbid such actions; in fact, it may recommend them. The theory insists only that in such cases the benefit to others is not what makes the act right. What makes the act right is, rather, the fact that it is to one's own advantage.

Finally, Ethical Egoism does not imply that in pursuing one's interests one ought always to do what one wants to do, or what gives one the most pleasure in the short run. Someone may want to drink a lot or smoke cigarettes or take drugs or waste his best years at the racetrack. Ethical Egoism would frown on all this, regardless of the momentary pleasure it brings. Ethical Egoism says that a person ought to do what really is in his or her own best interests, over the long run. It endorses selfishness, but it doesn't endorse foolishness.

6.2. Three Arguments in Favor of Ethical Egoism

What arguments can be advanced to support this doctrine? Unfortunately, the theory is asserted more often than it is argued for—many of its supporters apparently think its truth is self-evident, so that arguments are not needed. When it is argued for, three lines of reasoning are most commonly used.

The Argument That Altruism Is Self-Defeating. The first argument has several variations, each suggesting the same general point:

- Each of us is intimately familiar with our own individual wants and needs. Moreover, each of us is uniquely placed to pursue those wants and needs effectively. At the same time, we know the desires and needs of other people only imperfectly, and we are not well situated to pursue them. Therefore, it is reasonable to believe that if we set out to be "our brother's keeper," we would often bungle the job and end up doing more harm than good.

- At the same time, the policy of "looking out for others" is an offensive intrusion into other people's privacy; it is essentially a policy of minding other people's business.

- Making other people the object of one's "charity" is degrading to them; it robs them of their individual dignity and self-respect. The offer of charity says, in effect, that they are not competent to care for themselves; and the statement is self-fulfilling. They cease to be self-reliant and become passively dependent on others. That is why the recipients of "charity" are so often resentful rather than appreciative.

Thus, the policy of "looking out for others" is said to be self-defeating. If we want to do what is best for people, we should not adopt so-called altruistic policies of behavior. On the contrary, if each person looks after his or her own interests, it is more likely that everyone will be better off. As Robert G. Olson says in his book *The Morality of Self-Interest* (1965), "The individual is most likely to contribute to social betterment by rationally pursuing his own best long-range interests." Or as Alexander Pope put it,

> Thus God and nature formed the general frame
> And bade self-love and social be the same.

It is possible to quarrel with this argument on a number of grounds. Of course no one favors bungling, butting in, or depriving people of their self-respect. But is that really what we are doing when we feed hungry children? Is the starving child in Somalia really harmed when we "intrude" into "her business" by supplying food? It hardly seems likely. Yet we can set this point aside, for considered as an argument for Ethical Egoism, this way of thinking has an even more serious defect.

The trouble is that it isn't really an argument for Ethical Egoism at all. The argument concludes that we should adopt certain policies of behavior; and on the surface they appear to be egoistic policies. However, the *reason* it is said we should adopt those policies is decidedly unegoistic. It is said that we should adopt those policies because doing so will promote the "betterment of society"—but according to Ethical Egoism, that is something we should not be concerned about. Spelled out fully, with everything laid on the table, the argument says:

(1) We ought to do whatever will best promote everyone's interests.

(2) The best way to promote everyone's interests is for each of us to adopt the policy of pursuing our own interests exclusively.

(3) Therefore, each of us should adopt the policy of pursuing our own interests exclusively.

If we accept this reasoning, then we are not Ethical Egoists. Even though we might end up behaving like egoists, our ultimate principle is one of beneficence—we are doing what we think will help everyone, not merely what we think will benefit ourselves. Rather than being egoists, we turn out to be altruists with a peculiar view of what in fact promotes the general welfare.

Ayn Rand's Argument. Ayn Rand is not much read by philosophers, largely because the leading ideas associated with her name—that capitalism is a morally superior economic system, and that morality demands absolute respect for the rights of individuals—are developed more rigorously by other writers. Nevertheless, she was a charismatic figure who attracted a devoted following during her lifetime, and today, two decades after her death, the Ayn Rand industry is still going strong. Among 20th-century writers, the idea of Ethical Egoism is probably more closely associated with her than with anyone else.

Ayn Rand regarded the ethics of "altruism" as a totally destructive idea, both in society as a whole and in the lives of individuals taken in by it. Altruism, to her way of thinking, leads to a denial of the value of the individual. It says to a person: Your life is merely something that may be sacrificed. "If a man accepts the ethics of altruism," she writes, "his first concern is not how to live his life, but how to sacrifice it." Those who promote the ethics of altruism are beneath contempt—they are parasites who, rather than working to build and sustain their own lives, leech off those who do. She writes:

> Parasites, moochers, looters, brutes and thugs can be of no value to a human being—nor can he gain any benefit from living in a society geared to *their* needs, demands and protections, a society that treats him as a sacrificial animal and penalizes him for his virtues in order to reward *them* for their vices, which means: a society based on the ethics of altruism.

By "sacrificing one's life" Rand does not mean anything so dramatic as dying. A person's life consists, in part, of projects undertaken and goods earned and created. Thus to demand that a person abandon his projects or give up his goods is an effort to "sacrifice his life."

Rand also suggests that there is a metaphysical basis for egoistic ethics. Somehow, it is the only ethics that takes seriously the *reality* of the individual person. She bemoans "the enormity of the extent to which altruism erodes men's capacity to grasp . . . the value of an individual life; it reveals a mind from which the reality of a human being has been wiped out."

What, then, of the hungry children? It might be argued that Ethical Egoism itself "reveals a mind from which the reality of a human being has been wiped out"—namely, the human being who is starving. But Rand quotes with approval the answer given by one of her followers: "Once, when Barbara Brandon was asked by a student: 'What will happen to the poor . . . ?' she answered: 'If *you* want to help them, you will not be stopped.' "

All these remarks are, I think, part of one continuous argument that can be summarized like this:

(1) A person has only one life to live. If we value the individual—that is, if the individual has moral worth— then we must agree that this life is of supreme importance. After all, it is all one has, and all one is.

(2) The ethics of altruism regards the life of the individual as something one must be ready to sacrifice for the good of others. Therefore, the ethics of altruism does not take seriously the value of the human individual.

(3) Ethical Egoism, which allows each person to view his or her own life as being of ultimate value, does take the human individual seriously—it is, in fact, the only philosophy that does so.

(4) Thus, Ethical Egoism is the philosophy that we ought to accept.

One problem with this argument, as you may already have noticed, is that it assumes we have only two choices: Either we accept the "ethics of altruism" or we accept Ethical Egoism. The choice is then made to look obvious by picturing "the ethics of altruism" as an insane doctrine that only an idiot would accept—"the ethics of altruism" is said to be the view that one's own interests have *no* value, and that one must be ready to sacrifice oneself *totally* any time *anybody* asks it. If this is the alternative, then any other view, including Ethical Egoism, will look good by comparison.

But that is hardly a fair picture of the choices. What we called the commonsense view stands between the two extremes. It says that one's own interests and the interests of others are *both* important and must be balanced against one another. Sometimes, when the balancing is done, it will turn out that one should act in the interests of others; at other times, it will turn out that one should take care for oneself. So even if we should reject the extreme "ethics of altruism," it does not follow that we must accept the other extreme of Ethical Egoism, because there is a middle way available.

Ethical Egoism as Compatible with Commonsense Morality. The third line of reasoning takes a different sort of approach. Ethical Egoism is usually presented as a *revisionist* moral philosophy, that is, as a philosophy that says our commonsense moral views are mistaken and need to be changed. It is possible, however, to interpret Ethical Egoism in a much less radical way, as a theory that accepts commonsense morality and offers a surprising account of its basis.

The less radical interpretation goes as follows. Ordinary morality consists in obeying certain rules. We must avoid doing harm to others, speak the truth, keep our promises, and so on. At first glance, these duties appear to have little in common—they are just a bunch of separate rules. Yet from a theoretical point of view, we may wonder whether there is not some hidden unity underlying the hodgepodge of separate duties. Perhaps there is some small number of fundamental principles that explain all the rest, just as in physics there are basic principles that bring together and explain diverse phenomena. From a theoretical point of view, the smaller the number of basic principles, the better. Best of all would be one fundamental principle, from which all the rest could be derived. Ethical Egoism, then, would be the theory that all these duties are ultimately derived from the one fundamental principle of self-interest.

Understood in this way, Ethical Egoism is not such a radical doctrine. It does not challenge commonsense morality; it only tries to explain and systematize it. And it does a surprisingly successful job. It can provide plausible explanations of the duties mentioned above, and more:

- *The duty not to harm others:* If we make a habit of doing things that are harmful to other people, people will not be reluctant to do things that harm us. We will be shunned and despised; others will not have us as friends and will not do us favors when we need them. If our offenses against others are serious enough, we may even end up in jail. Thus it is to our own advantage to avoid harming others.
- *The duty not to lie:* If we lie to other people, we will suffer all the ill effects of a bad reputation. People will distrust us and avoid doing business with us. We will often need for people to be honest with us, but we can hardly expect them to feel much of an obligation to be honest with us if we have not been honest with them. Thus it is to our own advantage to be truthful.
- *The duty to keep our promises:* It is to our own advantage to enter into mutually beneficial arrangements with other people. To benefit from those arrangements, we need to be able to rely on them to keep their bargains—we need to be able to rely on them to keep their promises to us.

But we can hardly expect others to keep their promises to us if we do not keep our promises to them. Therefore, from the point of view of self-interest, we should keep our promises.

Pursuing this line of reasoning, Thomas Hobbes suggested that the principle of Ethical Egoism leads to nothing less than the Golden Rule: We should "do unto others" because if we do, others will be more likely to "do unto us."

Does this argument succeed in establishing Ethical Egoism as a viable theory of morality? It is, in my opinion at least, the best try. But there are two serious problems with it. In the first place, the argument does not prove quite as much as it needs to prove. At best, it shows only that *mostly* it is to one's advantage to avoid harming others. It does not show that this is *always* to one's advantage. And it could not show that, for even though it may usually be to your advantage to avoid harming others, sometimes it is not. Sometimes you can gain from treating another person badly. In that case, the obligation not to harm the other person could not be derived from the principle of Ethical Egoism. Thus it appears that not all our moral obligations can be explained as derivable from self-interest.

But set that point aside. There is a still more fundamental problem. Suppose it is true that, say, contributing money for famine relief is somehow to one's own advantage. It does not follow that this is the only reason, or even the most basic reason, why doing so is a good thing. For example, the most basic reason might be *in order to help the starving people*. The fact that doing so is also to one's own advantage might be only a secondary, less important consideration. Thus, although Ethical Egoism says that self-interest is the *only* reason why you should help others, nothing in the present argument really supports that.

6.3. Three Arguments against Ethical Egoism

Ethical Egoism haunts moral philosophy. It is not a popular doctrine; the most important philosophers have rejected it outright. But it has never been very far from their minds. Although no thinker of consequence has defended it, almost everyone has felt it necessary to explain why he was rejecting it, as though the very possibility that it might be correct was hanging in the air, threatening to smother their other ideas. As the merits of the various "refutations" have been debated, philosophers have returned to it again and again.

Curiously, philosophers have not paid much attention to what you might think is the most obvious argument against Ethical Egoism, namely that it would endorse wicked actions— provided, of course, that those actions benefit the person who does them. Here are some examples, taken from various newspapers: To increase his profits, a pharmacist filled prescriptions for cancer-patients using watered-down drugs. A nurse raped two patients while they were unconscious. A paramedic gave emergency patients injections of sterile water rather than morphine, so that he could sell the morphine. Parents fed a baby acid so that they could fake a lawsuit, claiming the baby's formula was tainted. A 13-year-old girl was kidnapped by a neighbor and kept shackled in an underground bomb-shelter for 181 days, while she was sexually abused.

Suppose that, by doing such things, someone could actually gain some benefit for himself. Of course, this means that he would have to avoid being caught. But if he could get away with it, wouldn't Ethical Egoism have to say that such actions are permissible? This seems enough by itself to discredit the doctrine. I believe this is a valid complaint; nonetheless, one might think that it begs the question against Ethical Egoism, because in saying that these actions are wicked, we are appealing to a nonegoistic conception of wickedness. So we might ask if there isn't some further problem with Ethical Egoism, that doesn't beg the question.

Thus, some philosophers have tried to show that there are deeper, logical problems with Ethical Egoism. The following arguments are typical of the refutations they have proposed.

The Argument That Ethical Egoism Cannot Handle Conflicts of Interest. In his book *The Moral Point of View* (1958), Kurt Baier argues that Ethical Egoism cannot be correct because it cannot provide solutions for conflicts of interest. We need moral rules, he says, only because our interests sometimes come into conflict— if they never conflicted, then there would be no problems to solve and hence no need for the kind of guidance that morality provides. But Ethical Egoism does not help to resolve conflicts of interest; it only exacerbates them. Baier argues for this by introducing a fanciful example:

Let B and K be candidates for the presidency of a certain country and let it be granted that it is in the interest of either to be elected, but that only one can succeed. It would then be in the interest of B but against the interest of K if B were elected, and vice versa, and therefore in the interest of B but against the interest of K if K were liquidated, and vice versa. But from this it would follow that B ought to liquidate K, that it is wrong for B not to do so, that B has not "done his duty" until he has liquidated K; and vice versa. Similarly K, knowing that his own liquidation is in the interest of B and therefore, anticipating B's attempts to secure it, ought to take steps to foil B's endeavors. It would be wrong for him not to do so. He would "not have done his duty" until he had made sure of stopping B . . .

This is obviously absurd. For morality is designed to apply in just such cases, namely, those where interests conflict. But if the point of view of morality were that of self-interest, then there could never be moral solutions of conflicts of interest.

Does this argument prove that Ethical Egoism is unacceptable? It does, *if* the conception of morality to which it appeals is accepted. The argument assumes that an adequate morality must provide solutions for conflicts of interest in such a way that everyone concerned can live together harmoniously. The conflict between B and K, for example, should be resolved so that they would no longer be at odds with one another. (One would not then have a duty to do something that the other has a duty to prevent.) Ethical Egoism does not do that, and if you think an ethical theory should, then you will not find Ethical Egoism acceptable.

But a defender of Ethical Egoism might reply that he does not accept this conception of morality. For him, life is essentially a long series of conflicts in which each person is struggling to come out on top; and the principle he accepts—the principle of Ethical Egoism—grants to each person the right to do his or her best to win. On this view, the moralist is not like a courtroom judge, who resolves disputes. Instead, he is like the Commissioner of Boxing, who urges each fighter to do his best. So the conflict between B and K will be "resolved" not by the application of an ethical principle but by one or the other of them winning the struggle. The egoist will not be embarrassed by this. On the contrary, he will think it is no more than a realistic view of the nature of things.

The Argument That Ethical Egoism Is Logically Inconsistent.
Some philosophers, including Baier, have leveled an even more
serious charge against Ethical Egoism. They have argued that it
leads to logical contradictions. If this is true, then Ethical Egoism is indeed a mistaken theory, for no theory can be true if it is
self-contradictory.

Consider B and K again. As Baier explains their predica-
ment, it is in B's interest to kill K, and obviously it is in K's interest to prevent it. But, Baier says,

> if K prevents B from liquidating him, his act must be said
> to be both wrong and not wrong—wrong because it is the
> prevention of what B ought to do, his duty, and wrong for
> B not to do it; not wrong because it is what K ought to do,
> his duty, and wrong for K not to do it. But one and the same
> act (logically) cannot be both morally wrong and not
> morally wrong.

Now, does *this* argument prove that Ethical Egoism is unacceptable? At first glance it seems persuasive. However, it is a
complicated argument, so we need to set it out with each step
individually identified. Then we will be in a better position to
evaluate it. Spelled out fully, it looks like this:

   (1) Suppose it is each person's duty to do what is in his
   own best interests.

   (2) It is in B's best interest to liquidate K.

   (3) It is in K's best interest to prevent B from liquidating
   him.

   (4) Therefore B's duty is to liquidate K, and K's duty is to
   prevent B from doing it.

   (5) But it is wrong to prevent someone from doing his duty.

   (6) Therefore it is wrong for K to prevent B from liquidating him.

   (7) Therefore it is both wrong and not wrong for K to prevent B from liquidating him.

   (8) But no act can be both wrong and not wrong; that is a
   self-contradiction.

   (9) Therefore, the assumption with which we started—
   that it is each person's duty to do what is in his own
   best interests—cannot be true.

When the argument is set out in this way, we can see its hidden flaw. The logical contradiction—that it is both wrong and not wrong for K to prevent B from liquidating him—does not follow simply from the principle of Ethical Egoism. It follows from that principle *together with* the additional premise expressed in step (5), namely, that "it is wrong to prevent someone from doing his duty." Thus we are not compelled by the logic of the argument to reject Ethical Egoism. Instead, we could simply reject this additional premise, and the contradiction would be avoided. That is surely what the ethical egoist would do, for the ethical egoist would never say, without qualification, that it is always wrong to prevent someone from doing his duty. He would say, instead, that whether one ought to prevent someone from doing his duty depends entirely on whether it would be to one's own advantage to do so. Regardless of whether we think this is a correct view, it is, at the very least, a consistent view, and so this attempt to convict the egoist of self-contradiction fails.

The Argument That Ethical Egoism Is Unacceptably Arbitrary.
Finally, we come to the argument that I think comes closest to an outright refutation of Ethical Egoism. It is also the most interesting of the arguments, because it provides some insight into why the interests of other people *should* matter to us. But before presenting this argument, we need to look briefly at a general point about moral values. So let us set Ethical Egoism aside for a moment and consider this related matter.

There is a whole family of moral views that have this in common: They all involve dividing people into groups and saying that the interests of some groups count for more than the interests of other groups. Racism is the most conspicuous example; racism divides people into groups according to race and assigns greater importance to the interests of one race than to others. The practical result is that members of one race are treated better than the others. Anti-Semitism works the same way, and so can nationalism. People in the grip of such views will think, in effect: "*My* race counts for more," or "Those who believe in *my* religion count for more," or "*My* country counts for more," and so on.

Can such views be defended? The people who accept such views are usually not much interested in argument—racists, for example, rarely try to offer rational grounds for their beliefs. But suppose they did. What could they say?

There is a general principle that stands in the way of any such defense, namely: *We can justify treating people differently only if we can show that there is some factual difference between them that is relevant to justifying the difference in treatment.* For example, if one person is admitted to law school while another is rejected, this might be justified by pointing out that the first graduated from college with honors and scored well on the admissions test, while the second dropped out of college and never took the test. However, if both graduated with honors and did well on the entrance examination—if they are in all relevant respects equally well qualified—then it is merely arbitrary to admit one but not the other.

So, we must ask: Can a racist point to any differences between, say, white people and black people that would justify treating them differently? In the past, racists have sometimes attempted to do this by picturing blacks as stupid, lacking in ambition, and the like. If this were true, then it might justify treating them differently, in at least some circumstances. (This is the deep purpose of racist stereotypes, to provide the "relevant differences" needed to justify differences in treatment.) But of course it is not true, and in fact there are no such general differences between the races. Thus racism is an arbitrary doctrine, in that it advocates treating people differently even though there are no differences between them to justify it.

Ethical Egoism is a moral theory of the same type. It advocates that each of us divide the world into two categories of people—ourselves and all the rest—and that we regard the interests of those in the first group as more important than the interests of those in the second group. But each of us can ask, what is the difference between me and everyone else that justifies placing myself in this special category? Am I more intelligent? Do I enjoy my life more? Are my accomplishments greater? Do I have needs or abilities that are so different from the needs or abilities of others? In short, *what makes me so special?* Failing an answer, it turns out that Ethical Egoism is an arbitrary doctrine, in the same way that racism is arbitrary. And this, in addition to explaining why Ethical Egoism is unacceptable, also sheds some light on the question of why we should care about others.

We should care about the interests of other people for the same reason we care about our own interests; for their needs and desires are comparable to our own. Consider, one last time, the starving children we could feed by giving up some of our luxuries. Why should we care about them? We care about ourselves, of course—if we were starving, we would go to almost any lengths to get food. But what is the difference between us and them? Does hunger affect them any less? Are they somehow less deserving than we? If we can find no relevant difference between us and them, then we must admit that if our needs should be met, so should theirs. It is this realization, that we are on a par with one another, that is the deepest reason why our morality must include some recognition of the needs of others, and why, then, Ethical Egoism fails as a moral theory.

CHAPTER 7

The Utilitarian Approach

Given our present perspective, it is amazing that Christian ethics down through the centuries could have accepted almost unanimously the sententious doctrine that "the end does not justify the means." We have to ask now, "If the end does not justify the means, what does?" The answer is, obviously, "Nothing!"
JOSEPH FLETCHER, *MORAL RESPONSIBILITY* (1967)

7.1. The Revolution in Ethics

Philosophers like to think their ideas can change the world. Usually, it is a vain hope: They write books that are read by a few other like-minded thinkers, while the rest of humanity goes on unaffected. On occasion, however, a philosophical theory can alter the way people think. Utilitarianism, a theory proposed by David Hume (1711–1776) but given definitive formulation by Jeremy Bentham (1748–1832) and John Stuart Mill (1806–1873), is a case in point.

The late 18th and 19th centuries produced an astonishing series of upheavals. The modern nation-state was emerging in the aftermath of the French Revolution and the wreckage of the Napoleonic empire; the revolutions of 1848 showed the continuing power of the new ideas of "liberty, equality, fraternity"; in America, a new country with a new kind of constitution was created, and its bloody civil war was to put an end, finally, to slavery in Western civilization; and all the while the industrial revolution was bringing about a complete restructuring of society.

It is not surprising that in the midst of all this change people might begin to think differently about ethics. The old ways of thinking were very much up in the air, open to challenge. Against this background, Bentham's argument for a new conception of morality had a powerful influence. Morality, he

91

urged, is not a matter of pleasing God, nor is it a matter of faithfulness to abstract rules. Morality is just the attempt to bring about as much happiness as possible in this world.

Bentham argued that there is one ultimate moral principle, namely "the Principle of Utility." This principle requires that whenever we have a choice between alternative actions or social policies, we must choose the one that has the best overall consequences for everyone concerned. Or, as he put it in his book *The Principles of Morals and Legislation,* published in the year of the French Revolution:

> By the Principle of Utility is meant that principle which approves or disapproves of every action whatsoever, according to the tendency which it appears to have to augment or diminish the happiness of the party whose interest is in question; or what is the same thing in other words, to promote or to oppose that happiness.

Bentham was the leader of a group of philosophical radicals whose aim was to reform the laws and institutions of England along utilitarian lines. One of his followers was James Mill, the distinguished Scottish philosopher, historian, and economist. James Mill's son, John Stuart Mill, would become the leading advocate of utilitarian moral theory for the next generation, so the Benthamite movement would continue unabated even after its founder's death.

Bentham was fortunate to have such disciples. John Stuart Mill's advocacy was, if anything, even more elegant and persuasive than the master's. In his little book *Utilitarianism* (1861), Mill presents the main idea of the theory in the following way. First, we envision a certain state of affairs that we would like to see come about—a state of affairs in which all people are as happy and well-off as they can be:

> According to the Greatest Happiness Principle . . . the ultimate end, with reference to and for the sake of which all other things are desirable (whether we are considering our own good or that of other people), is an existence exempt as free as possible from pain, and as rich as possible in enjoyments.

The primary rule of morality can, then, be stated simply. It is to act so as to bring about this state of affairs, insofar as that is possible:

This, being, according to the utilitarian opinion, the end
of human action, is necessarily also the standard of morality, which may accordingly be defined, as the rules and precepts for human conduct, by the observance of which an
existence such as has been described might be, to the
greatest extent possible, secured to all mankind, and not to
them only, but, so far as the nature of things admits, to the
whole of sentient creation.

In deciding what to do, we should, therefore, ask what course of
conduct would promote the greatest amount of happiness for
all those who will be affected. Morality requires that we do what
is best from that point of view.

At first glance, this may not seem like such a radical idea; in
fact it may seem a mild truism. Who could argue with the proposition that we should oppose suffering and promote happiness?
Yet in their own way Bentham and Mill were leading a revolution
as radical as either of the other two great intellectual revolutions
in the 19th century, those of Marx and Darwin. To understand
the radicalness of the Principle of Utility, we have to appreciate
what it *leaves out* of its picture of morality: Gone are all references
to God or to abstract moral rules "written in the heavens." Morality is no longer to be understood as faithfulness to some divinely
given code or to some set of inflexible rules. The point of morality is seen as the happiness of beings in this world, and nothing
more; and we are permitted—even required— to do whatever is
necessary to promote that happiness. That, in its time, was a revolutionary idea.

The utilitarians were, as I said, social reformers as well as
philosophers. They intended their doctrine to make a difference, not only in thought but in practice. To illustrate this, we
will briefly examine the implications of their philosophy for two
rather different practical issues: euthanasia and the treatment
of nonhuman animals. These matters do not by any means exhaust the practical applications of Utilitarianism; nor are they
necessarily the issues that utilitarians would find most pressing.
But they do give a good indication of the kind of distinctive approach that Utilitarianism provides.

7.2. First Example: Euthanasia

Matthew Donnelly was a physicist who had worked with X-rays for
30 years. Perhaps as a result of too much exposure, he contracted

cancer and lost part of his jaw, his upper lip, his nose, and his left hand, as well as two fingers from his right hand. He was also left blind. Mr. Donnelly's physicians told him that he had about a year to live, but he decided that he did not want to go on living in such a state. He was in constant pain. One writer said that "at its worst, he could be seen lying in bed with teeth clinched and beads of perspiration standing out on his forehead." Knowing that he was going to die eventually anyway, and wanting to escape this misery, Mr. Donnelly begged his three brothers to kill him. Two refused, but one did not. The youngest brother, 36-year-old Harold Donnelly, carried a .30-caliber pistol into the hospital and shot Matthew to death.

This, unfortunately, is a true story, and the question naturally arises whether Harold Donnelly did wrong. On the one hand, we may assume that he was motivated by noble sentiments; he loved his brother and wanted only to relieve his misery. Moreover, Matthew had asked to die. All this argues for a lenient judgment. Nevertheless, according to the dominant moral tradition in our society, what Harold Donnelly did was unacceptable.

The dominant moral tradition in our society is, of course, the Christian tradition. Christianity holds that human life is a gift from God, so that only he may decide when it will end. The early church prohibited all killing, believing that Jesus' teachings on this subject permitted no exceptions to the rule. Later, some exceptions were made, chiefly to allow capital punishment and killing in war. But other kinds of killing, including suicide and euthanasia, remained forbidden. To summarize the church's doctrine, theologians formulated a rule saying that *the intentional killing of innocent people is always wrong.* This conception has, more than any other single idea, shaped Western attitudes about the morality of killing. That is why we are so reluctant to excuse Harold Donnelly, even though he may have acted from noble motives. He intentionally killed an innocent person; therefore, according to our moral tradition, what he did was wrong.

Utilitarianism takes a very different approach. It would have us ask: Considering the choices available to Harold Donnelly, which one would have the best overall consequences? What action would produce the greatest balance of happiness over unhappiness for all concerned? The person who would be most affected would, of course, be Matthew Donnelly himself. If Harold does not kill him, he will live on, for perhaps a year, blind, mutilated, and in continuing pain. How much unhappiness would this involve? It is hard to say precisely; but Matthew Donnelly's own testimony was that he was so unhappy in this condition that he preferred death. Killing him would provide an escape from this misery. Therefore, utilitarians have concluded that euthanasia may, in such a case, be morally right.

Although this kind of argument is very different from what one finds in the Christian tradition—as I said before, it depends on no theological conceptions, and it has no use for inflexible "rules"—the classical utilitarians did not think they were advocating an atheistic or antireligious philosophy. Bentham suggests that religion would endorse, not condemn, the utilitarian viewpoint if only its adherents would take seriously their view of God as a *benevolent* creator. He writes:

> The dictates of religion would coincide, in all cases, with those of utility, were the Being, who is the object of religion, universally supposed to be as benevolent as he is supposed to be wise and powerful . . . But among the votaries of religion (of which number the multifarious fraternity of Christians is but a small part) there seem to be but few (I will not say how few) who are real believers in his benevolence. They call him benevolent in words, but they do not mean that he is so in reality.

The morality of mercy killing might be a case in point. How, Bentham might ask, could a benevolent God forbid the killing of Matthew Donnelly? If someone were to say that God is kind but that he requires Mr. Donnelly to suffer for the additional year before finally dying, this would be exactly what Bentham means by "calling him benevolent in words, but not meaning that he is so in reality."

But the majority of religious people do not agree with Bentham, and not only our moral tradition but our legal tradition has evolved under the influence of Christianity. Euthanasia is illegal in every Western nation except Holland. In the United States, it is simply murder, and Harold Donnelly was duly arrested and charged. (I do not know what happened in court, although it is common in such cases for the defendant to be found guilty of a lesser charge and given a light sentence.) What would Utilitarianism say about this? If, on the utilitarian view, euthanasia is moral, should it also be made legal?

This question is connected with the more general question of what the purpose of the law ought to be. Bentham was trained in the law, and he thought of the Principle of Utility as a guide for legislators as well as for ordinary people making individual moral decisions. The purpose of the law is the same as that of morals: It should promote the general welfare of all citizens. Bentham thought it obvious that if the law is to serve this purpose, it should not restrict the freedom of citizens any more than necessary. In particular, no type of activity should be prohibited unless, in engaging in that activity, one is doing harm to others. Bentham objected to laws regulating the sexual conduct of "consenting adults," for example, on the grounds that such conduct is not harmful to others, and because such laws diminish rather than increase happiness. But it was Mill who gave this principle its most eloquent expression, when he wrote in his essay *On Liberty* (1859):

> The sole end for which mankind are warranted, individually or collectively, in interfering with the liberty of action of any of their number, is self-protection. The only purpose for which power can be rightfully exercised over any member of a civilized community, against his will, is to prevent harm to others. His own good, physical or moral, is not a sufficient warrant . . . Over himself, over his own body and mind, the individual is sovereign.

Thus, for the classical utilitarians, laws prohibiting euthanasia are not only contrary to the general welfare, they are also unjustifiable restrictions on people's right to control their own lives. When Harold Donnelly killed his brother, he was assisting him in concluding his own life in a manner that he had chosen. No harm was caused to anyone else, and so it was none of their business. Most Americans seem to agree with this point of view, at least when it is a practical issue for them. In a 2000 study conducted by the National Institutes of Health, 60% of terminally ill patients said that euthanasia or physician-assisted suicide should be available upon request. Consistent with his philosophy, Bentham himself is said to have requested euthanasia in his final days, although we do not know whether this request was granted.

7.3. Second Example: Nonhuman Animals

The treatment of nonhumans has not traditionally been re-garded as presenting much of a moral issue. The Christian tradition says that man alone is made in God's image and that mere animals do not even have souls. Thus the natural order of things permits humans to use animals for any purpose they see fit. St. Thomas Aquinas summed up the traditional view when he wrote:

> Hereby is refuted the error of those who said it is sinful for a man to kill dumb animals: for by divine providence they are intended for man's use in the natural order. Hence it is no wrong for man to make use of them, either by killing them or in any other way whatever.

But isn't it wrong to be *cruel* to animals? Aquinas concedes that it is, but he says the reason has to do with human welfare, not the welfare of the animals themselves:

> If any passages of Holy Writ seem to forbid us to be cruel to dumb animals, for instance to kill a bird with its young: this is either to remove man's thoughts from being cruel to other men, and lest through being cruel to animals one becomes cruel to human beings: or because injury to an animal leads to the temporal hurt of man, either the doer of the deed, or of another.

Thus people and animals are in separate moral categories. Strictly speaking, animals have no moral standing of their own. We are free to treat them in any way that might seem to our advantage.

When it is spelled out as baldly as this, the traditional doctrine might make one a little nervous: It seems rather extreme in its lack of concern for the animals, many of whom are, after all, intelligent and sensitive creatures. Yet only a little reflection is needed to see how much our conduct is actually guided by this doctrine. We eat animals; we use them as experimental subjects in our laboratories; we use their skins for clothing and their heads as wall ornaments; we make them the objects of our amusement in zoos and rodeos; and, indeed, there is a popular sport that consists in tracking them down and killing them just for the fun of it.

If one is uncomfortable with the theological "justification" for these practices, Western philosophers have offered an abundance of secular ones. It is said, variously, that animals are not *rational,* that they lack the ability to *speak,* or that they simply are not *human*—and all these are given as reasons why their interests are outside the sphere of moral concern.

The utilitarians, however, would have none of this. On their view, what matters is not whether an individual has a soul, is rational, or any of the rest. All that matters is whether he is capable of experiencing happiness and unhappiness, pleasure and pain. If an individual is capable of suffering, then we have a duty to take that into account when we are deciding what to do, even if the individual in question is not human. In fact, Bentham argues, whether the individual is human or nonhuman is just as irrelevant as whether he is black or white. Bentham writes:

> The day *may* come when the rest of the animal creation may acquire those rights which never could have been witholden from them but by the hand of tyranny. The French have already discovered that the blackness of the skin is no reason why a human being should be abandoned without redress to the caprice of a tormentor. It may one day come to be recognized that the number of the legs, the villosity of the skin, or the termination of the *os sacrum* are reasons equally insufficient for abandoning a sensitive being to the same fate. What else is it that should trace the insuperable line? Is it the faculty of reason, or perhaps the faculty of discourse? But a full-grown horse or dog is beyond comparison a more rational, as well as a more conversable animal, than an infant of a day or a week or even a month old. But suppose they were otherwise, what would it avail? The question is not, Can they *reason?* nor Can they *talk?* but, *Can they suffer?*

Because both humans and nonhumans can suffer, we have the same reason for not mistreating both. If a human is tormented, why is it wrong? Because she suffers. Similarly, if a nonhuman is tormented, she also suffers, and so it is equally wrong for the same reason. To Bentham and Mill, this line of reasoning was conclusive. Humans and nonhumans are equally entitled to moral concern.

However, this view may seem as extreme, in the opposite direction, as the traditional view that gives animals no independent moral standing at all. Are animals really to be regarded as the equals of humans? In some ways Bentham and Mill thought so, but they were careful to point out that this does not mean that animals and humans must always be treated in the same way. There are factual differences between them that often will justify differences in treatment. For example, because humans have intellectual capacities that animals lack, they are able to take pleasure in things that nonhumans cannot enjoy—humans can do mathematics, appreciate literature, and so on. And similarly, their superior capacities might make them capable of frustrations and disappointments that other animals are not able to experience. Thus our duty to promote happiness entails a duty to promote those special enjoyments for them, as well as to prevent any special unhappinesses to which they are vulnerable. At the same time, however, insofar as the welfare of other animals is affected by our conduct, we have a strict moral duty to take that into account, and their suffering counts equally with any similar suffering experienced by a human.

Contemporary utilitarians have sometimes resisted this aspect of the classical doctrine, and that is not surprising. Our "right" to kill, experiment on, and otherwise use animals as we please seems to most of us so obvious that it is hard to believe we really are behaving as badly as Bentham and Mill suggest. Some contemporary utilitarians, however, have produced powerful arguments that Bentham and Mill were right. The philosopher Peter Singer, in a book with the odd-sounding title *Animal Liberation* (1975), has urged, following the principles laid down by Bentham and Mill, that our treatment of nonhuman animals is deeply objectionable.

Singer asks how we can possibly justify experiments such as this one:

> At Harvard University R. Solomon, L. Kamin, and L. Wynne tested the effects of electric shock on the behavior of dogs. They placed forty dogs in a device called a "shuttlebox" which consists of a box divided into two compartments, separated by a barrier. Initially the barrier was set at the height of the dog's back. Hundreds of intense electric shocks were delivered to the dogs' feet through a grid floor. At first the dogs could escape the shock if they learned to jump the barrier into the other compartment. In an attempt to "discourage" one dog from jumping, the experimenters forced the dog to jump *into* shock 100 times. They said that as the

dog jumped he gave a "sharp anticipatory yip which turned into a yelp when he landed on the electrified grid." They then blocked the passage between the compartments with a piece of plate glass and tested the same dog again. The dog "jumped forward and smashed his head against the glass." Initially dogs showed symptoms such as "defecation, urination, yelping and shrieking, trembling, attacking the apparatus" and so on, but after ten or twelve days of trials dogs that were prevented from escaping shock ceased to resist. The experimenters reported themselves "impressed" by this, and concluded that a combination of the plate glass barrier and foot shock were "very effective" in eliminating jumping by dogs.

The utilitarian argument is simple enough. We should judge actions right or wrong depending on whether they cause more happiness or unhappiness. The dogs in this experiment are obviously being caused terrible suffering. Is there any compensating gain in happiness elsewhere that justifies it? Is greater unhappiness being prevented, for other animals or for humans? If not, the experiment is not morally acceptable.

We may note that this style of argument does not imply that all such experiments are immoral—it suggests judging each one individually, on its own merits. The experiment with the dogs, for example, was part of a study of "learned helplessness," a topic that psychologists regard as very important. Psychologists say that finding out about learned helplessness will lead to long-term benefits for the mentally ill. The utilitarian principle does not, by itself, tell us what the truth is about particular experiments; but it does insist that the harm done to the animals *requires justification*. We cannot simply assume, because they are not human, that anything goes.

But criticizing such experiments is too easy for most of us. Because we do not do such research, we may feel superior or self-righteous. Singer points out, however, that none of us is free of blame in this area. We are all involved in cruelty just as serious as that perpetrated in any laboratory, because we all (or, at least most of us) eat meat. The facts about meat production are at least as harrowing as the facts about animal experimentation.

Most people believe, in a vague way, that while the slaughterhouse may be an unpleasant place, animals raised for food are otherwise treated well enough. But, Singer points out, nothing could be further from the truth. Veal calves, for example, spend their lives in pens too small to allow them to turn around or even to lie down comfortably—but from the producers' point of view, that is good, because exercise toughens the muscles, which reduces the "quality" of the meat; and besides, allowing the animals adequate living space would be prohibitively expensive. In these pens the calves cannot perform such basic actions as grooming themselves, which they naturally desire to do, because there is not room for them to twist their heads around. It is clear that the calves miss their mothers, and like human infants they want something to suck: They can be seen trying vainly to suck the sides of their stalls. In order to keep their meat pale and tasty, they are fed a liquid diet deficient in both iron and roughage. Naturally they develop cravings for these things. The calf's craving for iron becomes so strong that if allowed to turn around, it will lick at its own urine, although calves normally find this repugnant. The tiny stall, which prevents the animal from turning, solves this "problem." The craving for roughage is especially strong, since without it the animal cannot form a cud to chew. It cannot be given any straw for bedding, since the animal would be driven to eat it, and that would affect the meat. So for these animals, the slaughterhouse is not an unpleasant end to an otherwise contented existence. As terrifying as the process of slaughter is, for them it may actually be a merciful release.

Once again, given these facts, the utilitarian argument is simple enough. The system of meat production causes great suffering for the animals. Because we do not need to eat them—vegetarian meals are also tasty and nourishing—the good that is done does not, on balance, outweigh the evil. Therefore, it is wrong. Singer concludes that we should become vegetarians.

What is most revolutionary in all this is simply the idea that the interests of nonhuman animals *count.* We normally assume, as the dominant tradition of our society teaches, that human beings alone are worthy of moral consideration. Utilitarianism challenges that basic assumption and insists that the moral community must be expanded to include all creatures whose interests are affected by what we do. Human beings are in many ways special; and an adequate morality must acknowledge that. But it is also true that we are only one species among many inhabiting this planet; and morality must acknowledge that as well.

CHAPTER 8

The Debate over Utilitarianism

The utilitarian doctrine is that happiness is desirable, and the only thing desirable, as an end; all other things being desirable as means to that end.

JOHN STUART MILL, *UTILITARIANISM* (1861)

Man does not strive after happiness; only the Englishman does that.

FRIEDRICH NIETZSCHE, *TWILIGHT OF THE IDOLS* (1889)

8.1. The Classical Version of the Theory

Classical Utilitarianism, the theory of Bentham and Mill, can be summarized in three propositions: First, actions are to be judged right or wrong solely by virtue of their consequences. Nothing else matters. Second, in assessing consequences, the only thing that matters is the amount of happiness or unhappiness that is created. Everything else is irrelevant. Third, each person's happiness counts the same. As Mill put it,

> the happiness which forms the utilitarian standard of what is right in conduct, is not the agent's own happiness, but that of all concerned. As between his own happiness and that of others, utilitarianism requires him to be as strictly impartial as a disinterested and benevolent spectator.

Thus, right actions are those that produce the greatest possible balance of happiness over unhappiness, with each person's happiness counted as equally important.

The appeal of this theory to philosophers, economists, and others who theorize about human decision making has been enormous. The theory continues to be widely accepted, even though it has been challenged by a number of apparently devastating arguments. These antiutilitarian arguments are so nu-
102

merous, and so persuasive, that many have concluded the theory must be abandoned. But the remarkable thing is that so many have not abandoned it. Despite the arguments, a great many thinkers refuse to let the theory go. According to these contemporary utilitarians, the antiutilitarian arguments only show that the classical theory needs to be improved; they say the basic idea is sound and should be preserved, but recast into a more satisfactory form.

In what follows, we will examine some of these arguments against Utilitarianism and consider whether the classical version of the theory may be revised satisfactorily to meet them. These arguments are of interest not only for the assessment of Utilitarianism but for their own sakes, as they raise some fundamental issues of moral philosophy.

8.2. Is Happiness the Only Thing That Matters?

The question *What things are good?* is different from the question *What actions are right?* and Utilitarianism answers the second question by referring back to the first one. Right actions, it says, are the ones that produce the most good. But what is good? The classical utilitarian reply is: one thing, and one thing only, namely happiness. As Mill put it, "The utilitarian doctrine is that happiness is desirable, and the only thing desirable, as an end; all other things being desirable as means to that end."

The idea that happiness is the one ultimate good (and unhappiness the one ultimate evil) is known as Hedonism. Hedonism is a perennially popular theory that goes back at least as far as the ancient Greeks. It has always been attractive because of its beautiful simplicity and because it expresses the intuitively plausible notion that things are good or bad on account of the way they make us *feel*. Yet a little reflection reveals serious flaws in this theory. The flaws stand out when we consider examples like these:

A promising young pianist's hands are injured in an automobile accident so that she can no longer play. Why is this bad for her? Hedonism would say it is bad because it causes her unhappiness. She will feel frustrated and upset whenever she thinks of what might have been, and *that* is her misfortune. But this way of explaining the misfortune seems to get things the wrong way around. It is not as though, by feeling unhappy, she has made an otherwise neutral situation into a bad one. On the contrary, her unhappiness is a rational response to a situation that *is* unfortunate. She could have had a career as a concert pianist, and now she cannot. That is the tragedy. We could not eliminate the tragedy just by getting her to cheer up.

You think someone is your friend, but he ridicules you behind your back. No one tells you, so you never know. Is this unfortunate for you? Hedonism would have to say no, because you are never caused any unhappiness. Yet we feel there is something bad going on. You think he is your friend, and you are "being made a fool," even though you are unaware of it and you suffer no unhappiness.

Both these examples make the same basic point. We value all sorts of things, such as artistic creativity and friendship, for their own sakes. It makes us happy to have them, but only because we already think them good. (We do not think them good because they make us happy—this is how Hedonism "gets things the wrong way around.") Therefore, it is a misfortune to lose them, independently of whether or not the loss is accompanied by unhappiness,

In this way, Hedonism misunderstands the nature of happiness. Happiness is not something that is recognized as good and sought for its own sake, with other things desired only as a means of bringing it about. Instead, happiness is a response we have to the attainment of things that we recognize *as* good, independently and in their own right. We think that friendship is a good thing, and so having friends makes us happy. That is very different from first setting out after happiness, then deciding that having friends might make us happy, and then seeking friends as a means to this end.

For this reason, there are not many hedonists among contemporary philosophers. Those sympathetic to Utilitarianism have therefore sought a way to formulate their view without assuming a hedonistic account of good and evil. Some, such as the English philosopher G. E. Moore (1873–1958), have tried to compile short lists of things to be regarded as good in themselves. Moore suggested that there are three obvious intrinsic goods—pleasure, friendship, and aesthetic enjoyment—and that right actions are those that increase the world's supply of these things. Other utilitarians have bypassed the question of how many things are good in themselves, leaving it an open question and saying only that right actions are the ones that have the best results, however that is measured. Still others bypass the question in another way, holding only that we should act so as to maximize the satisfaction of people's *preferences*. It is beyond the scope of this book to discuss the merits or demerits of these varieties of Utilitarianism. I mention them only in order to note that, although the hedonistic assumption of the classical utilitarians has largely been rejected, contemporary utilitarians have not found it difficult to carry on. They do so by urging that Hedonism was never a necessary part of the theory in the first place.

8.3. Are Consequences All That Matter?

The idea that only consequences matter is, however, a necessary part of Utilitarianism. The theory's most fundamental idea is that in order to determine whether an action would be right, we should look at *what will happen as a result of doing it.* If it were to turn out that some other matter is also important in determining rightness, then Utilitarianism would be undermined at its very foundation.

Some of the most serious antiutilitarian arguments attack the theory at just this point: They urge that various other considerations, in addition to utility, are important in determining right and wrong. Here are three such arguments.

Justice. Writing in the academic journal *Inquiry* in 1965, H. J. McCloskey asks us to consider the following case:

> Suppose a utilitarian were visiting an area in which there was racial strife, and that, during his visit, a Negro rapes a white woman, and that race riots occur as a result of the crime, white mobs, with the connivance of the police, bashing and killing Negroes, etc. Suppose too that our utilitarian is in the area of the crime when it is committed such that his testimony would bring about the conviction of a particular Negro. If he knows that a quick arrest will stop the riots and lynchings, surely, as a Utilitarian, he must conclude that he has a duty to bear false witness in order to bring about the punishment of an innocent person.

This is a fictitious example, of course, although it was obviously inspired by the lynch-law that prevailed at one time in some parts of the United States. In any case, the argument is that if someone were in this position, then on utilitarian grounds he should bear false witness against the innocent person. This might have some bad consequences—the innocent man might be executed—but there would be enough good consequences to outweigh them: The riots and lynchings would be stopped. The best outcome would be achieved by lying; therefore, according to Utilitarianism, lying is the thing to do. But, the argument continues, it would be wrong to bring about the execution of an innocent person. Therefore, Utilitarianism, which implies it would be right, must be incorrect.

According to the critics of Utilitarianism, this argument illustrates one of the theory's most serious shortcomings: namely, that it is incompatible with the ideal of justice. Justice requires that we treat people fairly, according to their individual needs and merits. McCloskey's example illustrates how the demands of justice and the demands of utility can come into conflict. Thus, an ethical theory that says utility is the whole story cannot be right.

Rights.   Here is a case that is not fictitious; it is from the records of the U.S. Court of Appeals, Ninth Circuit (Southern District of California), 1963, in the case of *York* v. *Story:*

> In October, 1958, appellant [Ms. Angelynn York] went to the police department of Chino for the purpose of filing charges in connection with an assault upon her. Appellee Ron Story, an officer of that police department, then acting under color of his authority as such, advised appellant that it was necessary to take photographs of her. Story then took appellant to a room in the police station, locked the door, and directed her to undress, which she did. Story then directed appellant to assume various indecent positions, and photographed her in those positions. These photographs were not made for any lawful purpose.
>
> Appellant objected to undressing. She stated to Story that there was no need to take photographs of her in the nude, or in the positions she was directed to take, because the bruises would not show in any photograph.
>
> Later that month, Story advised appellant that the pictures did not come out and that he had destroyed them. Instead, Story circulated these photographs among the personnel of the Chino police department. In April, 1960,

two other officers of that police department, appellee
Louis Moreno and defendant Henry Grote, acting under
color of their authority as such, and using police photo-
graphic equipment located at the police station made additional prints of the photographs taken by Story. Moreno
and Grote then circulated these prints among the personnel of the Chino police department.

Ms. York brought suit against these officers and won. Her legal
rights had clearly been violated. But what of the *morality* of the
officers' behavior? Utilitarianism says that actions are defensible if they produce a favorable balance of happiness over unhappiness. This suggests that we consider the amount of unhappiness caused to Ms. York and compare it with the amount
of pleasure taken in the photographs by Officer Story and his
cohorts. It is at least possible that more happiness than unhappiness was caused. In that case, the utilitarian conclusion apparently would be that their actions were morally all right. But
this seems to be a perverse way of thinking. Why should the
pleasure afforded Story and his cohorts matter at all? Why
should it even count? They had no right to treat Ms. York in this
way, and the fact that they enjoyed doing so hardly seems a relevant defense.

Here is an (imaginary) related case. Suppose a Peeping
Tom spied on Ms. York by peering through her bedroom window, and secretly took pictures of her undressed. Further suppose that he did this without ever being detected and that he
used the photographs entirely for his own amusement, without
showing them to anyone. Now under these circumstances, it
seems clear that the only consequence of his action is an increase in his own happiness. No one else, including Ms. York, is
caused any unhappiness at all. How, then, could Utilitarianism
deny that the Peeping Tom's actions are right? But it is evident
to moral common sense that they are not right. Thus, Utilitarianism appears to be unacceptable.

The moral to be drawn from this argument is that Utilitarianism is at odds with the idea that people have *rights* that may
not be trampled on merely because one anticipates good results. In these cases, it is Ms. York's right to privacy that is violated; but it would not be difficult to think of similar cases in
which other rights are at issue—the right to freedom of religion, to free speech, or even the right to life itself. It may

happen that good purposes are served, from time to time, by violating these rights. But we do not think that our rights should be set aside so easily. The notion of a personal right is not a utilitarian notion. Quite the opposite: It is a notion that places limits on how an individual may be treated, regardless of the good purposes that might be accomplished.

Backward-Looking Reasons. Suppose you have promised someone you will do something—say, you promised to meet her downtown this afternoon. But when the time comes to go, you don't want to do it; you need to do some work and you would rather stay home. What should you do? Suppose you judge that the utility of getting your work accomplished slightly outweighs the inconvenience your friend would be caused. Appealing to the utilitarian standard, you might then conclude that it is right to stay home. However, this does not seem correct. The fact that you promised imposes an obligation on you that you cannot escape so easily. Of course, if a great deal was at stake—if, for example, your mother had just been stricken with a heart attack and you had to rush her to the hospital—you would be justified in breaking the promise. But a *small* gain in utility cannot overcome the obligation imposed by the fact that you promised. Thus Utilitarianism, which says that consequences are the only things that matter, once again seems to be mistaken.

There is an important general lesson to be learned from this argument. Why is Utilitarianism vulnerable to this sort of criticism? It is because the only kinds of considerations that the theory holds relevant to determining the rightness of actions are considerations having to do with the future. Because of its exclusive concern with consequences, Utilitarianism has us confine our attention to what *will happen* as a result of our actions. However, we normally think that considerations about the past are also important. (The fact that you promised your friend to meet her is a fact about the past.) Therefore, Utilitarianism seems to be faulty because it excludes backward-looking considerations.

Once we understand this point, other examples of backward-looking considerations come easily to mind. The fact that someone did not commit a crime is a good reason why he should not be punished. The fact that someone once did you a favor may be a good reason why you should now do him a favor. The fact that you did something to hurt someone may be a reason why you should now make it up to her. These are all facts about the past that are relevant to determining our obligations. But Utilitarianism makes the past irrelevant, and so it seems deficient for just that reason.

8.4. Should We Be Equally Concerned for Everyone?

The final component of utilitarian morality is the idea that we must treat each person's welfare as equally important—as Mill put it, that we must be "as strictly impartial as a disinterested and benevolent spectator." This sounds plausible when it is stated abstractly, but it has troublesome implications. One problem is that the requirement of "equal concern" places too great a demand on us; another problem is that it disrupts our personal relationships.

The Charge That Utilitarianism Is Too Demanding. Suppose you are on your way to the theater when someone points out that the money you are about to spend could be used to provide food for starving people or inoculations for third-world children. Surely, those people need food and medicine more than you need to see a play. So you forgo your entertainment and give the money to a charitable agency. But that is not the end of it. By the same reasoning, you cannot buy new clothes, a car, a computer, or a camera. Probably you should move into a cheaper apartment. After all, what is more important—your having these luxuries or children having food?

In fact, faithful adherence to the utilitarian standard would require you to give away your resources until you have lowered your own standard of living to the level of the neediest people you could help. We might admire people who do this, but we do not regard them as simply doing their duty. Instead, we regard them as saintly people whose generosity goes *beyond* what duty requires. We distinguish actions that are morally required from actions that are praiseworthy but not strictly required. (Philosophers call the latter *supererogatory* actions.) Utilitarianism seems to eliminate this distinction.

But the problem is not merely that Utilitarianism would require us to give up most of our material resources. Equally important, abiding by Utilitarianism's mandates would make it impossible for us to carry on our individual lives. Each of our lives includes projects and activities that give it character and meaning; these are what make our lives worth living. But an ethic that requires the subordination of everything to the impartial promotion of the general welfare would require us to abandon those projects and activities. Suppose you are a cabinetmaker, not getting rich but making a comfortable living; you have two children that you love; and on weekends you like to perform with an amateur theater group. In addition you are interested in history and you read a lot. How could there be anything wrong with this? But judged by the utilitarian standard, you are leading a morally unacceptable life. After all, you could be doing a lot more good if you spent your time in other ways.

Personal Relationships. In practice, none of us is willing to treat all people as equals, for it would require that we abandon our special relationships with friends and family. We are all deeply partial where our friends and family are concerned. We love them and we go to great lengths to help them. To us, they are not just members of the great crowd of humanity—they are special. But all this is inconsistent with impartiality. When you are impartial, intimacy, love, affection, and friendship fly out the window.

The fact that Utilitarianism undermines our personal relationships seems to many critics to be its single greatest fault. Indeed, at this point Utilitarianism seems to have lost all touch with reality. What would it be like to be no more concerned for one's husband or wife than for strangers whom one has never met? The very idea is absurd; not only is it profoundly contrary to normal human emotions, but the institution of marriage could not even exist apart from understandings about special responsibilities and obligations. Again, what would it be like to treat one's children with no greater love than one has for strangers? As John Cottingham puts it, "A parent who leaves his child to burn, on the ground that the building contains someone else whose future contribution to the general welfare promises to be greater, is not a hero; he is (rightly) an object of moral contempt, a moral leper."

8.5. The Defense of Utilitarianism

These arguments add up to an overwhelming indictment of Utilitarianism. The theory, which at first seemed so progressive and commonsensical, now seems indefensible: It is at odds with such fundamental moral notions as justice and individual rights, and it seems unable to account for the place of backward-looking reasons in justifying conduct. It would have us abandon our ordinary lives and spoil the personal relationships that mean everything to us. Not surprisingly, the combined weight of these arguments has prompted many philosophers to abandon the theory altogether.

Many thinkers, however, continue to believe that Utilitarianism, in some form, is true. In reply to the above arguments, three general defenses have been offered.

The First Line of Defense: Fanciful Examples Don't Matter. The first line of defense is to argue that the antiutilitarian arguments make unrealistic assumptions about how the world works. The arguments about rights, justice, and backward-looking reasons share a common strategy. A case is described, and then it is said that from a utilitarian point of view a certain action is required—bearing false witness, violating someone's rights, or breaking a promise. It is then said that these things are not right. Therefore, it is concluded, the utilitarian conception of rightness cannot be correct.

But this strategy succeeds only if we agree that the actions described really would have the best consequences. But why should we agree with that? In the real world, bearing false witness does *not* have good consequences. Suppose, in the case described by McCloskey, the "utilitarian" tried to incriminate the innocent man in order to stop the riots. He probably would not succeed; his lie might be found out, and then the situation would be even worse than before. Even if the lie did succeed, the real culprit would remain at large, to commit additional crimes. Moreover, if the guilty party were caught later on, which is always a possibility, the liar would be in deep trouble, and confidence in the criminal justice system would be undermined. The moral is that although one might *think* that one can bring about the best consequences by such behavior, one can by no means be certain of it. In fact, experience teaches the contrary: Utility is not served by framing innocent people.

The same goes for the other cases cited in the antiutilitarian arguments. Violating people's rights, breaking one's promises, and lying all have bad consequences. Only in philosophers' imaginations is it otherwise. In the real world, Peeping Toms are caught, just as Officer Story and his cohorts were caught; and their victims suffer. In the real world, when people lie, others are hurt and their own reputations are damaged; and when people break their promises, and fail to return favors, they lose their friends.

Therefore, far from being incompatible with the idea that we should not violate people's rights, or lie, or break our promises, Utilitarianism explains why we should not do those things. Moreover, apart from the utilitarian explanation, these duties would remain mysterious and unintelligible. What could be more mysterious than the notion that some actions are right "in themselves," severed from any notion of a good to be produced by them? Or what could be more unintelligible than the idea that people have "rights" unconnected with any benefits derived from the acknowledgment of those rights? Utilitarianism is not incompatible with common sense; on the contrary, Utilitarianism is commonsensical.

So that is the first line of defense. How effective is it? Unfortunately, it contains more bluster than substance. While it can plausibly be maintained that *most* acts of false witness and the like have bad consequences in the real world, it cannot reasonably be asserted that *all* such acts have bad consequences. Surely, at least once in a while, one can bring about a good result by doing something that moral common sense condemns. Therefore, in at least some real-life cases Utilitarianism will come into conflict with common sense. Moreover, even if the antiutilitarian arguments had to rely exclusively on fictitious examples, those arguments would nevertheless retain their power; for showing that Utilitarianism has unacceptable consequences in hypothetical cases is a valid way of pointing up its theoretical defects. The first line of defense, then, is weak.

The Second Line of Defense: The Principle of Utility Is a Guide for Choosing Rules, Not Individual Acts. The second line of defense admits that the classical version of Utilitarianism is inconsistent with moral common sense and proposes to save the theory by giving it a new formulation which *will* be in line with our commonsense evaluations. In revising a theory, the trick is to identify precisely which of its features is causing the trouble and to change that, leaving the rest of the theory undisturbed. What is it about the classical version that generates all the unwelcome results?

The troublesome aspect of classical Utilitarianism, it was said, is its assumption that *each individual action* is to be evaluated by reference to the Principle of Utility. If on a certain occasion you are tempted to bear false witness, the classical version of the theory says that whether it would be wrong is determined by the consequences of *that particular lie;* similarly, whether you should keep a promise depends on the consequences of *that particular promise;* and so on for each of the examples we have considered. This is the assumption that caused all the trouble; it is what leads to the conclusion that you can do any sort of questionable thing if it has the best consequences.

Therefore, the new version of Utilitarianism modifies the theory so that individual actions will no longer be judged by the Principle of Utility. Instead, we first ask what *set of rules* is optimal, from a utilitarian point of view. What rules should we prefer to have current in our society, if the people in our society are to flourish? Individual acts are then judged right or wrong according to whether they are acceptable or unacceptable by those rules. This new version of the theory is called *Rule-Utilitarianism,* to distinguish it from the original theory, now commonly called *Act-Utilitarianism.* Richard Brandt was perhaps the most prominent defender of Rule-Utilitarianism; he suggested that "morally wrong" means that an action

> would be prohibited by any moral code which all fully rational persons would tend to support, in preference to all others or to none at all, for the society of the agent, if they expected to spend a lifetime in that society.

Rule-Utilitarianism has no difficulty coping with the antiutilitarian arguments. An act-utilitarian, faced with the situation described by McCloskey, would be tempted to bear false witness against the innocent man because the consequences of *that particular act* would be good. But the rule-utilitarian would not reason in that way. He would first ask, "What general rules of conduct tend to promote the greatest happiness?" Suppose we imagine two societies, one in which the rule "Don't bear false witness against the innocent" is faithfully adhered to, and one in which this rule is not followed. In which society are people likely to be better off? From the point of view of utility, the first society is preferable. Therefore, the rule against incriminating the innocent should be accepted, and by appealing to this rule, we conclude that the person in McCloskey's example should not testify against the innocent man.

Analogous reasoning can be used to establish rules against violating people's rights, breaking promises, lying, and all the rest. Rules governing personal relationships—requiring loyalty to friends, loving care of one's children, and so on—can also be established in this manner. We should accept such rules because following them, as a regular practice, promotes the general welfare. But once having appealed to the Principle of Utility to establish the rules, we do not have to invoke the principle again to determine the rightness of particular actions. Individual actions are justified simply by appeal to the already-established rules.

Thus Rule-Utilitarianism cannot be convicted of violating our moral common sense. In shifting emphasis from the justification of acts to the justification of rules, the theory has been brought into line with our intuitive judgments to a remarkable degree.

The Third Line of Defense: "Common Sense" Can't Be Trusted. Finally, a small group of contemporary utilitarians has had a very different response to the antiutilitarian arguments. Those arguments point out that the classical theory is at odds with ordinary notions of justice, individual rights, and so on; and this group responds: "So what?" In 1961 the Australian philosopher J. J. C. Smart published a monograph entitled *An Outline of a System of Utilitarian Ethics;* reflecting on his position in that book, Smart said:

> Admittedly utilitarianism does have consequences which are incompatible with the common moral consciousness, but I tended to take the view "so much the worse for the common moral consciousness." That is, I was inclined to reject the common methodology of testing general ethical principles by seeing how they square with our feelings in particular instances.

Our moral common sense is, after all, not necessarily reliable. It may incorporate various irrational elements, including prejudices absorbed from our parents, our religion, and the general culture. Why should we simply assume that our feelings are always correct? And why should we reject a plausible, rational theory of ethics simply because it conflicts with those feelings? Perhaps it is the feelings, not the theory, that should be discarded. In light of this, consider again McCloskey's example of the person tempted to bear false witness. McCloskey argues that it would be wrong to have a man convicted of a crime he did not commit because it would be unjust. But wait: Such a judgment serves *that man's* interests well enough, but what of the *other* innocent people who will be hurt if the rioting and lynchings continue? Surely we might hope that we never have to face a situation like this. All the options are terrible. But if we must choose between (a) securing the conviction of one innocent person and (b) allowing the deaths of several innocent people, is it so unreasonable to think that the first option, bad as it is, is preferable to the second?

And consider again the objection that Utilitarianism is too demanding because it would require us to use our resources to feed starving children rather than go to movies and buy cars and cameras. Is it unreasonable to believe that continuing our affluent lives is less important than those children?

On this way of thinking, Act-Utilitarianism is a perfectly defensible doctrine and does not need to be modified. Rule-Utilitarianism, by contrast, is an unnecessarily watered-down version of the theory, which gives rules a greater importance than they merit. There is a serious problem with Rule-Utilitarianism, which can be brought out if we ask whether its rules have *exceptions*. After the rule-utilitarian's "ideal social code" has been established, are its rules to be followed no matter what? There will inevitably be cases where an act that is prohibited by the code would nevertheless maximize utility, maybe even by a considerable amount. Then what is to be done? If the rule-utilitarian says that in such cases we may violate the code, it looks like he has fallen back into act-utilitarianism. On the other hand, if he says that we may not do the "forbidden" act, then, as Smart puts it, the utilitarian's original concern for promoting welfare has been replaced by an irrational "rule worship." What sort of utilitarian would allow the sky to fall for the sake of a rule?

Act-Utilitarianism engages in no such rule-worship. It is, however, recognized to be a radical doctrine that implies that many of our ordinary moral feelings may be mistaken. In this respect, it does what good philosophy always does—it challenges us to rethink matters that we have heretofore taken for granted. If we consult what Smart calls our "common moral consciousness," it seems that many considerations other than utility are morally important. But Smart is right to warn us that "common sense" cannot be trusted. That may turn out to be Utilitarianism's greatest contribution. The deficiencies of moral common sense are obvious, once we think for only a moment. Many white people once felt that there is an important difference between whites and blacks, so that the interests of whites are somehow more important. Trusting the "common sense" of their day, they might have insisted that an adequate moral theory should accommodate this "fact." Today, no one worth listening to would say such a thing, but who knows how many other irrational prejudices are still a part of our moral common sense? At the end of his classic study of race relations, *An American Dilemma* (1944), the Swedish sociologist Gunnar Myrdal reminds us:

> There must be still other countless errors of the same sort that no living man can yet detect, because of the fog within which our type of Western culture envelops us. Cultural influences have set up the assumptions about the mind, the body, and the universe with which we begin; pose the questions we ask; influence the facts we seek; determine the interpretation we give these facts; and direct our reaction to these interpretations and conclusions.

Could it be, for example, that future generations will look back in disgust at the way affluent people in the 21st century enjoyed their comfortable lives while third-world children died of easily preventable diseases? Or at the way we slaughtered and ate helpless animals? If so, they might note that utilitarian philosophers of the day were criticized as simple-minded for advancing a moral theory that straightforwardly condemned such things.

CHAPTER **9**

Are There Absolute Moral Rules?

You may not do evil that good may come.

ST. PAUL, *LETTER TO THE ROMANS* (CA. A.D. 50)

9.1. Harry Truman and Elizabeth Anscombe

Harry Truman, the 33rd President of the United States, will always be remembered as the man who made the decision to drop the atomic bombs on Hiroshima and Nagasaki. When he became President in 1945, following the death of Franklin D. Roosevelt, Truman knew nothing about the development of the bomb; he had to be filled in by the presidential advisers. The Allies were winning the war in the Pacific, they said, but at a terrible cost. Plans had been prepared for an invasion of the Japanese home islands, which would be even bloodier than the Normandy invasion. Using the atomic bomb on one or two Japanese cities, however, might bring the war to a speedy end, making the invasion unnecessary.

Truman was at first reluctant to use the new weapon. The problem was that each bomb would obliterate an entire city—not just the military targets, but hospitals, schools, and civilian homes. Women, children, old people, and other noncombatants would be wiped out along with the military personnel. Although the Allies had bombed cities before, Truman sensed that the new weapon made the issue of noncombatants even more acute. Moreover, the U.S. was on record condemning attacks on civilian targets. In 1939, before the U.S. had entered the war, President Roosevelt had sent a message to the governments of France, Germany, Italy, Poland, and England, denouncing the

bombardment of cities in the strongest terms. He had called it
"inhuman barbarism":

> The ruthless bombing from the air of civilians . . . which
> has resulted in the maiming and in the death of thousands
> of defenseless men, women, and children, has sickened the
> hearts of every civilized man and woman, and has pro-
> foundly shocked the conscience of humanity. If resort is
> had to this form of inhuman barbarism during the period
> of the tragic conflagration with which the world is now con-
> fronted, hundreds of thousands of innocent human beings
> who have no responsibility for, and who are not even re-
> motely participating in, the hostilities which have now bro-
> ken out, will lose their lives.

When he decided to authorize the bombings, Truman expressed
similar thoughts. He wrote in his diary that "I have told the Sec.
of War, Mr. Stimson, to use it so that military objectives and soldiers and sailors are the target and not women and children. . . .
He and I are in accord. The target will be a purely military one."
It is hard to know what to make of this, since Truman knew the
bombs would destroy whole cities. Nonetheless, it is clear that he
was worried about the issue of noncombatants. It is also clear
that he was satisfied he was doing the right thing. He told an aide
that, after signing the order, he "slept like a baby."

Elizabeth Anscombe, who died in 2001 at the age of 81, was
a 20-year-old student at Oxford University when World War II
began. In that year she co-authored a controversial pamphlet arguing that Britain should not go to war because it would end up
fighting by unjust means, such as attacks upon civilians. "Miss
Anscombe," as she was always known, despite her 50-year marriage and her seven children, would go on to become one of the
20th century's most distinguished philosophers, and the greatest woman philosopher in history.

Miss Anscombe was also a Catholic, and her religion was
central to her life. Her ethical views, especially, reflected traditional Catholic teachings. In 1968 she celebrated Pope Paul VI's
affirmation of the church's ban on contraception and wrote a
pamphlet explaining why artificial birth-control is wrong. Late
in her life she was arrested while protesting outside a British
abortion clinic. She also accepted the church's teaching about
the ethical conduct of war, which brought her into conflict with
Mr. Truman.

Harry Truman and Elizabeth Anscombe crossed paths in 1956 when he was awarded an honorary degree by Oxford University. The degree was a way of thanking Truman for America's wartime help. Those proposing the honor thought it would be uncontroversial. But Anscombe and two other members of the faculty opposed awarding the degree, and although they lost, they forced a vote on what would otherwise have been a rubber-stamp approval. Then, while the degree was being conferred, Anscombe knelt outside the hall, praying.

Anscombe wrote another pamphlet, this time explaining that Truman was a murderer because he had ordered the bombings of Hiroshima and Nagasaki. Of course, Truman thought the bombings were justified—they had shortened the war and saved lives. For Anscombe, this was not good enough. "For men to choose to kill the innocent as a means to their ends," she wrote, "is always murder." To the argument that the bombings saved more lives than they took, she retorted: "Come now. If you had to choose between boiling one baby and letting some frightful disaster befall a thousand people—or a million people, if a thousand is not enough—what would you do?"

The point is that, according to Anscombe, *there are some things that may not be done, no matter what.* It does not matter if you could accomplish some great good by boiling a baby; it simply must not be done. (Considering what happened to the babies in Hiroshima, "boiling a baby" is not so far off.) That we may not intentionally kill innocent people is one inviolable rule, but there are others as well:

> [I]t has been characteristic of [the Hebrew-Christian] ethic to teach that there are certain things forbidden whatever *consequences* threaten, such as: choosing to kill the innocent for any purpose, however good; vicarious punishment; treachery (by which I mean obtaining a man's confidence in a grave matter by promises of trustworthy friendship and then betraying him to his enemies); idolatry; sodomy; adultery; making a false profession of faith.

Of course, many philosophers do not agree; they insist that any rule may be broken, if the circumstances demand it. Anscombe says of them,

> It is noticeable that none of these philosophers displays any consciousness that there is such an ethic, which he is

contradicting: it is pretty well taken for obvious among them all that a prohibition such as that on murder does not operate in face of some consequences. But of course the strictness of the prohibition has as its point that *you are not to be tempted by fear or hope of consequences.*

Anscombe and her husband, Peter Geach, who was also a distinguished philosopher, were the 20th century's foremost philosophical champions of the doctrine that moral rules are absolute.

9.2. The Categorical Imperative

The idea that moral rules hold without exception is hard to defend. It is easy enough to explain why we *should* make an exception to a rule—we can simply point out that, in some circumstances, following the rule would have terrible consequences. But how can we explain why we should *not* make an exception to the rule, in such circumstances? It is a daunting assignment. One way would be to say that moral rules are God's inviolable commands. Apart from that, what can be said?

Prior to the 20th century, there was one major philosopher who believed that moral rules are absolute, and he offered a famous argument for this view. Immanuel Kant (1724–1804) was one of the seminal figures in modern thought. He argued, to take one example, that lying is never right, no matter what the circumstances. He did not appeal to theological considerations; he held, instead, that reason requires that we never lie. To see how he reached this remarkable conclusion, we will begin with a brief look at his general theory of ethics.

Kant observed that the word *ought* is often used nonmorally. For example,

1. If you want to become a better chess player, you ought to study the games of Garry Kasparov.
2. If you want to go to law school, you ought to sign up for the entrance examination.

Much of our conduct is governed by such "oughts." The pattern is: We have a certain desire (to become a better chess player, to go to law school); we recognize that a certain course of action would help us get what we want (studying Kasparov's games, signing up for the entrance examination); and so we conclude that we should follow the indicated plan.

Kant called these "hypothetical imperatives" because they tell us what to do *provided that* we have the relevant desires. A person who did not want to improve his or her chess would have no reason to study Kasparov's games; someone who did not want to go to law school would have no reason to take the entrance examination. Because the binding force of the "ought" depends on our having the relevant desire, we can escape its force simply by renouncing the desire. Thus if you no longer want to go to law school, you can escape the obligation to take the exam.

Moral obligations, by contrast, do not depend on our having particular desires. The form of a moral obligation is not "*If* you want so-and-so, then you ought to do such-and-such." Instead, moral requirements are *categorical:* they have the form, "You ought to do such-and-such, *period.*" The moral rule is not, for example, that you ought to help people *if* you care for them or *if* you have some other purpose that helping them might serve. Instead, the rule is that you should be helpful to people *regardless of* your particular wants and desires. That is why, unlike hypothetical "oughts," moral requirements cannot be escaped simply by saying "But I don't care about that."

Hypothetical "oughts" are easy to understand. They merely require us to adopt the means necessary to achieve the ends we seek. Categorical "oughts," on the other hand, are mysterious. How can we be obligated to behave in a certain way regardless of the ends we wish to achieve? Much of Kant's moral philosophy is an attempt to explain how this is possible.

Kant holds that, just as hypothetical "oughts" are possible because we have *desires,* categorical "oughts" are possible because we have *reason.* Categorical "oughts" are binding on rational agents simply because they are rational. How can this be so? It is, Kant says, because categorical oughts are derived from a principle that every rational person must accept. He calls this principle the Categorical Imperative. In his *Foundations of the Metaphysics of Morals* (1785), he expresses the Categorical Imperative like this: it is a rule which says,

> Act only according to that maxim by which you can at the same time will that it should become a universal law.

This principle summarizes a procedure for deciding whether an act is morally permissible. When you are contemplating doing a particular action, you are to ask what rule you would be follow-ing if you were to do that action. (This will be the "maxim" of the act.) Then you are to ask whether you would be willing for that rule to be followed by everyone all the time. (That would make it a "universal law" in the relevant sense.) If so, the rule may be followed, and the act is permissible. However, if you would not be willing for everyone to follow the rule, then you may not follow it, and the act is morally impermissible.

Kant gives several examples to explain how this works. Suppose, he says, a man needs to borrow money, and he knows that no one will lend it to him unless he promises to repay. But he also knows that he will be unable to repay. He therefore faces this problem: Should he promise to repay the debt, knowing that he cannot do so, in order to persuade someone to make the loan? If he were to do that, the "maxim of the act" (the rule he would be following) would be: Whenever you need a loan, promise to repay it, regardless of whether you believe you actu-ally can repay it. Now, could this rule become a universal law? Obviously not, because it would be self-defeating. Once this be-came a universal practice, no one would any longer believe such promises, and so no one would make loans because of them. As Kant himself puts it, "no one would believe what was promised to him but would only laugh at any such assertion as vain pretense."

Another of Kant's examples has to do with giving charity. Suppose, he says, someone refuses to help others in need, saying to himself, "What concern of mine is it? Let each one be happy as heaven wills, or as he can make himself, I will not take any-thing from him or even envy him; but to his welfare or to his as-sistance in time of need I have no desire to contribute." This, again, is a rule that one cannot will to be a universal law. For at some time in the future this man will himself be in need of as-sistance from others, and he would not want others to be so in-different to him.

9.3. Absolute Rules and the Duty Not to Lie

Being a moral agent, then, means guiding one's conduct by "universal laws"—moral rules that hold, without exception, in all circumstances. Kant thought that the rule against lying was one such rule. Of course, this was not the only absolute rule Kant defended—he thought there are many others; morality is full of them. But it will be useful to focus on the rule against lying as a convenient example. Kant devoted considerable space to discussing this rule, and it is clear that he felt especially strongly about it. He said that lying in any circumstances is "the obliteration of one's dignity as a human being." Kant offered two main arguments for this view.

1. His primary reason for thinking that lying is always wrong was that the prohibition of lying follows straightaway from the Categorical Imperative. We could not will that it be a universal law that we should lie, because it would be self-defeating; people would quickly learn that they could not rely on what other people said, and so the lies would not be believed. Surely there is something to this: In order for lies to be successful, people must generally believe that others tell the truth; so the success of a lie depends on there not being a "universal law" permitting it.

There is, however, a problem with this argument, which will become clear if we spell out Kant's line of thought more fully. Suppose it was necessary to lie to save someone's life. Should we do it? Kant would have us reason as follows:

(1) We should do only those actions that conform to rules that we could will to be adopted universally.

(2) If we were to lie, we would be following the rule "It is permissible to lie."

(3) This rule could not be adopted universally, because it would be self-defeating: people would stop believing one another, and then it would do no good to lie.

(4) Therefore, we should not lie.

The problem with this way of reasoning was nicely summarized by Elizabeth Anscombe when she wrote about Kant in the academic journal *Philosophy* in 1958:

> His own rigoristic convictions on the subject of lying were so intense that it never occurred to him that a lie could be relevantly described as anything but just a lie (e.g., as "a lie in such-and-such circumstances"). His rule about universalizable maxims is useless without stipulations as to what shall count as a relevant description of an action with a view to constructing a maxim about it.

In this respect, Anscombe was a model of intellectual integrity: Although she agreed with Kant's conclusion, she was quick to point out the error in his reasoning. The difficulty arises in step (2) of the argument. Exactly what rule would you be following if you lied? The crucial point is that there are many ways to formulate the rule; some of them might not be "universalizable" in Kant's sense, but some would be. Suppose we said you were following this rule (R): "It is permissible to lie when doing so would save someone's life." We could will that (R) be made a "universal law," and it would not be self-defeating.

2. Many of Kant's contemporaries thought that his insistence on absolute rules was strange, and they said so. One reviewer challenged him with this example: Imagine that someone is fleeing from a murderer and tells you he is going home to hide. Then the murderer comes, playing innocent, and asks where the first man went. You believe that if you tell the truth, the murderer will find the man and kill him. Furthermore, suppose the murderer is already headed in the right direction, and you believe that if you simply remain silent, he will find the man and kill him. What should you do? We might call this the Case of the Inquiring Murderer. In this case, most of us would think it is obvious that we should lie. After all, we might say, which is more important, telling the truth or saving someone's life?

Kant responded in an essay with the charmingly old-fashioned title "On a Supposed Right to Lie from Altruistic Motives," in which he discusses the Inquiring Murderer and gives a second argument for his view about lying. He writes:

> After you have honestly answered the murderer's question as to whether his intended victim is at home, it may be that he has slipped out so that he does not come in the way of the murderer, and thus the murder may not be committed. But if you had lied and said he was not at home when he had really gone out without your knowing it, and if the murderer had then met him as he went away and murdered him, you might justly be accused as the cause of his death. For if you had told the truth as far as you knew it, perhaps the murderer might have been apprehended by the neighbors while he searched the house and thus the deed might have been prevented. Therefore, whoever tells

a lie, however well intentioned he might be, must answer
for the consequences, however unforeseeable they were,
and pay the penalty for them . . .
    To be truthful (honest) in all deliberations, there-
fore, is a sacred and absolutely commanding decree of reason, limited by no expediency.

This argument may be stated in a more general form: We are
tempted to make exceptions to the rule against lying because in
some cases we think the consequences of truthfulness would be
bad and the consequences of lying good. However, we can never
be certain about what the consequences of our actions will be—
we cannot *know* that good results will follow. The results of lying
might be unexpectedly bad. Therefore, the best policy is to
avoid the known evil, lying, and let the consequences come as
they will. Even if the consequences are bad, they will not be our
fault, for we will have done our duty.

A similar argument, we may note, would apply to Truman's
decision to drop the atomic bombs on Hiroshima and Nagasaki.
The bombs were dropped in the hope that the war could be
swiftly concluded. But Truman did not know for sure that this
would happen. The Japanese might have hunkered down and
the invasion might still have been necessary. So, Truman was
betting hundreds of thousands of lives on the mere hope that
good results might ensue.

The problems with this argument are obvious enough—so
obvious, in fact, that it is surprising a philosopher of Kant's
stature was not more sensitive to them. In the first place, the argument depends on an unreasonably pessimistic view of what we
can know. Sometimes we can be quite confident of what the consequences of our actions will be, in which case we need not hes-
itate because of uncertainty. Moreover—and this is a more interesting matter, from a philosophical point of view—Kant seems
to assume that although we would be morally responsible for any
bad consequences of lying, we would not be similarly responsible for any bad consequences of telling the truth. Suppose, as a
result of our telling the truth, the murderer found his victim and
killed him. Kant seems to assume that we would be blameless.
But can we escape responsibility so easily? After all, we aided the
murderer. This argument, then, is not very convincing.

9.4. Conflicts between Rules

The idea that moral rules are absolute, allowing no exceptions, is implausible in light of such cases as the Case of the Inquiring Murderer, and Kant's arguments for it are unsatisfactory. But are there any convincing arguments *against* the idea, apart from its being implausible?

The principal argument against absolute moral rules has to do with the possibility of conflict cases. Suppose it is held to be absolutely wrong to do A in any circumstances and also wrong to do B in any circumstances. Then what about the case in which a person is faced with the choice between doing A and doing B, when he must do something and there are no other alternatives available? This kind of conflict case seems to show that it is logically untenable to hold that moral rules are absolute.

Is there any way that this objection can be met? One way would be to deny that such cases ever actually occur. Peter Geach took just this view, appealing to God's providence. We can describe fictitious cases in which there is no way to avoid violating one of the absolute rules, he said, but God will not permit such circumstances to exist in the real world. In his book *God and the Soul* (1969) Geach writes:

> "But suppose circumstances are such that observance of one Divine law, say the law against lying, involves breach of some other absolute Divine prohibition?"—If God is rational, he does not command the impossible; if God governs all events by his providence, he can see to it that circumstances in which a man is inculpably faced by a choice between forbidden acts do not occur. Of course such circumstances (with the clause "and there is no way out" written into their description) are consistently describable; but God's providence could ensure that they do not in fact arise. Contrary to what nonbelievers often say, belief in the existence of God does make a difference to what one expects to happen.

Do such cases actually occur? There is no doubt that serious moral rules do sometimes clash. During the Second World War, Dutch fishermen smuggled Jewish refugees to England in their boats, and the fishing boats with refugees in the hold would sometimes be stopped by Nazi patrol boats. The Nazi captain would call out and ask the Dutch captain where he was bound, who was on board, and so forth. The fishermen would lie and be allowed to pass. Now it is clear that the fishermen had only two alternatives, to lie or to allow their passengers (and themselves) to be taken and killed. No third alternative was available; they could not, for example, remain silent or outrun the Nazis.

Now suppose the two rules "It is wrong to lie" and "It is wrong to facilitate the murder of innocent people" are both taken to be absolute. The Dutch fishermen would have to do one of these things; therefore, a moral view that absolutely prohibits both is incoherent. Of course this difficulty could be avoided if one holds that at least one of these rules is not absolute. But it is doubtful that this way out will be available every time there is a conflict. It is also hard to understand, at the most basic level, why some serious moral rules should be absolute, if others are not.

9.5. Another Look at Kant's Basic Idea

In his book *A Short History of Ethics* (1966), Alasdair MacIntyre remarks that "For many who have never heard of philosophy, let alone of Kant, morality is roughly what Kant said it was"—that is, a system of rules that one must follow from a sense of duty, regardless of one's wants or desires. Yet at the same time, few contemporary philosophers would defend the central idea of his ethics, the Categorical Imperative, as Kant formulated it. As we have seen, the Categorical Imperative is beset by serious, perhaps insurmountable, problems. Nonetheless, it might be a mistake to give up on Kant's principle too quickly. Is there some basic idea underlying the Categorical Imperative that we might accept, even if we do not accept Kant's particular way of expressing it? I believe that there is, and that the power of this idea accounts, at least in part, for Kant's vast influence.

Remember that Kant thinks the Categorical Imperative is binding on rational agents simply because they are rational—in other words, a person who did not accept this principle would be guilty not merely of being immoral but of being irrational. This is a compelling idea, that there are rational as well as moral constraints on what a good person may believe and do. But what exactly does this mean? In what sense would it be irrational to reject the Categorical Imperative?

The basic idea is related to the thought that a moral judgment must be backed by good reasons—if it is true that you ought (or ought not) to do such-and-such, then there must be a reason why you should (or should not) do it. For example, you may think that you ought not to set forest fires because property would be destroyed and people would be killed. The Kantian twist is to point out that *if you accept any considerations as reasons in one case, you must also accept them as reasons in other cases.* If there is another case where property would be destroyed and people killed, you must accept this as a reason for action in that case, too. It is no good saying that you accept reasons some of the time, but not all the time; or that other people must respect them, but not you. Moral reasons, if they are valid at all, are binding on all people at all times. This is a requirement of consistency; and Kant was right to think that no rational person may deny it.

This is the Kantian idea—or, I should say, one of the Kantian ideas—that has been so influential. It has a number of important implications. It implies that a person cannot regard herself as special, from a moral point of view: She cannot consistently think that she is permitted to act in ways that are forbidden to others, or that her interests are more important than other people's interests. As one commentator remarked, I cannot say that it is all right for me to drink your beer and then complain when you drink mine. Moreover, it implies that there are rational constraints on what we may do: We may want to do something—say, drink someone else's beer—but recognize that we cannot consistently do it because we cannot at the same time accept the implication that he may drink our beer. If Kant was not the first to recognize this, he was the first to make it the cornerstone of a fully worked-out system of morals. That was his great contribution.

But Kant went one step further and said that consistency requires rules that have no exceptions. It is not hard to see how his basic idea pushed him in that direction; but the extra step was not necessary, and it has caused trouble for his theory ever since. Rules, even within a Kantian framework, need not be regarded as absolute. All that Kant's basic idea requires is that when we violate a rule, we do so for a reason that we would be willing for anyone to accept, were they in our position. In the Case of the Inquiring Murderer, this means that we may violate the rule against lying only if we would be willing for anyone to do so were he faced with the same situation. And most of us would readily agree to that.

Harry Truman, too, would no doubt agree that anyone else in his particular circumstances would have good reason to drop the bomb. Thus, even if Truman was wrong, Kant's arguments do not prove it. One might say, instead, that Truman was wrong because other options available to him would have had better consequences—many people have argued, for example, that he should have negotiated an end to the war on terms that the Japanese could have accepted. But saying that negotiating would have been better, because of its consequences, is very different from saying that Truman's actual course violated an absolute rule.

CHAPTER 10

Kant and Respect for Persons

Are there any who would not admire man?

GIOVANNI PICO DELLA MIRANDOLA, *ORATION
ON THE DIGNITY OF MAN* (1486)

10.1. The Idea of Human Dignity

Kant thought that human beings occupy a special place in creation. Of course he was not alone in thinking this. It is an old idea: From ancient times, humans have considered themselves to be essentially different from all other creatures—and not just different, but better. In fact, humans have traditionally thought themselves to be quite fabulous. Kant certainly did. On his view, human beings have "an intrinsic worth, i.e., *dignity*," which makes them valuable "above all price." Other animals, by contrast, have value only insofar as they serve human purposes. In his *Lectures on Ethics* (1779), Kant wrote:

> But so far as animals are concerned, we have no direct duties. Animals . . . are there merely as means to an end. That end is man.

We can, therefore, use animals in any way we please. We do not even have a "direct duty" to refrain from torturing them. Kant admits that it probably is wrong to torture them, but the reason is not that they would be hurt; the reason is only that humans might suffer indirectly as a result of it, because "He who is cruel to animals becomes hard also in his dealings with men." Thus, on Kant's view, mere animals have no moral importance. Human beings are, however, another story entirely. According to Kant, humans may never be "used" as means to an end. He even went so far as to suggest that this is the ultimate law of morality.

Like a number of other philosophers, Kant believed that morality can be summed up in one ultimate principle, from which all our duties and obligations are derived. He called this principle the Categorical Imperative. In the *Foundations of the Metaphysics of Morals* (1785) he expressed it like this:

> Act only according to that maxim by which you can at the same time will that it should become a universal law.

However, Kant also gave another formulation of the Categorical Imperative. Later in the same book, he said that the ultimate moral principle may be understood as saying:

> Act so that you treat humanity, whether in your own person or in that of another, always as an end and never as a means only.

Scholars have wondered ever since why Kant thought these two rules were equivalent. They seem to express different moral conceptions. Are they, as he apparently believed, two versions of the same basic idea, or are they really different ideas? We will not pause over this question. Instead we will concentrate on Kant's belief that morality requires us to treat persons "always as an end and never as a means only." What exactly does this mean, and why should we think it true?

When Kant said that the value of human beings "is above all price," he did not intend this as mere rhetoric but as an objective judgment about the place of human beings in the scheme of things. Two important facts about people, in his view, support this judgment.

First, because people have desires and goals, other things have value *for* them, in relation to their projects. Mere "things" (and this includes nonhuman animals, whom Kant considered unable to have self-conscious desires and goals) have value only as means to ends, and it is human ends that *give* them value. Thus if you want to become a better chess player, a book of chess instruction will have value for you; but apart from such ends the book has no value. Or if you want to travel about, a car will have value for you; but apart from such a desire the car will have no value.

Second, and even more important, humans have "an intrinsic worth, i.e., dignity," because they are *rational agents,* that is, free agents capable of making their own decisions, setting their own goals, and guiding their conduct by reason. Because the moral law is the law of reason, rational beings are the embodiment of the moral law itself. The only way that moral goodness can exist is for rational creatures to apprehend what they should do and, acting from a sense of duty, do it. This, Kant thought, is the only thing that has "moral worth." Thus if there were no rational beings, the moral dimension of the world would simply disappear.

It makes no sense, therefore, to regard rational beings merely as one kind of valuable thing among others. They are the beings for whom mere "things" have value, and they are the beings whose conscientious actions have moral worth. So Kant concludes that their value must be absolute, and not comparable to the value of anything else.

If their value is "beyond all price," it follows that rational beings must be treated "always as an end and never as a means only." This means, on the most superficial level, that we have a strict duty of beneficence toward other persons: We must strive to promote their welfare; we must respect their rights, avoid harming them, and generally "endeavor, so far as we can, to further the ends of others."

But Kant's idea also has a somewhat deeper implication. The beings we are talking about are rational beings, and "treating them as ends-in-themselves" means *respecting their rationality.* Thus we may never manipulate people, or use people, to achieve our purposes, no matter how good those purposes may be. Kant gives this example, which is similar to one he uses to illustrate the first version of his Categorical Imperative: Suppose you need money, and you want a loan, but you know you will not be able to repay it. In desperation, you consider making a false promise to repay in order to trick a friend into giving you the money. May you do this? Perhaps you need the money for a good purpose—so good, in fact, that you might convince yourself the lie would be justified. Nevertheless, if you lied to your friend, you would merely be manipulating him and using him "as a means."

On the other hand, what would it be like to treat your friend "as an end"? Suppose you told the truth, that you need the money for a certain purpose but will not be able to repay it. Then your friend could make up his own mind about whether to let you have the money. He could exercise his own powers of reason, consulting his own values and wishes, and make a free, autonomous choice. If he did decide to give the money for the stated purpose, he would be choosing *to make that purpose his own.* Thus you would not be using him as a means to achieving your goal, for it would now be his goal, too. This is what Kant meant when he said, "Rational beings . . . must always be esteemed at the same time as ends, i.e., only as beings who must be able to contain in themselves the end of the very same action."

Kant's conception of human dignity is not easy to grasp; it is probably the most difficult notion discussed in this book. We need to find a way to make the idea clearer. In order to do that, we will consider in some detail one of its most important applications. This may be better than a dry, theoretical discussion. Kant believed that if we take the idea of human dignity seriously, we will be able to understand the practice of criminal punishment in a new and revealing way. The rest of this chapter will be devoted to an examination of this example.

10.2. Retribution and Utility in the Theory of Punishment

Jeremy Bentham, the great utilitarian theorist, said that "all punishment is mischief: all punishment in itself is evil." By this he meant that punishment always involves treating people badly, whether by taking away their freedom (imprisonment), their property (fines), or even their life (capital punishment). Since these things are all evils, they require justification. How can it be right to treat people like this?

The traditional answer is that punishment is justified as a way of "paying back" the offender for his evil deed. Those who have committed crimes, such as stealing from other people or assaulting other people, deserve to be treated badly in return. It is essentially a matter of justice: If someone harms other people, justice requires that he be harmed also. As the ancient saying has it, "An eye for an eye, a tooth for a tooth."

This view is known as Retributivism. Retributivism was, on Bentham's view, a wholly unsatisfactory idea, because it advocated the infliction of suffering without any compensating gain in happiness. Retributivism would have us increase, not decrease, the amount of suffering in the world. This is not a "hidden" implication of Retributivism. Kant, who was a retributivist, was aware of this implication and openly embraced it. In *The Critique of Practical Reason* (1788), he wrote:

> When someone who delights in annoying and vexing peace-loving folk receives at last a right good beating, it is certainly an ill, but everyone approves of it and considers it as good in itself even if nothing further results from it.

Thus punishing people may increase the amount of misery in the world; but according to Kant that is all right, for the extra suffering is borne by the criminal who, after all, deserves it. Utilitarianism takes a very different approach. According to Utilitarianism, our duty is to do whatever will increase the amount of happiness in the world. Punishment is, on its face, "an evil" because it makes someone—the person who is punished—unhappy. Thus Bentham says, "If it ought at all to be admitted, it ought to be admitted in as far as it promises to exclude some greater evil." In other words, it can be justified only if it will have good results that, on balance, outweigh the evil done.

So for the utilitarian, the question is whether a good purpose is served by punishing criminals, other than simply making them suffer. Utilitarians have traditionally answered in the affirmative. There are two ways in which the practice of punishing lawbreakers benefits society.

First, punishing criminals helps to prevent crime, or at least to reduce the level of criminal activity in a society. People who are tempted to misbehave can be deterred from doing so if they know they will be punished. Of course, the threat of punishment will not always be efficacious. Sometimes people will break the law anyway. But there will be *less* misconduct if punishments are threatened. Imagine what it would be like if the police did not stand ready to arrest thieves; one would have to be a hopeless romantic not to recognize that there would be a lot more thievery. Since criminal misconduct causes unhappiness to its victims, in preventing crime (by providing punishments) we are preventing unhappiness—in fact we are undoubtedly preventing more unhappiness than we are causing. Thus, because there is a net gain in happiness, the utilitarian would see punishment as justified.

Second, a well-designed system of punishment might have the effect of rehabilitating wrongdoers. Criminals are often people with emotional problems, who find it difficult to function well in society. They are often ill educated and unable to hold down jobs. Considering this, why should we not respond to crime by attacking the problems that give rise to it? If a person is breaking society's rules, he is a danger to society and may first be imprisoned to remove the danger. But while he is there, his problems should be addressed with psychological therapy, educational opportunities, or job training, as appropriate. If he can eventually be returned to society as a productive citizen, rather than as a criminal, both hc and society will benefit.

The logical outcome of this way of thinking is that we should abandon the notion of *punishment* and replace it with the more humane notion of *treatment*. Karl Menninger, the distinguished psychologist, drew this conclusion when he wrote in 1959:

> We, the agents of society, must move to end the game of tit-for-tat and blow-for-blow in which the offender has foolishly engaged himself and us. We are not driven, as he is, to wild and impulsive actions. With knowledge comes power, and with power there is no need for the frightened vengeance of the old penology. In its place should go a quiet, dignified, therapeutic program for the rehabilitation of the disorganized one, if possible, the protection of society during the treatment period, and his guided return to useful citizenship, as soon as this can be effected.

These utilitarian ideas have dominated Anglo-American law for the past century, and today the utilitarian theory of punishment is the reigning orthodoxy. Prisons, once mere places of confinement, have been redesigned (in theory, at least) as centers for rehabilitation, complete with psychologists, libraries, educational programs, and vocational training. The shift in thinking has been so great that the term *prison* is no longer in favor; the preferred nomenclature is *correctional facility*, and the people who work there are called *corrections officers*. Notice the implications of the new terminology—inmates are there not to be "punished" but to be "corrected." In fact, prisons remain brutal places and more often than not the programs of rehabilitation have been dismally unsuccessful. Nevertheless, the programs are *supposed to be* rehabilitative. The victory of the utilitarian ideology has been virtually complete.

10.3. Kant's Retributivism

Like all orthodoxies, the utilitarian theory of punishment has generated opposition. Much of the opposition is practical in nature; the programs of rehabilitation, despite all the efforts that have been put into them, have not worked very well. In California, for example, more has been done to "rehabilitate" criminals than anywhere else; yet the rate of recidivism is higher there than in most other states. But some of the opposition is also based on purely theoretical considerations that go back at least to Kant.

Kant abjured "the serpent-windings of Utilitarianism" because, he said, the theory is incompatible with human dignity. In the first place, it has us calculating how to use people as means to an end, and this is not permissible. If we imprison the criminal in order to secure the well-being of society, we are merely using him for the benefit of others. This violates the fundamental rule that "one man ought never to be dealt with merely as a means subservient to the purpose of another."

Moreover, the aim of "rehabilitation," although it sounds noble enough, is actually no more than the attempt to mold people into what we think they should be. As such, it is a violation of their rights as autonomous beings to decide for themselves what sort of people they will be. We do have the right to respond to their wickedness by "paying them back" for it, but we do not have the right to violate their integrity by trying to manipulate their personalities.

Thus Kant would have no part of utilitarian justifications of punishment. Instead, he argued that punishment should be governed by two principles. First, people should be punished simply because they have committed crimes, and for no other reason:

> Juridical punishment can never be administered merely as a means for promoting another good either with regard to the criminal himself or to civil society, but must in all cases be imposed only because the individual on whom it is inflicted has committed a crime.

And second, Kant says it is important to punish the criminal *proportionately* to the seriousness of his crime. Small punishments may suffice for small crimes, but big punishments are necessary in response to big crimes:

But what is the mode and measure of punishment which public justice takes as its principle and standard? It is just the principle of equality, by which the pointer of the scale of justice is made to incline no more to the one side than to the other . . . Hence it may be said: "If you slander another, you slander yourself; if you steal from another, you steal from yourself; if you strike another, you strike yourself; if you kill another, you kill yourself." This is . . . the only principle which . . . can definitely assign both the quality and the quantity of a just penalty.

This second principle leads Kant inevitably to endorse capital punishment; for in response to murder, only death is a sufficiently stern penalty. In a notorious passage, Kant says:

Even if a civil society resolved to dissolve itself with the consent of all its members—as might be supposed in the case of a people inhabiting an island resolving to separate and scatter throughout the whole world—the last murderer lying in prison ought to be executed before the resolution was carried out. This ought to be done in order that every one may realize the desert of his deeds, and that blood-guiltiness may not remain on the people; for otherwise they will all be regarded as participants in the murder as a public violation of justice.

It is worth noting that Utilitarianism has been faulted for violating both of Kant's principles. There is nothing in the basic idea of Utilitarianism that limits punishment to the guilty, or that limits the amount of punishment to the amount deserved. If the purpose of punishment is to secure the general welfare, as Utilitarianism says, it could sometimes happen that the general welfare will be served by "punishing" someone who has not committed a crime—an innocent person. Similarly, it might happen that the general welfare is promoted by punishing people excessively—a greater punishment might have a greater deterrent effect. But both of these are, on their face, violations of justice, which Retributivism would not allow.

Now Kant's two principles do not constitute an argument in favor of punishment or a justification of it. They merely describe limits on what punishment can justly involve: Only the guilty may be punished, and the injury done to the person punished must be comparable to the injury he has inflicted on others. We still need an argument to show that the practice of punishment, conceived in this way, would be a morally good thing. We have already noted that Kant regards punishment as a matter of justice. He says that, if the guilty are not punished, justice is not done. This is one argument. But Kant also provides an additional argument, based on his conception of treating people as "ends-in-themselves." This additional argument is Kant's distinctive contribution to the theory of Retributivism.

On the face of it, it seems unlikely that we could describe punishing someone as "respecting him as a person" or as "treating him as an end-in-himself." How could taking away someone's freedom, by sending him to prison, be a way of "respecting" him? Yet that is exactly what Kant suggests. Even more paradoxically, he implies that executing someone may also be a way of treating him "as an end." How can this be?

Remember that, for Kant, treating someone as an "end-in-himself" means treating him *as a rational being*. Thus we have to ask, What does it mean to treat someone as a rational being? A rational being is someone who is capable of reasoning about his conduct and who freely decides what he will do, on the basis of his own conception of what is best. Because he has these capacities, a rational being is responsible for his actions.

We need to bear in mind the difference between:

1. Treating someone as a responsible being

and

2. Treating someone as a being who is not responsible for his conduct.

Mere animals, who lack reason, are not responsible for their actions; nor are people who are mentally ill and not in control of themselves. In such cases it would be absurd to "hold them accountable." We could not properly feel gratitude or resentment toward them, for they are not responsible for any good or ill they cause. Moreover, we cannot expect them to understand *why* we treat them as we do, any more than they understand why they behave as they do. So we have no choice but to deal with them by manipulating them, rather than by addressing them as autonomous individuals. When we spank a dog who has urinated on the rug, for example, we may do so in an attempt to prevent him from doing it again; but we are merely trying to "train" him. We could not reason with him even if we wanted to. The same goes for mentally deranged humans.

On the other hand, rational beings are responsible for their behavior and so they are accountable for what they do. We may feel gratitude when they behave well and resentment when they behave badly. Reward and punishment—not "training" or other manipulation—are the natural expressions of this gratitude and resentment. Thus in punishing people, we are holding them responsible for their actions in a way in which we cannot hold mere animals responsible. We are responding to them not as people who are "sick" or who have no control over themselves, but as people who have freely chosen their evil deeds.

Furthermore, in dealing with responsible agents, we may properly allow their conduct to determine, at least in part, how we respond to them. If someone has been kind to you, you may respond by being generous in return; and if someone is nasty to you, you may also take that into account in deciding how to deal with him or her. And why shouldn't you? Why should you treat everyone alike, regardless of how *they* have chosen to behave?

Kant gives this last point a distinctive twist. There is, on his view, a deep logical reason for responding to other people "in kind." The first formulation of the Categorical Imperative comes into play here. When we decide what to do, we in effect proclaim our wish that our conduct be made into a "universal law." Therefore, when a rational being decides to treat people in a certain way, he decrees that in his judgment *this is the way people are to be treated.* Thus if we treat him the same way in return, we are doing nothing more than treating him *as he has decided* people are to be treated. If he treats others badly, and we treat him badly, we are complying with his own decision. (And of course, if he treats others well, and we treat him well in return, we are also complying with the choice he has made.) We are allowing him to decide how he is to be treated and so we are, in a perfectly clear sense, respecting his judgment, by allowing it to control our treatment of him. Thus Kant says of the criminal, "His own evil deed draws the punishment upon himself."

By associating punishment with the idea of treating people as rational beings, Kant gave the retributive theory a new depth. What we ultimately think of the theory will depend on what we think about the big issues Kant has identified—on what we judge the nature of crime, and the nature of criminals, to be. If lawbreakers are, as Menninger suggests, "disorganized personalities" who are "driven to wild and impulsive actions" over which they have no control, then the therapeutic model will inevitably have greater appeal than Kant's sterner attitude. In fact, Kant himself would insist that if criminals are not responsible agents, it would make no sense to resent their behavior and "punish" them for it. But to the extent that they are regarded as responsible people, without excuse, who simply choose to violate the rights of others for no rationally acceptable motive, Kantian Retributivism will continue to have great persuasive power.

CHAPTER 11

The Idea of a Social Contract

> The passions that incline men to peace, are fear of death; desire of such things as are necessary to commodious living; and a hope by their industry to obtain them. And reason suggesteth convenient articles of peace, upon which men may be drawn to agreement. These articles, are they, which otherwise are called the Laws of Nature.
>
> THOMAS HOBBES, *LEVIATHAN* (1651)

11.1. Hobbes's Argument

Suppose we take away all the traditional props for morality. Assume, first, that there is no God to issue commands and reward virtue; and second, that there are no "moral facts" built into the nature of things. Further, suppose we deny that human beings are naturally altruistic—we see people as essentially motivated to pursue their own interests. Where, then, does morality come from? If we cannot appeal to God, moral facts, or natural altruism, is there anything left on which morality might be founded?

Thomas Hobbes, the foremost British philosopher of the 17th century, tried to show that morality does not depend on any of those things. Instead, morality should be understood as the solution to a practical problem that arises for self-interested human beings. We all want to live as well as possible; but none of us can flourish unless we have a peaceful, cooperative social order. And we cannot have a peaceful, cooperative social order without rules. The moral rules, then, are simply the rules that are necessary if we are to gain the benefits of social living. That—not God, altruism, or "moral facts"—is the key to understanding ethics.

Hobbes begins by asking what it would be like if there were no social rules and no commonly accepted mechanism

141

for enforcing them. Imagine, if you will, that there was no such thing as government—no laws, no police, and no courts. In this situation, each of us would be free to do as we pleased. Hobbes called this *the state of nature*. What would it be like? Hobbes thought it would be dreadful. In the *Leviathan* he wrote that there would be

> no place for industry, because the fruit thereof is uncertain: and consequently no culture of the earth; no navigation, nor use of the commodities that may be imported by sea; no commodious building; no instruments of moving, and removing, such things as require much force; no knowledge of the face of the earth; no account of time; no arts; no letters; no society; and which is worst of all, continual fear, and danger of violent death; and the life of man, solitary, poor, nasty, brutish, and short.

Why would things be so bad? It is not because people are bad. Rather, it is because of four basic facts about the conditions of human life:

- First, there is the fact of *equality of need*. Each of us needs the same basic things in order to survive—food, clothing, shelter. Although we may differ in some of our needs (diabetics need insulin, others don't), we are all essentially alike.
- Second, there is the fact of *scarcity*. We do not live in the Garden of Eden, where milk flows in streams and every tree hangs heavy with fruit. The world is a hard, inhospitable place, where the things we need to survive do not exist in plentiful supply. We have to work hard to produce them, and even then there often is not enough to go around.
- If there are not enough essential goods to go around, who will get them? Since each of us wants to live, and to live as well as possible, each of us will want as much as we can get. But will we be able to prevail over the others, who also want the scarce goods? Hobbes thinks not, because of the third fact about our condition, the fact of *the essential equality of human power*. No one is so superior to everyone else, in strength and cunning, that he or she can prevail over them indefinitely. Of course, some people are smarter and stronger than others; but

even the strongest can be brought down by others acting together.

- If we cannot prevail by our own strength, what hope do
  we have? Can we, for example, rely on the charity or
  good will of other people to help us? We cannot. The
  fourth and final fact is the fact of *limited altruism*. Even if
  people are not wholly selfish, they nevertheless care very
  much about themselves; and we cannot simply assume
  that whenever our vital interests conflict with theirs, they
  will step aside.

When we put these facts together, a grim picture emerges. We
all need the same basic things, and there aren't enough of them
to go around. Therefore, we will be in a kind of competition for
them. But no one has what it takes to prevail in this competition,
and no one—or almost no one—will be willing to forgo the satisfaction of his or her needs in favor of others. The result, as
Hobbes puts it, is a "constant state of war, of one with all." And
it is a war no one can hope to win. The reasonable person who
wants to survive will try to seize what he needs and prepare to
defend it from attack. But others will be doing the same thing.
This is why life in the state of nature would be intolerable.

Hobbes did not think this a mere speculation. He pointed
out that this is what actually happens when governments collapse, as during a civil insurrection. People begin desperately to
hoard food, arm themselves, and lock out their neighbors.
(What would you do if tomorrow morning you woke up to discover that because of some great catastrophe the government
had collapsed so that there were no functioning laws, police, or
courts?) Moreover, the nations of the world, without any mean-
ingful international law, exist in relation to one another very
much like individuals in the "state of nature," and they are constantly at one another's throats, armed and distrustful.

Clearly, to escape the state of nature, some way must be
found for people to cooperate with one another. In a stable and
cooperative society, the amount of essential goods can be increased and distributed to all who need them. But two things
are required for this to happen. First, there must be guarantees
that people will *not harm one another*—people must be able to
work together without fear of attack, theft, or treachery. And
second, people must be able to rely on one another to *keep their*

agreements. Only then can there be a division of labor. If one person grows food and another spends his time helping the sick, while still another builds houses, with each expecting to share in the benefits created by the others, each person in the chain must be able to count on the others to perform as expected.

Once these assurances are in place, a society can develop in which everyone is better off than they were in the state of nature. There can then be "commodities imported by the sea, commodious building, arts, letters," and the like. But—and this is one of Hobbes's main points—in order for this to happen, government must be established; for it is government, with its system of laws, police, and courts, that ensures that people can live with a minimum fear of attack and that people will have to keep their bargains with one another. Government is an indispensable part of the scheme.

To escape the state of nature, then, people must agree to the establishment of rules to govern their relations with one another, and they must agree to the establishment of an agency— the state—with the power necessary to enforce those rules. According to Hobbes, such an agreement actually exists, and it makes social living possible. This agreement, to which every citizen is a party, is called *the social contract.*

In addition to explaining the purpose of the state, the Social Contract Theory explains the nature of morality. The two are closely linked: The state exists to enforce the most important rules necessary for social living, while morality *consists in* the whole set of rules that facilitate social living.

It is only within the context of the social contract that we can become beneficent beings, because the contract creates the conditions under which we can afford to care about others. In the state of nature, it is every man for himself; it would be foolish for anyone to adopt the policy of "looking out for others," because one could do so only at the cost of putting one's own interests in continual jeopardy. But in society, altruism becomes possible. By releasing us from "the continual fear of violent death," the social contract frees us to take heed of others. Jean-Jacques Rousseau (1712–1778), the French thinker who after Hobbes is most closely identified with this theory, went so far as to say that we become *different kinds of creatures* when we enter civilized relations with others. In his most famous work, *The Social Contract* (1762), Rousseau wrote:

The passage from the state of nature to the civil state pro-
duces a very remarkable change in man . . . Then only, when
the voice of duty takes the place of physical impulses and
right to appetite, does man, who so far had considered only
himself, find that he is forced to act on different principles,
and to consult his reason before listening to his inclinations
. . . His faculties are so stimulated and developed, his ideas
so extended, his feelings so ennobled, and his whole soul so
uplifted, that, did not the abuses of this new condition often degrade him below that which he left, he would be
bound to bless continually the happy moment which took
him from it forever, and, instead of a stupid and unimagi-
native animal, made him an intelligent being and a man.

And what does the "voice of duty" require this new man to do?
It requires him to set aside his private, self-centered "inclinations" in favor of rules that impartially promote the welfare of
everyone alike. But he is able to do this only because others have
agreed to do the same thing—that is the essence of the "contract." Thus we can summarize the social contract conception of
morality as follows:

*Morality consists in the set of rules, governing how people are to
treat one another, that rational people will agree to accept, for their mutual benefit, on the condition that others follow those rules as well.*

11.2. The Prisoner's Dilemma

Hobbes's argument is one way of arriving at the Social Contract
Theory. There is another line of thought, however, that has also
impressed many philosophers in recent years. This line of
thought is connected with a problem in decision theory known
as the Prisoner's Dilemma. The Prisoner's Dilemma may be
stated first in the form of a puzzle; you may want to see if you
can solve it before looking at the answer.

Suppose you live in a totalitarian society, and one day, to
your astonishment, you are arrested and charged with treason.
The police say that you have been plotting against the government with a man named Smith, who has also been arrested and
is being held in a separate cell. The interrogator demands that
you confess. You protest your innocence; you don't even know
Smith. But this does no good. It soon becomes clear your cap-
tors are not interested in the truth; for reasons of their own,

they merely want to convict someone. They offer you the following deal:

- If Smith does not confess, but you confess and testify against him, they will release you. You will go free, whereas Smith, who did not cooperate, will be put away for 10 years.
- If Smith confesses and you do not, the situation will be reversed—he will go free while you get 10 years.
- If you both confess, however, you will each be sentenced to 5 years.
- But if neither of you confesses, there won't be enough evidence to convict either of you. They can hold you for a year, but then they will have to let both of you go.

Finally, you are told that Smith is being offered the same deal; but you cannot communicate with him and you have no way of knowing what he will do.

The problem is this: Assuming that your only goal is to spend as little time in jail as possible, what should you do? Confess or not confess? For the purposes of this problem, you should forget about maintaining your dignity, standing up for your rights, and other such notions. That is not what this problem is about. You should also forget about trying to help Smith. This problem is strictly about calculating what is in your own interests. The question is: What will get you free the quickest? Confessing or not confessing?

At first glance it may seem that the question cannot be answered unless you know what Smith will do. But that is an illusion. The problem has a perfectly clear solution: No matter what Smith does, you should confess. This can be shown by the following reasoning.

(1) Either Smith will confess or he won't.

(2) Suppose Smith confesses. Then, if you confess you will get 5 years, whereas if you do not confess you will get 10. Therefore, if he confesses, you are better off confessing as well.

(3) On the other hand, suppose Smith does not confess. Then you are in this position: If you confess you will go free, whereas if you do not confess you will remain imprisoned for a year. Clearly, then, even if Smith does not confess, you will still be better off if you do.

(4) Therefore, you must confess. That will get you out of jail the soonest, regardless of what Smith does.

So far, so good. But there is a catch. Remember that Smith is being offered the same deal. Assuming that he is not stupid, he will also conclude from the very same reasoning that he should confess. Thus the outcome will be that you will both confess, and this means that you will both be given 5-year sentences. *But if you had both done the opposite, each of you could have gotten out in only one year.* That's the catch. By rationally pursuing your own interests, you both end up worse off than if you had acted differently. That is what makes the Prisoner's Dilemma a dilemma. It is a paradoxical situation: You and Smith will both be better off if you simultaneously do what is *not* in your own individual self-interests.

If you could communicate with Smith, of course, you could make an agreement with him. You could agree that neither of you would confess; then you could both get the one-year detention. By cooperating you would both be better off than if you acted independently. Cooperating will not get either of you the optimum result—immediate freedom—but it will get both of you a better result than either of you could obtain if you did not cooperate.

It would be vital, however, that any agreement between you be enforceable, because if he reneged and confessed, while you kept the bargain, then you would end up serving the maximum 10 years while he went free. Thus, in order for it to be rational for you to keep your part of such a bargain, you would have to be assured that he will have to keep his part. (And of course he would have the same worry about you reneging.) Only an enforceable agreement could provide a way out of the dilemma, for either of you.

Morality as the Solution to a Prisoner's-Dilemma-Type Problem.
The Prisoner's Dilemma is not just a clever puzzle. Although the story we have told is fictitious, the pattern it exemplifies comes up often in real life. Prisoner's-Dilemma-type situations occur whenever two conditions are present:

1. It must be a situation in which people's interests are affected not only by what they do but by what other people do as well;

and

2. It must be a situation in which, paradoxically, everyone will end up worse off if they individually pursue their own interests than if they simultaneously do what is not in their own individual interests.

This kind of situation comes up in real life much more often than you might think.

Consider, for example, the choice between two general strategies of living. First, you could pursue your own self-interests exclusively—in every situation, you could do whatever will benefit yourself, taking no notice of how others might be affected. Let us call this "acting egoistically." Alternatively, you could be concerned with other people's welfare as well as your own, balancing the two against one another, and sometimes forgoing your own interests in order to benefit them. Let us call this strategy "acting benevolently."

But it is not only you who has to decide how to live. Other people will also have to choose which policy to adopt. There are four possibilities: First, you could be an egoist while other people are benevolent; second, others could be egoists while you are benevolent; third, everyone could be egoistic; and fourth, everyone could be benevolent. How would you fare in each of these situations? Purely from the point of view of advancing your own welfare, you might assess the possibilities like this:

- You would be best off in the situation in which you were an egoist while other people were benevolent. You would get the benefit of their generosity, without having to return the favor. (In this situation you would be, in the terminology of decision theory, a "free rider.")
- Second-best would be the situation in which everyone was benevolent. You would no longer have the advantage of being able to ignore other people's interests, but at least you would have the advantages that go with considerate treatment by others. (This is the situation of "ordinary morality.")
- A bad situation, but not the worst, would be one in which everyone was egoistic. You would try to protect your own interests, although you would get little help from anyone else. (This is Hobbes's "state of nature.")

- And finally, you would be worst off in a situation in which you were benevolent while others are egoists. Other people could knife you in the back when it was to their advantage, but you would not be free to do the same. You would come out on the short end every time. (We might say that in this situation you are a "sucker.")

Now this is exactly the kind of array that gives rise to the Prisoner's Dilemma. Based on these assessments, you should adopt the egoistic strategy:

(1) Either other people will respect your interests or they won't.

(2) If they do respect your interests, you will be better off not respecting theirs, at least whenever it is to your advantage not to do so. This will be the optimum situation—you get to be a free rider.

(3) If they do not respect your interests, then it would be foolish for you to respect theirs—that would land you in the worst possible situation. You would be a sucker.

(4) Therefore, regardless of what other people do, you are better off adopting the policy of looking out for yourself. You should be an egoist.

And now we come to the catch: Other people, of course, can reason in the same way, and the result will be that we end up back in Hobbes's state of nature. Everyone will be an egoist, willing to knife everyone else whenever they see some advantage in it for themselves. And in this situation each of us is obviously worse off than we would be if we cooperated. To escape the dilemma, we need another enforceable agreement, this time an agreement to obey the rules of mutually respectful social living. As before, cooperation would not yield the optimum outcome (we being egoists while others are benevolent), but it would lead to a better result than could be obtained by each of us independently pursuing our own interests. We need, in David Gauthier's words, to "bargain our way into morality." We can do that if we can establish sufficient sanctions to ensure that, if we respect other people's interests, they must respect ours as well.

11.3. Some Advantages of the Social Contract Theory of Morals

The Social Contract Theory of Morals is, as we have seen, the idea that *morality consists in the set of rules governing how people are to treat one another that rational people will agree to accept, for their mutual benefit, on the condition that others follow those rules as well.* The strength of this theory is due, in large measure, to the fact that it provides simple and plausible answers to some difficult questions that have always perplexed philosophers.

1. *What moral rules are we bound to follow, and how are those rules justified?* The key idea is that morally binding rules are the ones that are necessary for social living. It is obvious, for example, that we could not live together very well if we did not accept rules prohibiting murder, assault, theft, lying, breaking promises, and the like. These rules are justified simply by showing that they are necessary if we are to cooperate for our mutual benefit. On the other hand, some rules that are often viewed as moral rules—such as the prohibition of prostitution, sodomy, and sexual promiscuity—are not obviously justifiable in this way. How is social living threatened by one person's engaging in private voluntary sexual activity with another? If this conduct does not threaten us in any way, then it is outside the scope of the social contract and is none of our business. Those rules, therefore, have only a doubtful claim on us.

2. *Why is it reasonable for us to follow the moral rules?* We agree to follow the moral rules because it is to our own advantage to live in a society in which the rules are accepted. Of course, it may sometimes be to our short-term benefit to break the rules. However, it is not reasonable for us to want an arrangement in which people may violate the rules any time it is advantageous for them to do so—the whole point of the social contract is that we want to be able to *count on* people to keep the rules, except perhaps in the most dire emergencies. Only then can we feel safe. Our own steady compliance is the reasonable price we pay in order to secure the compliance of others.

3. *Under what circumstances are we allowed to break the rules?* This is a somewhat more complicated matter. The key idea here is the idea of reciprocity—we agree to obey the rules on the condition that others obey them as well. Thus, when someone violates the condition of reciprocity, he releases us, at least to some

extent, from our obligation toward him. Suppose someone refuses to be helpful to you, in circumstances in which he clearly should help you. Then, if later on he needs your help, you may rightly feel that you have less of a duty to help him. The same basic point explains why it is permissible to punish those who have broken the criminal law. Lawbreakers are treated differently from normal citizens—in punishing them, we treat them in ways that are not normally permitted. How can this be justified? The answer has two parts. In the first place, the purpose of the state is to enforce the primary rules necessary for social living. If we are to live together without fear, it cannot be left to the individual's discretion whether he or she will attack others, steal from them, and so on. Attaching sanctions to the violation of these rules is the only workable means of enforcing them. It follows that we need to punish. But why is it *permissible* to punish? The answer is that the criminal has violated the fundamental condition of reciprocity: We recognize the rules of social living as limiting what we can do only on the condition that others accept the same restrictions on what they can do. Therefore, by violating the rules with respect to us, criminals release us from our obligation toward them and leave themselves open to retaliation.

Finally, there is an even more dramatic circumstance in which one may violate the moral rules. In normal circumstances, morality requires us to be impartial, that is, to give no greater weight to our own interests than to the interests of others. But suppose you face a situation in which you must choose between your own death and the deaths of five other people. Impartiality, it seems, would require you to choose your own death; after all, there are five of them and only one of you. Are you morally bound to sacrifice yourself?

Philosophers have often felt uneasy about this sort of example; they have felt instinctively that somehow there are limits to what morality can demand of us. Therefore, they have traditionally said that such heroic actions are supererogatory—that is, they are actions above and beyond the call of duty, admirable when they occur, but not strictly required. Yet it is hard to explain why such actions are not strictly required. If morality demands impartial decisions, and impartial reason decrees it is better for one to die than five, why is one not required to sacrifice oneself?

The Social Contract Theory has an explanation. It is rational to accept the social contract because it is to our own advantage. We give up our unconditional freedom, but in return we get the benefits of social living. However, if we are then required by the contract to give up our lives, we are no better off than we were in the state of nature; so we no longer have any reason to abide by the contract. Thus there is a natural limit on the amount of self-sacrifice that can be expected from anyone: We may not exact a sacrifice so profound that it negates the very point of the contract. In this way the Social Contract Theory explains a feature of morality that on other theories remains mysterious.

4. *Does morality have an objective basis?* Are there moral "facts"? Are moral judgments objectively true? Philosophers have long wondered whether our moral opinions represent anything more than our subjective feelings or the customs of our society. They have felt that there must be something more to morality than customs and feelings, but it is hard to say just what that something is. If there are moral "facts," what kind of thing could they be?

One of the main attractions of the Social Contract Theory is that it sweeps aside all these worries so easily. No long explanation is needed. Morality is not merely a matter of custom or feeling; it has an objective basis. But the theory does not need to postulate any special kinds of "facts" to explain that basis. Morality is the set of rules that rational people would agree to accept for their mutual benefit. We can determine what those rules are by rational investigation and then determine whether a particular act is morally acceptable by seeing whether it conforms to the rules. Once this is understood, the old worries about moral "objectivity" simply vanish.

11.4. The Problem of Civil Disobedience

Moral theories should provide help in understanding particular moral issues. The Social Contract Theory is based on an important insight about the nature of society and its institutions, so it is especially well suited to help us deal with issues involving those institutions. As a result of the social contract, we have an obligation to obey the law. But are we ever justified in defying the law? And if so, when?

The classic modern examples of civil disobedience are, of course, the actions taken in connection with the Indian independence movement led by Mohandas K. Gandhi and the American civil rights movement led by Martin Luther King, Jr. Both movements were characterized by public, conscientious, nonviolent refusal to comply with the law. But the goals of the movements were importantly different. Gandhi and his followers did not recognize the right of the British to govern India; they wanted to replace British rule with an entirely different system. King and his followers, on the other hand, did not question the legitimacy of the basic institutions of American government. They objected only to particular laws and social policies that they regarded as unjust—so unjust, in fact, that they felt released from any obligation to obey them.

In his *Letter from the Birmingham City Jail* (1963), King detailed the frustration and anger that arises

> when you have seen vicious mobs lynch your mothers and fathers at will and drown your sisters and brothers at whim; when you have seen hate-filled policemen curse, kick, brutalize and even kill your black brothers and sisters with impunity; when you see the vast majority of your twenty million Negro brothers smothering in an air-tight cage of poverty in the midst of an affluent society; when you suddenly find your tongue twisted and your speech stammering as you seek to explain to your six-year-old daughter why she can't go to the public amusement park that has just been advertised on television, and see tears welling up in her little eyes when she is told that Funtown is closed to colored children, and see the depressing clouds of inferiority begin to distort her little personality.

The problem was not only that racial segregation, with all its attendant evils, was enforced by social custom; it was a matter of *law* as well, a law that black citizens were denied a voice in formulating. When urged to rely on ordinary democratic processes, King first pointed out that there had been many attempts at negotiation, but these efforts had met with little success; and as for "democracy," the word had no meaning to Southern blacks: "Throughout the state of Alabama all types of conniving methods are used to prevent Negroes from becoming registered voters and there are some counties without a single Negro registered to vote despite the fact that the Negro constitutes a majority of the population." King believed, therefore, that blacks had no choice but to put their case before the public by defying the unjust laws.

Today, with King acclaimed as one of the giants of American history, and with the civil rights movement remembered as a great moral crusade, it takes an effort to recall how controversial the strategy of civil disobedience was. Many liberals, while expressing sympathy for the goals of the movement, nevertheless denied that disobeying the law was a legitimate means of pursuing those goals. An article published in the *New York State Bar Journal* in 1965 expressed the typical worries. After assuring his readers that "long before Dr. King was born, I espoused, and still espouse, the cause of civil rights for all people," Louis Waldman, a prominent New York lawyer, argued:

> Those who assert rights under the Constitution and the laws made thereunder must abide by that Constitution and the law, if that Constitution is to survive. They cannot pick and choose; they cannot say they will abide by those laws which they think are just and refuse to abide by those laws which they think are unjust . . .
>
> The country, therefore, cannot accept Dr. King's doctrine that he and his followers will pick and choose, knowing that it is illegal to do so. I say, such doctrine is not only illegal and for that reason alone should be abandoned, but that it is also immoral, destructive of the principles of democratic government, and a danger to the very civil rights Dr. King seeks to promote.

Waldman had a point: If the legal system is basically decent, then defying the law is on its face a bad thing, because such defiance weakens respect for the values that the law protects. To meet this objection, those who advocated civil disobedience needed an argument to show why defiance of the law was justified. One such argument, which King often used, was that the evils being opposed were so serious, so numerous, and so resistant to remedy by less drastic means that civil disobedience was justified as a "last resort." The end justifies the means, even though the means are regrettable. This, in the opinion of many moralists, was a sufficient reply to the point made by Waldman. But there is a more profound reply available, suggested by the Social Contract Theory.

Why do we have an obligation to obey the law in the first place? According to the Social Contract Theory, it is because each of us participates in a complicated arrangement whereby we gain certain benefits in return for accepting certain burdens. The benefits are the benefits of social living: We escape the state of nature and live in a society in which we are secure and enjoy basic rights under the law. In order to gain these benefits, we agree to do our part to uphold the institutions that make them possible. This means that we must obey the law, pay our taxes, and so forth—these are the burdens we accept in return.

But what if things are arranged so that one group of people within the society is not accorded the rights enjoyed by others? What if, instead of protecting them, "hate-filled policemen curse, kick, brutalize and even kill with impunity"? What if some citizens are "smothered in an air-tight cage of poverty" by being denied the opportunity to acquire decent education or decent jobs? If the denial of these rights is sufficiently widespread and sufficiently systematic, we are forced to conclude that the terms of the social contract are not being honored. Thus, if we continue to demand that the disadvantaged group obey the law and otherwise respect society's institutions, we are demanding that they accept the burdens imposed by the social arrangement even though they are denied its benefits.

This line of reasoning suggests that, rather than civil disobedience being an undesirable "last resort" for socially disenfranchised groups, it is in fact the most natural and reasonable means of expressing protest. For when they are denied a fair share of the benefits of social living, the disenfranchised are in effect released from the contract that otherwise would require them to support the arrangements that make those benefits possible. This is the deepest reason that justifies civil disobedience, and it is to the credit of the Social Contract Theory that it exposes this point so clearly.

11.5. Difficulties for the Theory

Social Contract Theory is one of four major options in current moral philosophy. (The others are Utilitarianism, Kantianism, and Virtue Theory.) It is not hard to see why; the theory explains a great deal about moral life in an economical, no-nonsense way.

What can be said against it? The following two objections seem to have the greatest weight.

1. The most common objection has been that Social Contract Theory is based on a historical fiction. We are asked to imagine that people once lived in isolation from one another; that they found this intolerable; and that they eventually banded together, agreeing to follow social rules of mutual benefit. But none of this ever happened. It is just a fantasy. So of what relevance is it? To be sure, if people *had* come together in this way, we could explain their obligations to one another as the theory suggests: They would be obligated to obey the rules because they would have contracted to do so. But even then, there would still be trouble. We would have to face such questions as the following: Was the agreement unanimous? If not, what of the people who did not sign up—are they not required to act morally? And if the contract was consummated a long time ago, are we supposed to be bound by the agreements of our ancestors? If not, how is the "contract" renewed in each new generation? Suppose someone says, "I didn't agree to any such contract, and I want no part of it"? But in fact there never was such a contract, and so nothing can sensibly be explained by appealing to it. As one critic wisecracked, the social contract "isn't worth the paper it's not written on."

In reply, it might be said that there is an *implicit* social contract by which we are all bound. To be sure, none of us ever actually signed a "real" contract—there is no piece of paper with signatures affixed. However, a social arrangement very much like the one described in the Social Contract Theory does exist: There is a set of rules that everyone recognizes as binding on them, and we all benefit from the fact that these rules are followed. Each of us accepts the benefits conferred by this arrangement; and more than that, we expect and encourage other people to continue observing the rules. This is a description of the actual state of affairs; it is not fictitious. And, the argument continues, by accepting the benefits of this arrangement, we incur an obligation to do our part in supporting it—in other words, to reciprocate. The contract is "implicit" because we become a part of it not through our words but through our actions, as we participate in social institutions and accept the benefits of social living.

Thus the story of the "social contract" need not be intended as a description of historical events. Rather, it is a useful analytical tool, based on the idea that we may understand our moral obligations *as if* they had arisen in this way. Consider the following situation. Suppose you were to come upon a group of people playing an elaborate game. It looks like fun, and so you join in. After a while, however, you begin to break some of the rules, because that looks like more fun. The others protest; they say that if you are going to play, you must follow the rules. You reply that you never promised to follow the rules. They may rightly respond that this is irrelevant. Perhaps nobody explicitly promised to obey; nevertheless, by joining the game, each person implicitly agrees to abide by the rules that make the game possible. It is *as though* they had all agreed. Morality is like this. The game is social living; we derive enormous benefits from it, and we do not want to forgo those benefits; but in order to play the game and get the benefits, we have to follow the rules.

It isn't clear to what extent the great social contract theorists, such as Hobbes and Rousseau, would accept this way of defending their view. But that doesn't matter; the reply seems to save the theory from what would otherwise be a devastating objection.

2. We have already observed that moral theories should provide help in dealing with practical moral issues. The important theories do this, but all too often a theory that clarifies one issue only confuses another. For each theory, there are some issues on which its pronouncements seem exactly right; but problems arise when, on other issues, the theory's implications seem unacceptable. When we considered the problem of civil disobedience, the Social Contract Theory seemed just right. But in connection with some other issues, its implications are more disturbing.

The second objection to the Social Contract Theory, which seems to me more powerful than the first, has to do with its implications for our duties toward beings who are not able to participate in the contract. Nonhuman animals, for example, lack the capacities necessary to enter into any sort of agreements with us, whether explicit or implicit. Therefore it seems impossible that they should be covered by any "rules of mutual benefit" established by such an agreement. Nevertheless, isn't it morally wrong to torture an animal, when there is no good reason for it? And isn't this wrong because of the pain caused to the animal itself? But the idea of moral duties with respect to beings who are *not parties to the contract* seems contrary to the most basic idea behind the theory. Thus the theory seems to be defective.

Hobbes was aware that, on his view, animals are excluded from moral consideration. He wrote that "to make covenants with brute beasts, is impossible." Apparently this did not bother him. Animals have never been treated well by humans, but in Hobbes's day they were held in especially low regard. Descartes and Malebranche, two of Hobbes's contemporaries, had popularized the idea that animals are not even capable of feeling pain. For Descartes, this was because, lacking souls, animal bodies are mere machines; for Malebranche, it was necessary for the theological reason that suffering is a consequence of Adam's sin, and animals are not descended from Adam. But regardless of the reason, their view was that animals cannot suffer, so animals are beyond the reach of moral consideration. This enabled 17th-century scientists to experiment on animals without worrying about their nonexistent "feelings." Nicholas Fontaine, an eyewitness, described a visit to one laboratory in his memoirs, published in 1738:

> They administered beatings to dogs with perfect indifference, and made fun of those who pitied the creatures as if they felt pain. They said the animals were clocks; that the cries they emitted when struck were only the noise of a little spring that had been touched, but that the whole body was without feeling. They nailed poor animals up on boards by their four paws to vivisect them and see the circulation of the blood which was a great subject of conversation.

If we do have a duty not to cause needless suffering to animals, it is difficult to see how that duty could be accommodated within the Social Contract Theory. However, many people, like Hobbes, might not find this so worrisome, for they might not regard the question of duties to mere animals as particularly urgent. But there is a further difficulty, of a similar kind, which may still give them pause.

Many humans are mentally impaired to such an extent that they cannot participate in the kind of agreements envisioned by the Social Contract Theory. They are certainly capable of suffering, and even of living simple human lives. But they are not sufficiently intelligent to understand the consequences of their actions. They may not even know when they are hurting others. Therefore, we may not hold them responsible for their conduct.

These humans pose exactly the same problem for the theory as nonhuman animals. Since they cannot participate in the agreements that, according to the theory, give rise to moral obligations, they are outside the realm of moral consideration. Yet we do think that we have moral obligations toward them. Moreover, our obligations toward them are often based on exactly the same reasons as our obligations toward normal humans—the primary reason we should not torture normal people, for example, is because it causes them terrible pain; and this is exactly the same reason we should not torture mentally impaired people. The Social Contract Theory can explain our duty in the one case but not in the other.

This problem does not concern some minor aspect of the theory; it goes right to the theory's heart. Therefore, unless some way can be found to remedy this difficulty, the verdict must be that the basic idea of the theory is flawed.

CHAPTER 12

*F*eminism and the
Ethics of Care

> But it is obvious that the values of women differ very often from the
> values which have been made by the other sex; naturally, this is so.
> Yet it is the masculine values that prevail.
> VIRGINIA WOOLF, *A ROOM OF ONE'S OWN* (1929)

12.1. Do Women and Men Think Differently about Ethics?

The idea that women and men think differently has traditionally been used to justify subjugating one to the other. Aristotle
said that women are not as rational as men, and so women are
naturally ruled by men. Kant agreed, adding that for this reason
women "lack civil personality" and should have no voice in public life. Rousseau tried to put a good face on it by emphasizing
that men and women merely possess different virtues; but of
course it turned out that men's virtues fit them for leadership,
whereas women's virtues fit them for home and hearth.

Against this background, it is not surprising that the bur-
geoning women's movement of the 1960s and '70s rejected the
idea of psychological differences between women and men altogether. The conception of men as rational and women as
emotional was dismissed as a mere stereotype. Nature makes no
mental or moral distinction between the sexes, it was said; and
when there seem to be such differences, it is only because
women have been conditioned by an oppressive system to behave in "feminine" ways.

More recently, however, feminist thinkers have reconsidered the matter, and some have concluded that women do indeed think differently than men. But, they add, women's ways of

160

thinking are not inferior to men's; nor do the differences justify subordinating anyone to anyone else. On the contrary, female ways of thinking yield insights that have been missed in male-dominated areas. Thus, by attending to the distinctive approach of women, progress can be made in subjects that were stalled. Ethics is said to be a leading candidate for this treatment.

Kohlberg's Stages of Moral Development. Consider the following problem, devised by the educational psychologist Lawrence Kohlberg. Heinz's wife was near death, and her only hope was a drug that had been discovered by a pharmacist who was selling it for an exorbitant price. The drug cost $200 to make, and the pharmacist was selling it for $2,000. Heinz could raise only $1,000. He offered this to the druggist, and when his offer was rejected, Heinz said he would pay the rest later. Still the druggist refused. In desperation, Heinz considered stealing the drug. Would it be wrong for him to do that?

This problem, known as "Heinz's Dilemma," was one of several used by Kohlberg in studying the moral development of children. Kohlberg interviewed children of various ages, presenting them with a series of dilemmas and asking questions designed to elicit their moral judgments and the supporting reasons. Analyzing their responses, Kohlberg concluded that there are six levels of moral development. Children begin with a self-centered view of "right" as whatever avoids punishment, and eventually they progress through six stages to the fully mature view of rightness as conformity to universal principles. (At least, the fortunate ones progress that far. Some people get stuck at lower levels.) Here are the six stages:

1. The earliest is the Stage of Punishment and Obedience, in which right is conceived as obeying authority and avoiding punishment.
2. Then the child moves on to the Stage of Individual Instrumental Purpose and Exchange—here, right is acting to meet one's own needs and allowing others to do the same, while making "fair deals" with others to further one's ends.
3. Next is the Stage of Mutual Interpersonal Expectations, Relationships, and Conformity. Right is defined in terms of the duties and responsibilities that go with

one's social roles and one's relationships with other people; a critical virtue is "keeping loyalty and trust with partners."

4. In the Stage of Social System and Conscience Maintenance, the idea of doing one's duty in society and maintaining the welfare of the group becomes paramount. (The demands of personal relationships are subordinated to following the rules of the social group.)

5. In the Stage of Prior Rights and Social Contract or Utility, right consists of upholding the basic rights, values, and legal arrangements of the society. (At this stage and at the next, personal relationships are subordinated to universal principles of justice.)

6. Finally, the most morally mature people reach the Stage of Universal Ethical Principles, in which full moral maturity is manifested through one's fidelity to abstract principles that all humanity should follow.

Heinz's dilemma was presented to an 11-year-old boy named Jake, who thought it was obvious that Heinz should steal the drug. Jake explained:

> For one thing, a human life is worth more than money, and if the druggist only makes $1,000, he is still going to live, but if Heinz doesn't steal the drug, his wife is going to die.
>
> *(Why is life worth more than money?)*
>
> Because the druggist can get a thousand dollars later from rich people with cancer, but Heinz can't get his wife again.
>
> *(Why not?)*
>
> Because people are all different and so you couldn't get Heinz's wife again.

But Amy, also 11, saw the matter differently. Should Heinz steal the drug? Compared to Jake's forthright statements, Amy seems hesitant and evasive:

> Well, I don't think so. I think there might be other ways besides stealing it, like if he could borrow the money or make a loan or something, but he really shouldn't steal the drug—but his wife shouldn't die either . . . If he stole the drug, he might save his wife then, but if he did, he might have to go to jail, and then his wife might get sicker again, and he couldn't get more of the drug, and it might not be

good. So, they should really just talk it out and find some other way to make the money.

The interviewer asks Amy further questions, making it clear that she is not being responsive—if Heinz does not steal the drug, his wife will die. But Amy will not budge; she refuses to accept the terms in which the problem is posed. Instead she recasts the issue as a conflict between Heinz and the druggist that must be resolved by further discussions.

In terms of Kohlberg's stages, Jake seems to have advanced one or two full levels beyond Amy. Amy's response is typical of people operating at Stage 3, where personal relationships are paramount—Heinz and the druggist must work things out between them. Jake, on the other hand, appeals to impersonal principles—"a human life is worth more than money." Jake appears to be operating at level 4 or 5.

Gilligan's Objection. Kohlberg began his studies of moral development in the 1950s, when psychology was dominated by behaviorism and the popular image of psychological research featured rats in mazes. His humanistic, cognitively oriented project showed a different way of pursuing psychological investigations. But there was a problem with Kohlberg's central idea. It is legitimate and interesting to study the different ways that people think at different ages—if children think differently at 5, 10, and 15, that is certainly worth knowing. It is also worthwhile to identify the best ways of thinking. But these are different projects. One involves observing how children in fact think. The other involves the assessment of ways of thinking as better or worse. Different kinds of evidence are relevant to each investigation, and there is no reason to assume in advance that the results will match. Contrary to the opinion of older people, it *could* turn out that age does not bring wisdom after all.

Kohlberg's theory has been a target of feminist thinkers, who have given this criticism a special twist. In 1982 Carol Gilligan, like Kohlberg a professor in Harvard's School of Education, published an influential book called *In a Different Voice: Psychological Theory and Women's Development,* in which she objects specifically to what Kohlberg says about Jake and Amy. The two children think differently, she says, but Amy's way of thinking is not inferior. When confronted with Heinz's Dilemma, Amy responds in a typically female fashion to the personal aspects of the situation, whereas Jake, thinking like a typical male, sees only "a conflict between life and property that can be resolved by a logical deduction."

Jake's response will be judged "at a higher level" only if one assumes, as Kohlberg does, that an ethic of principle is superior to an ethic that emphasizes intimacy, caring, and personal relationships. But why should we make any such assumption? Most moral philosophers have favored an ethic of principle, but that is only because most moral philosophers have been males.

The "male way of thinking"—the appeal to impersonal principles—abstracts away the details that give each situation its special flavor. Women, Gilligan says, find it harder to ignore these details. Amy worries that "If [Heinz] stole the drug, he might save his wife then, but if he did, he might have to go to jail, and then his wife might get sicker again, and he couldn't get more of the drug." Jake, who reduces the situation to "a human life is worth more than money," ignores all this.

Gilligan suggests that women's basic moral orientation is caring for others—"taking care" of others in a personal way, not just being concerned for humanity in general—and attending to their needs. This explains why Amy's response seems, at first, confused and uncertain. Sensitivity to the needs of others leads women to "attend to voices other than their own and to include in their judgment other points of view." Thus Amy could not simply reject the druggist's point of view; she could only insist upon further talking with him and trying somehow to accommodate him. "Women's moral weakness," says Gilligan, "manifest in an apparent diffusion and confusion of judgment, is thus inseparable from women's moral strength, an overriding concern with relationships and responsibilities."

Other feminist thinkers have taken up this theme and developed it into a distinctive view about the nature of ethics. In 1990 Virginia Held summed up the central feminist idea: "Caring, empathy, feeling with others, being sensitive to each other's feelings," she said, "all may be better guides to what morality requires in actual contexts than may abstract rules of reason, or rational calculation, or at least they may be necessary components of an adequate morality."

Before turning to the implications of this idea for ethics and ethical theory, we may pause to consider how "feminine" it really is. Is it true that women and men think differently about ethics? And if it is true, what accounts for the difference?

Is It True That Women and Men Think Differently? Since Gilligan's book was published, there has been a great deal of research on "women's voices," but it remains unclear whether women and men really think differently. One thing seems certain, however: Even if they do think differently, the differences cannot be very great. In the first place, they will be differences of emphasis rather than differences in fundamental values. It is not as though women make judgments that are incomprehensible to men, or vice versa. Men can understand the value of caring relationships, empathy, and sensitivity easily enough, even if they sometimes have to be reminded; and they can agree with Amy that the happiest solution to Heinz's Dilemma would be for the two men somehow to work it out. (Not even the most reprobate male thinks theft would be the *best* thing that could happen.) For their part, women will hardly disagree with such notions as human life being worth more than money. Plainly, the two sexes do not inhabit different moral universes.

Suppose we concede, however, that there is a difference in style between people who are more inclined to think in terms of principles and people who are more inclined to adopt a "caring perspective." Is the former style exclusively male and the latter exclusively female? Plainly not. There are women who are devoted to principles and men who care. So, even if there are different styles of moral thinking, there is no style that is exclusively male or female.

Still, we should not be too quick to dismiss the notion that there are typically male and female perspectives. There are plenty of general differences between men and women that don't apply to every individual. Women are typically smaller than men, but that doesn't mean that every woman is smaller than every man.

The difference in moral thinking could be like that: Women might typically be more attracted to a caring perspective, even though not every woman is more caring than every man. To many people, including a large number of feminist writers, this seems plausible. Its plausibility would be increased, however, if we could explain *why* there should be such a difference. Why should women be more caring?

What Could Account for Such a Difference between the Sexes?
There seem to be two possibilities. One is that women think differently because of the social role to which they are assigned.

Women have traditionally been given responsibility for home and hearth; even if this is nothing but a sexist outrage, the fact remains that women have occupied this role. It is easy to see how being assigned to such duties and coming to understand this as "one's place" could induce one to adopt the values that go with it. Thus, the ethics of care could be just part of the psychological conditioning that girls routinely receive. (This theory could be tested by looking at girls raised in nontraditional homes. Would they still be natural caregivers? What about boys raised in nonstandard ways?)

The second possibility is that there is some sort of intrinsic connection between being female and having an ethic of caring. What could this connection be? Since the obvious natural difference between the sexes is that women are the childbearers, we might conjecture that women's nature as mothers somehow makes them natural caregivers. Even girls like Amy, who at age 11 has had no experience mothering, might come equipped by nature for the task, psychologically as well as physically.

The theory of evolutionary psychology might explain how nature works this trick. Evolutionary psychology, a controversial theory developed in the last third of the 20th century, interprets major features of human psychological life as the products of natural selection—people today have the emotions and behavioral tendencies that enabled their ancestors to survive and reproduce in the distant past. This could have produced different patterns of behavior and emotional response in men and women.

We may think of the Darwinian "struggle for survival" as a competition to reproduce in the next generation as many copies of one's genes as possible. Any traits that help one to do this will be preserved in future generations; while traits that put one at a disadvantage in this competition will tend to disappear.

From this point of view, the overwhelmingly important difference between males and females is that men can father hundreds of children during their reproductive lifetimes, while women can have only one baby each nine months. This means that the optimum reproductive strategies for males and females will be different. For males, the optimum strategy will be to impregnate as many females as possible, investing in each infant only whatever resources are necessary for the maximum number to survive. For females, the optimum strategy is to invest heavily in each child and to choose as partners males who are willing to stay around and make a similar investment. This obviously creates a tension between male and female interests, and that may explain why the sexes could have evolved different attitudes. It explains, notoriously, why men are more promiscuous than women; but at the same time it explains what we are interested in here, namely, why women are more attracted than men to the values of the nuclear family.

This kind of explanation is often misunderstood. The point is not that people consciously calculate how to propagate their genes; no one does that. Nor is the point that people *should* calculate in this way; from an ethical point of view, they should not. The point is just to explain, if we can, the phenomena we observe.

12.2. Implications for Moral Judgment

Not all women philosophers have been self-consciously feminist; nor have all feminists embraced the ethics of care. Nonetheless, this is the ethical view most closely identified with modern feminist philosophy. As Annette Baier put it, " 'Care' is the new buzzword."

One way of understanding and assessing an ethical view is to ask what difference it would make in one's moral judgments and whether that difference would be an improvement over the alternatives. So, suppose one adopts an ethic of care. Would this lead to different moral judgments than if one adopted a principled "male" approach? Here are three examples.

Family and Friends. Traditional theories of obligation are notoriously ill-suited to describing life among family and friends. Those theories take the notion of obligation as morally fundamental: They provide an account of what we *ought* to do. But, as Annette Baier observes, when we try to construe "being a loving parent" as a duty, we immediately encounter problems. A loving parent acts from motives other than duty. If you care for your children because you feel it is your duty, it will be a disaster. Your children will sense it and realize they are unloved. Parents who act from a sense of duty are bad parents.

Moreover, the ideas of equality and impartiality that pervade theories of obligation seem deeply antagonistic to the values of love and friendship. John Stuart Mill said that a moral

agent must be "as strictly impartial as a disinterested and benevolent spectator." But that is not the standpoint of a parent or
friend. We do not regard our family and friends merely as members of the great crowd of humanity. We think of them as special, and we treat them as special.

The ethics of care, on the other hand, is perfectly suited to
describe such relations. The ethics of care does not take "obligation" as fundamental; nor does it require that we impartially
promote the interests of everyone alike. Instead, it begins with
a conception of moral life as a network of relationships with specific other people, and it sees "living well" as caring for those
people, attending to their needs, and keeping faith with them.

These outlooks lead to different judgments about what we
may do. May I devote my time and resources to caring for my
own friends and family, even if this means ignoring the needs of
other people whom I could also help? From an impartial point
of view, our duty is to promote the interests of everyone alike.
But few of us accept that view. The ethics of care confirms the
priority that we naturally give to our family and friends, and so
it seems a more plausible moral conception.

It is not surprising that the ethics of care appears to do a
good job explaining the nature of our moral relations with
friends and family. After all, those relationships are its primary
inspiration.

Disadvantaged Children. Each year over 10 million children
die from easily preventable causes—disease, malnutrition, and
bad drinking water. Organizations such as UNICEF work to save
these children, but they never have enough money. By contributing to their work, we could prevent at least some of these
deaths. For $17, for example, UNICEF can vaccinate a third-
world child against measles, polio, diphtheria, whooping
cough, tetanus, and tuberculosis.

A traditional "ethics of principle," such as Utilitarianism,
would conclude from this that we have a substantial duty to support UNICEF. The reasoning is straightforward: Almost all of
us have resources that we waste on relatively trivial things—we
buy fancy clothes, carpets, and television sets. None of these is
as important as vaccinations for children. Therefore, we should
give at least some of our resources to UNICEF. Of course, if we
try to fill in all the details and answer all the objections, this

simple reasoning can become complicated. But its basic idea is clear enough. One might think that an ethic of care would reach a similar conclusion—after all, shouldn't we care for those disadvantaged children? But that misses the point. An ethic of care focuses on small-scale, personal relationships. If there is no such relationship, "caring" cannot take place. Nel Noddings, whose book *Caring: A Feminine Approach to Ethics and Moral Education* is one of the best-known works of feminist moral theory, explains that the caring relation can exist only if the "cared-for" can interact with the "one-caring," at a minimum by receiving and acknowledging the care in a personal, one-to-one encounter. Otherwise, on her view, there is no obligation: "We are not obliged to act as one-caring if there is no possibility of completion in the other." For this reason, Noddings concludes that we have no obligation to help "the needy in the far regions of the earth."

Even though it might come as a relief to learn that we are free to spend our money as we please, it is hard to avoid the feeling that something has gone wrong here. Making personal relationships the whole of ethics seems as wrong-headed as ignoring them altogether. A more sensible approach might be to say that the ethical life includes both caring personal relationships *and* a benevolent concern for people generally. The obligation to support UNICEF might then be seen as falling under the latter heading rather than the former. If we were to take this approach, we would interpret the ethics of care as a supplement to traditional theories of obligation rather than as a replacement for them. Annette Baier seems to have this in mind when she writes that, eventually, "women theorists will need to connect their ethics of love with what has been the men theorists' preoccupation, namely, obligation."

Animals. Do we have obligations to nonhuman animals? Should we, for example, be vegetarians? One argument from "rational principles" says that we should because the business of raising and slaughtering animals for food causes them great suffering, and by becoming vegetarians we could nourish ourselves without the cruelty. Since the modern animal rights movement began in the mid-1970s, this sort of argument has persuaded many people (probably more women than men) to stop eating meat.

Nel Noddings suggests that this is a good issue "to test the basic notions on which an ethic of caring rests." What are those basic notions? First, such an ethic appeals to intuition and feeling rather than to principle. This leads to a different conclusion, for most people do not feel that meat-eating is wrong or that the suffering of livestock is important. Noddings observes that because we are human, our emotional responses to other humans are different from our responses to nonhumans.

A second "basic notion on which an ethic of caring rests" is the idea of an individual relationship between the one who cares and the one who is cared for. As we have noted, the cared-for must be able to participate in the relationship at least by responding to the care. Noddings believes that people do have this sort of relationship with some animals, namely pets, and this can be the basis of an obligation:

> When one is familiar with a particular animal family, one comes to recognize its characteristic form of address. Cats, for example, lift their heads and stretch toward the one they are addressing. . . . When I enter my kitchen in the morning and my cat greets me from her favorite spot on the counter, I understand her request. This is the spot where she sits and "speaks" in her squeaky attempt to communicate her desire for a dish of milk.

A relationship is established, and the attitude of care must be summoned. But one has no such relationship with the cow in the slaughterhouse, and so, Noddings concludes, even though we might wish for a world in which animals did not suffer, we have no obligation to do anything for the cow's sake, not even to refrain from eating him.

What are we to make of this? If we use this issue "to test the basic notions on which an ethic of caring rests," does the ethic pass or fail the test? The opposing arguments are impressive. First, intuitions and feelings are not reliable guides—at one time, people's intuitions told them that slavery was acceptable and that the subordination of women was God's own plan. And second, whether the animal is in a position to respond "personally" to you may have a lot to do with the satisfaction you get from helping, but it has nothing to do with the animal's needs or the good that you could accomplish. (Much the same, of course, may be said of the distant child's inability to thank you personally for the vaccination.) These arguments, of course, appeal to principles that are said to be typical of male reasoning. Therefore, if the ethics of caring is taken to be the whole of morality, such arguments will be ignored. On the other hand, if caring is only one part of morality, the arguments from principle still have considerable force. Livestock animals might come within the sphere of moral concern, not because of our caring relation with them, but for other reasons.

12.3. Implications for Ethical Theory

It is easy to see the influence of men's experience in the ethical theories they have created. Men dominate public life, and in politics and business, one's relations with other people are typically impersonal and contractual. Often the relationship is adversarial—others have interests that conflict with our own. So we negotiate; we bargain and make deals. Moreover, in public life our decisions may affect large numbers of people we do not even know. So we may try to calculate, in an impersonal way, which decisions will have the best overall outcome for the most people. And what do men's moral theories emphasize? Impersonal duty, contracts, the harmonization of competing interests, and the calculation of costs and benefits.

Little wonder, then, that feminists believe modern moral philosophy incorporates a male bias. The concerns of private life—the realm in which women traditionally dominate—are almost wholly absent, and the "different voice" of which Gilligan speaks is silent. A moral theory that accounted for women's concerns would look very different. In the smaller-scale world of home and hearth, we deal with family and friends, with whom our relationships are personal and intimate. Bargaining and calculating play a much smaller role, while love and caring dominate. Once the point is made, there is no denying that this side of life must also have a place in our understanding of morality.

This side of life, however, is not easy to accommodate within the traditional theories. As we noted, "being a loving parent" is not a matter of calculating how one ought to behave. The same might be said about being a loyal friend or a dependable colleague. To be loving, loyal, and dependable is to be *a certain kind of person,* and neither as a parent nor as a friend is it the kind of person who impartially "does his duty."

The contrast between "being a certain kind of person" and "doing one's duty" is at the heart of a larger conflict between two kinds of ethical theory. Virtue Theory sees being a moral person as having certain traits of character: being kind, generous, courageous, just, prudent, and so on. Theories of obligation, on the other hand, emphasize impartial duty: They typically picture the moral agent as one who listens to reason, figures out the right thing to do, and does it. One of the chief arguments in favor of Virtue Theory is that it seems well suited to accommodate the values of both public and private life. The two spheres require different virtues. Public life requires justice and beneficence, while the virtues of private life include love and caring.

The ethics of care, therefore, turns out to be one part of the ethics of virtue. Most feminist philosophers view it in this light. Although Virtue Theory is not exclusively a feminist project, it is so closely tied to feminist ideas that Annette Baier dubs its male promoters "honorary women." The verdict on the ethics of care will depend, ultimately, on the viability of the ethics of virtue.

CHAPTER 13

The Ethics of Virtue

> The concepts of obligation, and duty—*moral* obligation and *moral* duty, that is to say—and of what is *morally* right and wrong, and of the *moral* sense of "ought," ought to be jettisoned. . . . It would be a great improvement if, instead of "morally wrong," one always named a genus such as "untruthful," "unchaste," "unjust."
>
> G. E. M. ANSCOMBE, *MODERN MORAL PHILOSOPHY* (1958)

13.1. The Ethics of Virtue and the Ethics of Right Action

In thinking about any subject it makes a great deal of difference what questions we begin with. In Aristotle's *Nicomachean Ethics* (ca. 325 B.C.), the central questions are about *character*. Aristotle begins by asking "What is the good of man?" and his answer is "an activity of the soul in conformity with virtue." To understand ethics, therefore, we must understand what makes someone a virtuous person, and Aristotle, with a keen eye for the details, devotes much space to discussing particular virtues such as courage, self-control, generosity, and truthfulness. Although this way of thinking about ethics is closely identified with Aristotle, it was not unique to him. Socrates, Plato, and a host of other ancient thinkers all approached ethics by asking: *What traits of character make one a good person?* As a result, "the virtues" occupied center stage in their discussions.

As time passed, however, this way of thinking came to be neglected. With the coming of Christianity a new set of ideas was introduced. The Christians, like the Jews, were monotheists who viewed God as a lawgiver, and for them righteous living meant obedience to the divine commandments. The Greeks had viewed reason as the source of practical wisdom—the virtuous life was, for them, inseparable from the life of reason. But

173

St. Augustine, the fourth-century Christian thinker who was to be enormously influential, distrusted reason and taught that moral goodness depends on subordinating oneself to the will of God. Therefore, when the medieval philosophers discussed the virtues, it was in the context of Divine Law. The "theological virtues" of faith, hope, charity, and, of course, *obedience* came to have a central place.

After the Renaissance, moral philosophy began to be secularized once again, but philosophers did not return to the Greek way of thinking. Instead, the Divine Law was replaced by its secular equivalent, something called the *Moral Law*. The Moral Law, which was said to spring from human reason rather than divine fiat, was conceived to be a system of rules specifying which actions are right. Our duty as moral persons, it was said, is to follow its directives. Thus modern moral philosophers approached their subject by asking a fundamentally different question than the one asked by the ancients. Instead of asking *What traits of character make one a good person?* they began by asking *What is the right thing to do?* This led them in a different direction. They went on to develop theories, not of virtue, but of rightness and obligation:

- Each person ought to do whatever will best promote his or her own interests. (Ethical Egoism)
- We ought to do whatever will promote the greatest happiness for the greatest number. (Utilitarianism)
- Our duty is to follow rules that we could consistently will to be universal laws—that is, rules that we would be willing to have followed by all people in all circumstances. (Kant's theory)
- The right thing to do is to follow the rules that rational, self-interested people can agree to establish for their mutual benefit. (Social Contract Theory)

And these are the familiar theories that have dominated modern moral philosophy from the 17th century on.

Should We Return to the Ethics of Virtue? Recently, however, a number of philosophers have advanced a radical idea: They have argued that modern moral philosophy is bankrupt and that, in order to salvage the subject, we should return to Aristotle's way of thinking.

This idea was put forth in 1958 when Elizabeth Anscombe published an article called "Modern Moral Philosophy" in the academic journal *Philosophy*. In that article she suggested that modern moral philosophy is misguided because it rests on the incoherent notion of a "law" without a lawgiver. The very concepts of obligation, duty, and rightness, on which modern moral philosophers have concentrated, are inextricably linked to this nonsensical notion. Therefore, she argued, we should stop thinking about obligation, duty, and rightness, and return to Aristotle's approach. The virtues should once again take center stage.

In the wake of Anscombe's article a flood of books and essays appeared discussing the virtues, and Virtue Theory soon became a major option in contemporary moral philosophy. There is, however, no settled body of doctrine on which all these writers agree. Compared to such theories as Utilitarianism, Virtue Theory is still in a relatively undeveloped state. Yet there is a common set of concerns that motivate this approach. In what follows we will first take a look at what the theory of virtue is like. Then we will consider some of the reasons that have been given for thinking that the ethics of virtue is superior to other, more modern ways of approaching the subject. Finally, we will consider whether a "return to the ethics of virtue" is really a viable option.

13.2. The Virtues

A theory of virtue should have several components. First, there should be an explanation of what a virtue is. Second, there should be a list specifying which character traits are virtues. Third, there should be an explanation of what these virtues consist in. Fourth, there should be an explanation of why these qualities are good ones for a person to have. Lastly, the theory should tell us whether the virtues are the same for all people or whether they differ from person to person or from culture to culture.

What Is a Virtue? Aristotle said that a virtue is a trait of character manifested in habitual action. The "habitual" is important. The virtue of honesty, for example, is not possessed by someone who tells the truth only occasionally or whenever it is to his own advantage. The honest person is truthful as a matter of course; his actions "spring from a firm and unchangeable character."

This is a start, but it is not enough. It does not distinguish virtues from vices, for vices are also traits of character manifested in habitual action. Edmund L. Pincoffs, a philosopher who taught at the University of Texas, made a suggestion that takes care of this problem. Pincoffs suggested that virtues and vices are qualities that we refer to in deciding whether someone is to be sought or avoided. "Some sorts of persons we prefer; others we avoid," he says. "The properties on our list [of virtues and vices] can serve as reasons for preference or avoidance."

We seek out people for different purposes, and this makes a difference to the virtues that are relevant. In looking for an auto mechanic, we want someone who is skillful, honest, and conscientious; in looking for a teacher, we want someone who is knowledgeable, articulate, and patient. Thus the virtues associated with auto repair are different from the virtues associated with teaching. But we also assess people *as people*, in a more general way, so we have the concept, not just of a good mechanic or a good teacher, but of a good person. The moral virtues are the virtues of persons as such. Taking our cue from Pincoffs, then, we may define a virtue as *a trait of character, manifested in habitual action, that it is good for a person to have.* And the moral virtues are the virtues that it is good for everyone to have.

What Are the Virtues? What, then, are the virtues? Which traits of character should be fostered in human beings? There is no short answer, but the following is a partial list:

benevolence	fairness	patience
civility	friendliness	prudence
compassion	generosity	reasonableness
conscientiousness	honesty	self-discipline
cooperativeness	industriousness	self-reliance
courage	justice	tactfulness
courteousness	loyalty	thoughtfulness
dependability	moderation	tolerance

The list could be expanded, of course, with other traits added. But this is a reasonable start.

What Do These Virtues Consist In? It is one thing to say, in a general way, that we should be conscientious, compassionate, and tolerant; it is another thing to say exactly what these character traits consist in. Each of the virtues has its own distinctive features and raises its own distinctive problems. We will look briefly at four of them.

1. *Courage.* According to Aristotle, virtues are means poised between extremes: A virtue is "the mean by reference to two vices: the one of excess and the other of deficiency." Courage is a mean between the extremes of cowardice and foolhardiness—it is cowardly to run away from all danger; yet it is foolhardy to risk too much.

Courage is sometimes said to be a military virtue because it is so obviously needed to accomplish the soldier's task. Soldiers do battle; battles are fraught with danger; so without courage the battle will be lost. But soldiers are not the only ones who need courage. Anyone who faces danger, and at different times this includes all of us, needs courage. A scholar who spends his timid and safe life studying medieval literature might seem the very opposite of a soldier. Yet even he might become ill and need courage to face a dangerous operation. As Peter Geach put it:

> Courage is what we all need in the end, and it is constantly needed in the ordinary course of life: by women who are with child, by all of us because our bodies are vulnerable, by coalminers and fishermen and steel-workers and lorry drivers.

So long as we consider only "the ordinary course of life," the nature of courage seems unproblematic. But unusual circumstances present more troublesome types of cases. Consider a Nazi soldier who fights valiantly—he faces great risk without flinching—but he does so in an evil cause. Is he courageous? Geach thinks that, contrary to appearances, the Nazi soldier does not really possess the virtue of courage at all. "Courage in an unworthy cause," he says, "is no virtue; still less is courage in an evil cause. Indeed I prefer not to call this nonvirtuous facing of danger 'courage.'"

It is easy to see Geach's point. Calling the Nazi soldier "courageous" seems to praise his performance, and we do not want to praise it. Instead we would rather he behaved differently.

Yet neither does it seem quite right to say that he is *not* courageous—after all, look at how he behaves in the face of danger. To get around this problem, perhaps we should just say that he displays two qualities of character, one that is admirable (steadfastness in facing danger) and one that is not (a willingness to defend a despicable regime). He is courageous all right, and courage is an admirable thing; but because his courage is deployed in an evil cause, his behavior is *on the whole* wicked.

2. *Generosity.* Generosity is the willingness to expend one's resources to help others. Aristotle says that, like courage, it is also a mean between extremes: It stands somewhere between stinginess and extravagance. The stingy person gives too little; the extravagant person gives too much. But how much is enough?

The answer will depend to some extent on what general ethical view we accept. Jesus, another important ancient teacher, said that we must give all we have to help the poor. The possession of riches, while the poor starve, was in his view unacceptable. This was regarded by those who heard him as a hard teaching and it was generally rejected. It is still rejected by most people today, even by those who consider themselves to be his followers.

The modern utilitarians are, in this regard at least, Jesus's moral descendants. They hold that in every circumstance it is one's duty to do whatever will have the best overall consequences for everyone concerned. This means that we should be generous with our money until the point has been reached at which further giving would be more harmful to us than it would be helpful to others.

Why do people resist this idea? Partly it may be a matter of selfishness; we do not want to make ourselves poor by giving away what we have. But there is also the problem that adopting such a policy would prevent us from living normal lives. Not only money but time is involved; our lives consist in projects and relationships that require a considerable investment of both. An ideal of "generosity" that demands spending our money and time as Jesus and the utilitarians recommend would require that we abandon our everyday lives and live very differently.

A reasonable interpretation of the demands of generosity might, therefore, be something like this: We should be as generous with our resources as is consistent with conducting our ordinary lives in a minimally satisfying way. Even this, though, will leave us with some awkward questions. Some people's "ordinary lives" are quite extravagant—think of a rich person whose everyday life includes luxuries without which she would feel deprived. The virtue of generosity, it would seem, cannot exist in the context of a life that is too sumptuous, especially when there are others whose basic needs are unmet. To make this a "reasonable" interpretation of the demands of generosity, we need a conception of ordinary life that is itself not too extravagant.

3. *Honesty.* The honest person is, first of all, someone who does not lie. But is that enough? There are other ways of misleading people than by lying. Geach tells the story of St. Athanasius, who "was rowing on a river when the persecutors came rowing in the opposite direction: 'Where is the traitor Athanasius?' 'Not far away,' the Saint gaily replied, and rowed past them unsuspected."

Geach approves of Athanasius's deception even though he thinks it would have been wrong to tell an outright lie. Lying, Geach thinks, is always forbidden: A person possessing the virtue of honesty will not even consider it. Honest people will not lie, and so they will have to find other ways to deal with difficult situations. Athanasius was clever enough to do so. He told the truth, even if it was a deceptive truth.

Of course, it is hard to see why Athanasius's deception was not also dishonest. What nonarbitrary principle would approve of misleading people by one means but not by another? But whatever we think about this, the larger question is whether virtue requires adherence to absolute rules. Concerning honesty, we may distinguish two views of the matter:

1. That an honest person will never lie

and

2. That an honest person will never lie except in rare circumstances when there are compelling reasons why it must be done.

There is no obvious reason why the first view must be accepted. On the contrary, there is reason to favor the second. To see why, we need only to consider why lying is a bad thing in the first place. The explanation might go like this:

Our ability to live together in communities depends on our capacities of communication. We talk to one another, read one another's writing, exchange information and opinions, express our desires to one another, make promises, ask and answer questions, and much more. Without these sorts of interchanges, social living would be impossible. But in order for these interchanges to be successful, we must be able to assume that there are certain rules in force: We must be able to rely on one another to speak honestly.

Moreover, when we accept someone's word, we make ourselves vulnerable to harm in a special way. By accepting what they say and modifying our beliefs accordingly, we place our welfare in their hands. If they speak truthfully, all is well. But if they lie, we end up with false beliefs; if we act on those beliefs, we end up doing foolish things. It is their fault. We trusted them, and they let us down. This explains why being given the lie is distinctively offensive. It is at bottom a violation of trust. It also explains why lies and "deceptive truths" seem morally indistinguishable. Both may violate trust in the same fashion.

None of this, however, implies that honesty is the only important value or that we have an obligation to deal honestly with everyone who comes along, regardless of who they are and what they are up to. Self-preservation is also an important matter, especially protecting ourselves from those who would harm us unjustly. When this comes into conflict with the rule against lying, it is not unreasonable to think it takes priority. Suppose St. Athanasius had told the persecutors "I don't know him," and as a result they went off on a wild goose chase. Later, could they sensibly complain that he had violated their trust? It seems natural to think that they forfeited any right they might have had to the truth from him when they set out unjustly to persecute him.

4. *Loyalty to Family and Friends.* At the beginning of Plato's dialogue *Euthyphro*, Socrates learns that Euthyphro, whom he has encountered near the entrance to the court, has come there to prosecute his father for murder. Socrates expresses surprise at this and wonders whether it is proper for a son to bring charges against his father. Euthyphro sees no impropriety: For him, a murder is a murder. Unfortunately, the question is left unresolved as their discussion moves on to other matters.

The idea that there is something morally special about family and friends is, of course, familiar. We do not treat our family and friends as we would treat strangers. We are bound to them by love and affection and we do things for them that we would not do for just anybody. But this is not merely a matter of our being nicer to people we like. The nature of our relationships with family and friends is different from our relationships with other people, and part of the difference is that our duties and responsibilities are different. This seems to be an integral part of what friendship is. How could I be your friend and yet not treat you with special consideration?

If we needed proof that humans are essentially social creatures, the existence of friendship would supply all we could want. As Aristotle said, "No one would choose to live without friends, even if he had all other goods":

> How could prosperity be safeguarded and preserved without friends? The greater it is the greater are the risks it brings with it. Also, in poverty and all other kinds of misfortune men believe that their only refuge consists in their friends. Friends help young men avoid error; to older people they give the care and help needed to supplement the failing powers of action which infirmity brings.

Friends give help, to be sure, but the benefits of friendship go far beyond material assistance. Psychologically, we would be lost without friends. Our triumphs seem hollow unless we have friends to share them, and our failures are made bearable by their understanding. Even our self-esteem depends in large measure on the assurances of friends: By returning our affection, they confirm our worthiness as human beings.

If we need friends, we need no less the qualities of character that enable us to *be* a friend. Near the top of the list is loyalty. Friends can be counted on. They stick by one another even when the going is hard, and even when, objectively speaking, the friend might deserve to be abandoned. They make allowances for one another; they forgive offenses and they refrain from harsh judgments. There are limits, of course. Sometimes a friend will be the only one who can tell us hard truths about ourselves. But criticism is acceptable from friends because we know that their scolding is not a sign of rejection, and even if they scold us privately, they will not embarrass us in front of others.

None of this is to say that we do not have duties to other people, even to strangers. But they are different duties, associated with different virtues. Generalized beneficence is a virtue, and it may demand a great deal, but it does not require the same level of concern for strangers that we have for friends. Justice is another such virtue; it requires impartial treatment for all. But because friends are loyal, the demands of justice apply less certainly between them.

That is why Socrates is surprised to learn that Euthyphro is prosecuting his father. The relationship that we have with members of our family is even closer than that of friendship; so as much as we might admire Euthyphro's passion for justice, we still may be startled that he could take the same attitude toward his father that he would take toward someone else who had committed the same crime. It seems inconsistent with the proper regard of a son. The point is still recognized by the law today: In the United States, as well as in some other countries, a wife cannot be compelled to testify in court against her husband, and vice versa.

Why Are the Virtues Important? We said that virtues are traits of character that are good for people to have. This only raises the further question of why the virtues are desirable. Why is it a good thing for a person to be courageous, generous, honest, or loyal? The answer, of course, may vary depending on the particular virtue in question. Thus:

- Courage is a good thing because life is full of dangers and without courage we would be unable to cope with them.
- Generosity is desirable because some people will inevitably be worse off than others and they will need help.
- Honesty is needed because without it relations between people would go wrong in myriad ways.
- Loyalty is essential to friendship; friends stick by one another, even when they are tempted to turn away.

Looking at this list suggests that each virtue is valuable for a different reason. However, Aristotle believed it is possible to give a more general answer to our question; namely, that the virtues are important because the virtuous person will fare better in life. The point is not that the virtuous will be richer—that is obviously not so, or at least it is not always so. The point is that the virtues are needed to conduct our lives well.

To see what Aristotle is getting at, consider the kinds of creatures we are and the kinds of lives we lead. On the most general level, we are rational and social beings who want and need the company of other people. So we live in communities among friends, family, and fellow citizens. In this setting, such qualities as loyalty, fairness, and honesty are needed for interacting with all those other people successfully. (Imagine the difficulties that would be experienced by someone who habitually manifested the opposite qualities in his or her social life.) On a more individual level, our separate lives might include working at a particular kind of job and having particular sorts of interests. Other virtues may be necessary for successfully doing that job or pursuing those interests—perseverance and industriousness might be important. Again, it is part of our common human condition that we must sometimes face danger or temptation, so courage and self-control are needed. The upshot is that, despite their differences, the virtues all have the same general sort of value: They are all qualities needed for successful human living.

Are the Virtues the Same for Everyone? Finally, we may ask whether a single set of traits is desirable for all people. Should we speak of *the* good person, as though all good people come from one mold? This assumption has often been challenged. Friedrich Nietzsche, for example, did not think that there is only one kind of human goodness. In his flamboyant way, Nietzsche observes:

> How naive it is altogether to say: "Man *ought* to be such-and-such!" Reality shows us an enchanting wealth of types, the abundance of a lavish play and change of forms—and some wretched loafer of a moralist comments: "No! Man ought to be different." He even knows what man should be like, this wretched bigot and prig: he paints himself on the wall and exclaims, "*Ecce homo!*"

There is obviously something to this. The scholar who devotes his life to understanding medieval literature and the professional soldier are very different kinds of people. A Victorian woman who would never expose a knee in public and a modern woman on a bathing-beach have very different standards of modesty. And yet all may be admirable in their own ways.

There is, then, an obvious sense in which the virtues may be thought of as differing from person to person. Because people lead different kinds of lives, have different sorts of personalities, and occupy different social roles, the qualities of character that they manifest may differ.

It is tempting to go even further and say that the virtues differ from society to society. After all, the kind of life that is possible for an individual will depend on the society in which he or she lives. A scholar's life is possible only in a society that has institutions, such as universities, that define and make possible the life of a scholar. The same could be said of a football player, a priest, a geisha, or a samurai warrior. Societies provide systems of values, institutions, and ways of life within which individual lives are fashioned. The traits of character that are needed to occupy these roles will differ, and so the traits needed to live successfully will differ. Thus the virtues will be different. In light of all this, why shouldn't we just say that which qualities are virtues will depend on the ways of life that are created and sustained by particular societies?

To this it may be countered that *there are some virtues that will be needed by all people in all times*. This was Aristotle's view, and he was probably right. Aristotle believed that we all have a great deal in common, despite our differences. "One may observe," he said, "in one's travels to distant countries the feelings of recognition and affiliation that link every human being to every other human being." Even in the most disparate societies, people face the same basic problems and have the same basic needs. Thus:

- Everyone needs courage, because no one (not even the scholar) is so safe that danger may not sometimes arise.
- In every society there will be property to be managed and decisions to be made about who gets what, and in every society there will be some people who are worse off than others; so generosity is always to be prized.
- Honesty in speech is always a virtue because no society can exist without communication among its members.
- Everyone needs friends, and to have friends one must be a friend; so everyone needs loyalty.

This sort of list could—and in Aristotle's hands it does—go on and on.

To summarize, then, it may be true that in different societies the virtues are given somewhat different interpretations, and different sorts of actions are counted as satisfying them; and it may be true that some people, because they lead particular sorts of lives in particular sorts of circumstances, have need of some virtues more than others. But it cannot be right to say simply that whether any particular character trait is a virtue is never anything more than a matter of social convention. The major virtues are mandated not by social convention but by basic facts about our common human condition.

13.3. Some Advantages of Virtue Ethics

Why do some philosophers believe that an emphasis on the virtues is superior to other ways of thinking about ethics? A number of reasons have been suggested. Here are two of the most important.

1. *Moral motivation.* First, virtue ethics is appealing because it provides a natural and attractive account of moral motivation. The other theories seem deficient on this score. Consider the following:

You are in the hospital recovering from a long illness. You are bored and restless, and so you are delighted when Smith arrives to visit. You have a good time chatting with him; his visit is just the tonic you needed. After a while you tell Smith how much you appreciate his coming—he really is a fine fellow and a good friend to take the trouble to come all the way across town to see you. But Smith demurs; he confesses that he is merely doing his duty. At first you think he is only being modest, but the more you talk, the clearer it becomes that he is speaking the literal truth. He is not visiting you because he wants to, or because he likes you, but only because he thinks it is his duty to "do the right thing," and on this occasion he has decided it is his duty to visit you—perhaps because he knows of no one else who is more in need of cheering up or no one easier to get to.

This example was suggested by Michael Stocker in an influential article that appeared in the *Journal of Philosophy* in 1976. Stocker comments that surely you would be very disappointed to learn Smith's motive; now his visit seems cold and calculating and it loses all value to you. You thought he was your friend, but now you learn otherwise. Stocker says about Smith's behavior: "Surely there is something lacking here—and lacking in moral merit or value."

Of course, there is nothing wrong with what Smith *did*. The problem is his motive. We value friendship, love, and respect, and we want our relationships with people to be based on mutual regard. Acting from an abstract sense of duty, or from a desire to "do the right thing," is not the same. We would not want to live in a community of people who acted only from such motives, nor would we want to be such a person. Therefore, the argument goes, theories of ethics that emphasize only right action will never provide a completely satisfactory account of the moral life. For that, we need a theory that emphasizes personal qualities such as friendship, love, and loyalty—in other words, a theory of the virtues.

2. *Doubts about the "ideal" of impartiality.* A dominant theme of modern moral philosophy has been impartiality—the idea that all persons are morally equal, and that in deciding what to do we should treat everyone's interests as equally important. (Of the four theories of "right action" listed above, only Ethical Egoism, a theory with few adherents, denies this.) John Stuart Mill put the point well when he wrote that "Utilitarianism requires [the moral agent] to be as strictly impartial as a benevolent and disinterested spectator." The book you are now reading also treats impartiality as a fundamental moral requirement: In the first chapter impartiality was included as a part of the "minimum conception" of morality.

It may be doubted, though, whether impartiality is really such an important feature of the moral life. Consider one's relationships with family and friends. Are we really impartial where their interests are concerned? And should we be? A mother loves her children and cares for them in a way that she does not care for other children. She is partial to them through and through. But is anything wrong with that? Isn't that exactly the way a mother should be? Again, we love our friends and we are willing to do things for them that we would not do for just anyone. Is anything wrong with that? On the contrary, it seems that the love of family and friends is an inescapable feature of the morally good life. Any theory that emphasizes impartiality will have a difficult time accounting for this.

A moral theory that emphasizes the virtues, however, can account for all this very comfortably. Some virtues are partial and some are not. Love and friendship involve partiality toward loved ones and friends; beneficence toward people in general is also a virtue, but it is a virtue of a different kind. What is needed is not some general requirement of impartiality, but an understanding of the nature of these different virtues and how they relate to one another.

13.4. The Problem of Incompleteness

The preceding arguments make an impressive case for two general points: first, that an adequate theory of ethics must provide an understanding of moral character; and second, that modern moral philosophers have failed to do this. Not only have they neglected the topic, their neglect has led them sometimes to embrace doctrines that *distort* the nature of moral character. Suppose we accept these conclusions. Where do we go from here?

One way of proceeding would be to develop a theory that combines the best features of the right action approach with insights drawn from the virtues approach—we might try to improve Utilitarianism, Kantianism, and the like by adding to them a better account of moral character. Our total theory would then include an account of the virtues, but that account would be offered only as a supplement to a theory of right action. This sounds sensible, and if such a project could be carried out successfully, there would obviously be much to be said in its favor.

Some virtue theorists, however, have suggested that we should proceed differently. They have argued that the ethics of virtue should be considered as an *alternative* to the other sorts of theories—as an independent theory of ethics that is complete in itself. We might call this "radical virtue ethics." Is this a viable view?

Virtue and Conduct. As we have seen, theories that emphasize right action seem incomplete because they neglect the question of character. Virtue Theory remedies this problem by making the question of character its central concern. But as a result, Virtue Theory runs the risk of being incomplete in the opposite way. Moral problems are frequently problems about what we should *do*. It is not obvious how, according to Virtue Theory, we should go about deciding what to do. What can this approach tell us about the assessment, not of character, but of action?

The answer will depend on the spirit in which Virtue Theory is offered. If a theory of the virtues is offered only as a supplement to a theory of right action, then when the assessment of action is at issue, the resources of the total theory will be brought into play and some version of utilitarian or Kantian policies (for example) will be recommended. On the other hand, if the theory of virtue is offered as an independent theory intended to be complete in itself, more drastic steps must be taken. Either the theory will have to jettison the notion of "right action" altogether or it will have to give some account of the notion derived from the conception of virtuous character.

Although it sounds at first like a crazy idea, some philosophers have in fact argued that we should get rid of such concepts as "morally right action." Anscombe says that "it would be a great improvement" if we stopped using such notions altogether. We could still assess conduct as better or worse, she says, but we would do so in other terms. Instead of saying that an action was "morally wrong," we would simply say that it was "untruthful" or "unjust"—terms derived from the vocabulary of virtue. In her view, we need not say anything more than this to explain why an action is to be rejected.

But it is not really necessary for radical virtue theorists to jettison such notions as "morally right." These ideas can be retained but given a new interpretation within the virtue framework. This might be done as follows. First, it could be said that actions are to be assessed as right or wrong in the familiar way, by reference to the reasons that can be given for or against them: We ought to do those actions that have the best reasons in their favor. However, *the reasons cited will all be reasons that are connected with the virtues*—the reasons in favor of doing an act will be that it is honest, or generous, or fair, and the like; while the reasons against doing it will be that it is dishonest, or stingy, or unfair, and the like. This analysis could be summed up by saying that our duty is to act virtuously—the "right thing to do," in other words, is whatever a virtuous person would do.

The Problem of Incompleteness. We have now sketched the radical virtue theorist's way of understanding what we ought to do. Is that understanding sufficient? The principal problem for the theory is the problem of incompleteness.

To see the problem, consider a typical virtue, such as honesty. Suppose a person is tempted to lie, perhaps because lying offers some advantage in a particular situation. The reason he or she should not lie, according to the radical virtue ethics approach, is because doing so would be dishonest. This sounds reasonable enough. But what does it mean to be honest? Isn't an honest person simply one who follows such rules as "Do not lie"? It is hard to see what honesty consists in if it is not the disposition to follow such rules.

But we cannot avoid asking why such rules are important. Why shouldn't a person lie, especially when there is some advantage to be gained from it? Plainly we need an answer that goes beyond the simple observation that doing so would be incompatible with having a particular character trait; we need an explanation of why it is better to have this trait than its opposite. Possible answers might be that a policy of truth-telling is on the whole to one's own advantage; or that it promotes the general welfare; or that it is needed by people who must live together relying on one another. The first explanation looks suspiciously like Ethical Egoism; the second is utilitarian; and the third recalls contractarian ways of thinking. In any case, giving any explanation at all seems to take us beyond the limits of unsupplemented Virtue Theory.

Moreover, it is difficult to see how unsupplemented Virtue Theory could handle cases of moral conflict. Suppose you must choose between A and B, when it would be dishonest but kind to do A, and honest but unkind to do B. (An example might be telling the truth in circumstances that would be hurtful to someone.) Honesty and kindness are both virtues, and so there are reasons both for and against each alternative. But you must do one or the other—you must either tell the truth and be unkind, or not tell the truth and be kind. So which should you do? The admonition to act virtuously does not, by itself, offer much help. It only leaves you wondering which virtue takes precedence. It seems that we need some more general guidance, beyond that which radical Virtue Theory can offer, to resolve such conflicts.

Is There a Virtue That Matches Every Morally Good Reason for Doing Something? Finally, the problem of incompleteness points toward a more general theoretical difficulty for the radical virtue ethics approach. As we have seen, according to this approach the reasons for or against doing an action must always be associated with one or more virtues. Thus radical virtue ethics is committed to the idea that *for any good reason that may be given in favor of doing an action, there is a corresponding virtue that* *consists in the disposition to accept and act on that reason.* But this does not appear to be true.

Suppose, for example, that you are a legislator and you must decide how to allocate funds for medical research—there isn't enough money for everything, and you must decide whether to invest resources in AIDS research or in some other worthy project. And suppose you decide it is best in these circumstances to do what will benefit the most people. Is there a virtue that matches the disposition to do this? If there is, perhaps it should be called "acting like a utilitarian." Or, to return to our example of moral conflicts, is there a virtue connected with every principle that can be invoked to resolve conflicts between the other virtues? If there is, perhaps it is the "virtue" of wisdom—which is to say, the ability to figure out and do what is on the whole best. But this gives away the game. If we posit such "virtues" only to make all moral decision making fit into the preferred framework, we will have saved radical virtue ethics, but at the cost of abandoning its central idea.

Conclusion. For these reasons, it seems best to regard the theory of virtue as part of an overall theory of ethics rather than as a complete theory in itself. The total theory would include an account of all the considerations that figure in practical decision making, together with their underlying rationale. The question, then, is whether such a total view can accommodate both an adequate conception of right action and a related conception of virtuous character in a way that does justice to both.

I can see no reason why this is not possible. Our overall theory might begin by taking human welfare—or the welfare of all sentient creatures, for that matter—as the surpassingly important value. We might say that, from a moral point of view, we should want a society in which all people can lead happy and satisfying lives. We could then go on to consider both the question of what sorts of actions and social policies would contribute to this goal *and* the question of what qualities of character are needed to create and sustain individual lives. An inquiry into the nature of virtue could profitably be conducted from within the perspective that such a larger view would provide. Each could illuminate the other, and if each part of the overall theory has to be adjusted a bit here and there to accommodate the other, so much the better for truth.

CHAPTER 14

What Would a Satisfactory Moral Theory Be Like?

Some people believe that there cannot be progress in Ethics, since everything has already been said . . . I believe the opposite . . . Compared with the other sciences, Non-Religious Ethics is the youngest and least advanced.

DEREK PARFIT, *REASONS AND PERSONS* (1984)

14.1. Morality without Hubris

Moral philosophy has a rich and fascinating history. A great many thinkers have approached the subject from a wide variety of perspectives and have produced theories that both attract and repel the thoughtful reader. Almost all the classical theories contain plausible elements, which is hardly surprising, considering that they were devised by philosophers of undoubted genius. Yet the various theories are not consistent with one another, and most are vulnerable to crippling objections. After reviewing them, one is left wondering what to believe. What, in the final analysis, is the truth? Of course, different philosophers would answer this question in different ways. Some might refuse to answer at all, on the grounds that we do not yet know enough to have reached the "final analysis." (In this, moral philosophy is not much worse off than any other subject of human inquiry—we do not know the "final" truth about most things.) But we do know a lot, and it may not be unduly rash to say something about what a satisfactory moral theory might be like.

A Modest Conception of Human Beings. A satisfactory theory would, first of all, be sensitive to the facts about human nature, and it would be appropriately modest about the place of human

191

beings in the scheme of things. The universe is some 15 billion years old—that is the time elapsed since the "big bang"—and the earth itself was formed about 4.6 billion years ago. The evolution of life on the planet was a slow process, guided largely by natural selection. The first humans appeared quite recently. The extinction of the great dinosaurs 65 million years ago (possibly as the result of a catastrophic collision between the earth and an asteroid) left ecological room for the evolution of the few little mammals that were about, and after 63 or 64 million more years, one line of that evolution finally produced us. In geological time, we arrived only yesterday.

But no sooner did our ancestors arrive than they began to think of themselves as the most important things in all creation. Some of them even imagined that the whole universe had been made for their benefit. Thus, when they began to develop theories of right and wrong, they held that the protection of their own interests had a kind of ultimate and objective value. The rest of creation, they reasoned, was intended for their use. We now know better. We now know that we exist by evolutionary accident, as one species among many, on a small and insignificant world in one little corner of the cosmos. The details of this picture are revised each year, as more is discovered; but the main outlines seem well established.

How Reason Gives Rise to Ethics. Hume, who knew only a little of this story, nevertheless realized that human *hubris* is largely unjustified. "The life of a man," he wrote, "is of no greater importance to the universe than that of an oyster." But he also recognized that our lives are important to *us*. We are creatures with desires, needs, plans, and hopes; even if "the universe" does not care about those things, we do.

Human *hubris* is largely unjustified, but it is not entirely unjustified. Compared to the other creatures, we do have impressive intellectual capacities. We have evolved as rational beings. This fact gives some point to our inflated opinion of ourselves; as it turns out, it is also what makes us capable of having a morality. Because we are rational, we are able to take some facts as reasons for behaving one way rather than another. We can articulate those reasons and think about them. Thus we take the fact that an action would help satisfy our desires, needs, and so on—in short, the fact that an action would *promote our interests*—as a reason in favor of doing it.

The origin of our concept of "ought" may be found in these facts. If we were not capable of considering reasons for and against actions, we would have no use for such a notion. Like the lower animals, we would act from impulse or habit, or as Kant put it, from "inclination." But the consideration of reasons introduces a new factor. Now we find ourselves impelled to act in certain ways as a result of deliberation, as a result of thinking about our behavior and its consequences. We use the word *ought* to mark this new element of the situation: We ought to do what there are the weightiest reasons for doing.

Once we consider morality as a matter of acting on reason, another important point emerges. In reasoning about what to do, we can be consistent or inconsistent. One way of being inconsistent is to accept a fact as a reason on one occasion, while refusing to accept a similar fact as a reason on another occasion, even though there is no difference between the two occasions that would justify distinguishing them. (At the end of Chapter 9, I referred to this as "Kant's basic idea.") This happens when a person unjustifiably places the interests of his own race or social group above the comparable interests of other races and social groups. Racism means counting the interests of the members of other races as less important than the interests of the members of one's own race, despite the fact that there is no general difference between the races that would justify doing so. It is an offense against morality because it is first an offense against reason. Similar remarks could be made about other doctrines that divide humanity into the morally favored and disfavored, such as egoism, sexism, and nationalism. The upshot is that reason requires impartiality: We ought to act so as to promote the interests of everyone alike.

If Psychological Egoism were true, this would mean that reason demands more of us than we can manage. But Psychological Egoism is not true; it gives an altogether false picture of human nature and the human condition. We have evolved as social creatures, living together in groups, wanting one another's company, needing one another's cooperation, and capable of caring about one another's welfare. So there is a pleasing theoretical "fit" between (a) what reason requires, namely impartiality; (b) the requirements of social living, namely adherence to a set of rules that, if fairly applied, would serve everyone's interests; and (c) our natural inclination to care about others, at least to a modest degree. All three work together to make morality not only possible, but in an important sense, *natural* for us.

14.2. Treating People as They Deserve and Other Motives

The idea that we should "promote the interests of everyone alike," when it is taken as a proscription of bigotry, is appealing; however, it may be objected that such a maxim ignores the fact that people have different merits. At least some of the time, we should treat individuals as they deserve to be treated, rather than dealing with them as if they were only members of the great crowd of humanity.

The idea that people should be treated as they deserve is connected with the idea that they are rational agents with the power of choice—if people were not rational and had no control over their actions, they would not be responsible for their conduct and they could not deserve good or ill on account of it. Rational beings, however, are responsible for what they freely choose to do, and those who choose to behave decently toward others deserve to be treated well in return, while those who treat others badly deserve to be treated badly in return.

This sounds harsh until we consider examples. Suppose Smith has always been generous, helping you whenever she could, and now she is in trouble and needs your help. There is now a special reason *she* should be helped, beyond the general obligation you have to be helpful to everyone. She is not just another member of the crowd, but a particular person who, by her own previous conduct, has earned your respect and gratitude. But now consider someone with the opposite history: Suppose Jones is your neighbor, and he has always refused to help you when you needed it. One day, for example, your car wouldn't start, and Jones wouldn't give you a lift to work—he had no particular excuse, he just wouldn't be bothered. Imagine that, after this episode, Jones has car trouble and he has the nerve to ask you for a ride. Perhaps you will think you should help him anyway, despite his own lack of helpfulness. (You might think this will teach him generosity.) Nevertheless, if we concentrate on what he *deserves*, we must conclude that he deserves to be left to fend for himself. Certainly, if circumstances arise in which you must choose between helping Smith and helping Jones, you have good reason to choose Smith.

Adjusting our treatment of individuals to match how they have chosen to treat others is not just a matter of rewarding friends and holding grudges against enemies. It is a matter of treating people as responsible agents, who by their own choices show themselves to be deserving of particular responses, and toward whom such emotions as gratitude and resentment are appropriate. There is an important difference between Smith and Jones; why shouldn't that be reflected in the way we respond to them? What would it be like if we did *not* tailor our responses to people in this way?

For one thing, we would be denying people (including ourselves) the ability to earn good treatment at the hands of others. This is an important matter. Because we live together with other people, how each of us fares depends not only on what we do but on what others do as well. If we are to flourish, we need to obtain the good treatment of others. A system of understandings in which desert is acknowledged gives us a way of doing that. Thus, acknowledging deserts is a way of granting people the power to determine their own fates.

Absent this, what are we to do? What are the alternatives? We might imagine a system in which the only way for a person to ensure good treatment by others is somehow to coerce that treatment from them, or we might imagine that good treatment always comes as charity. But the practice of acknowledging deserts is different. The practice of acknowledging deserts gives people control over whether others will treat them well or badly, by saying to them: If you behave well, you will be *entitled* to good treatment from others. You will have earned it. Without this control, people would be impotent. Respecting people's right to choose their own conduct, and then adjusting our treatment of them according to how they choose, is ultimately a matter of "respect for persons" in a sense somewhat like Kant's.

Other Motives. There are other ways in which the idea of "promoting the interests of everyone alike" apparently fails to capture the whole of moral life. (I say "apparently" because I want to return later to the question of whether the failure is apparent or real.) Certainly, people should sometimes be motivated by an impartial concern for "the interests of everyone alike." But this is not the only morally praiseworthy motive:

- A mother loves and cares for her children: She is not concerned to "promote their interests" simply because they are people she can help. Her attitude toward them is entirely different from her attitude toward other children. While she might feel that she should help other children when she can, that vaguely benevolent feeling is nothing like the love she has for her own.

• A woman is loyal to her friends: Again, she is not concerned with their interests only as part of her benevolent concern for people generally. They are her friends, and friendship makes them special.

As we noted in Chapter 13, only a philosophical idiot would propose to eliminate love, loyalty, and the like from our understanding of the moral life. If such motives were eliminated, and instead people simply calculated what was for the best, we would all be much worse off. And in any case, who would want to live in a world without love and friendship?

There are, of course, many other valuable sorts of motives that come into play as people go about their lives:

• A composer is concerned, above all else, to finish her symphony. She pursues this even though she might do "more good" by doing something else.

• A teacher devotes great effort to preparing his classes, even though more overall good might be accomplished if he directed part of this energy elsewhere.

While these are not usually considered "moral" motives, they are motives that, from a moral point of view, we should not want to eliminate from human life. The desire to create, pride in doing one's job well, and other such motives contribute both to personal happiness (think of the joy of having created something beautiful or the satisfaction of having done a job well) and to the general welfare (think how much worse off we would be without music and good teachers). We should no more want to eliminate them than we would want to eliminate love and friendship.

14.3. Multiple-Strategies Utilitarianism

On the basis of some remarks about human nature and reason, we gave a sketchy justification of the principle that "we ought to act so as to promote the interests of everyone alike." But then we noted that this cannot be the whole story concerning our moral obligations because (at least sometimes) we should treat people according to their individual deserts. And then we noted that there are other morally important motives that apparently have nothing to do with the impartial promotion of interests. Yet it may be possible to see these diverse concerns as related to one another. At first blush it seems that treating people according to their individual deserts is quite different from seeking to promote the interests of everyone alike. But when we asked why deserts are important, the answer turned out to be that *we would all be much worse off* if the acknowledgment of deserts was not part of our moral scheme. And when we ask why love, friendship, artistic creativity, and pride in one's work are important, the answer is that *our lives would be so much poorer* were it not for such things. This suggests that there is a single standard at work in the assessment of all these different things.

Perhaps, then, the single moral standard is human welfare (or as Mill put it, the welfare of "the whole of sentient creation"— I will return to this complication in a moment). What is important is that people be as happy and well-off as possible. And this standard is to be used in assessing a wide variety of things, including actions, policies, social customs, laws, rules, motives, and traits of character. When we reflect about rules, motives, and the like, we refer to the standard of welfare. But this does not mean that we should always be motivated by that standard in the ordinary course of our lives. Our lives will go better if, instead, we love our children, enjoy our friends, take pride in our work, keep our promises, and so on. An ethic that values "the interests of everyone alike" will endorse this conclusion.

This is not a new idea. Henry Sidgwick, the great utilitarian theorist of the Victorian era, made the same point when he wrote:

> the doctrine that Universal Happiness is the ultimate *standard* must not be understood to imply that Universal Benevolence is the only right or always best *motive* of action . . . it is not necessary that the end which gives the criterion of rightness should always be the end at which we consciously aim: and if experience shows that the general happiness will be more satisfactorily attained if men frequently act from other motives than pure universal philanthropy, it is obvious that these other motives are reasonably to be preferred on Utilitarian principles.

Sidgwick's thought has been cited in support of a view called Motive Utilitarianism, the central idea of which is that we should act from the combination of motives that best promote the general welfare.

Yet the most plausible view of this type does not focus exclusively on motives; nor does it focus entirely on acts or rules, as other varieties of Utilitarianism have done. The most plausible view might be called *Multiple-Strategies Utilitarianism.* The ultimate end is the general welfare, but diverse strategies may be endorsed as means of achieving that end. Sometimes we aim directly at it, as when a legislator enacts laws for the general welfare, or an individual calculates that sending money to UNICEF would do more good than anything else available. But sometimes we don't think of it at all; instead we simply care for our children, work at our jobs, obey the law, and keep our promises.

Right Action as Living according to the Best Plan. We can make the idea behind Multiple-Strategies Utilitarianism a little more specific.

Suppose we had a fully specified list of the virtues, motives, and methods of decision making that would characterize a person whose life is both satisfying to himself or herself and contributes positively to the welfare of others. And suppose, further, that this is the *optimum* list for that person; there is no other combination of virtues, motives, and methods of decision making that would do the job better. The list would include at least the following:

- The virtues that are needed to make one's life go well;
- The motives on which one will act;
- The commitments and personal relationships that one will have to friends, family, and others;
- The social roles that one will occupy, with the responsibilities and demands that go with them;
- The duties and concerns associated with the projects one will undertake, such as being a musician or a soldier or an undertaker;
- The everyday rules that one will follow most of the time without even thinking; and
- A strategy, or group of strategies, about when to consider making exceptions to the rules, and the grounds on which exceptions can be made.

The list would also include a specification of the relations between the other items on the list—what takes priority over what, how to adjudicate conflicts, and so on. It might be extremely hard to construct such a list. As a practical matter, it might even be impossible. But we can be pretty sure that it would include endorsements of friendship, honesty, and other familiar useful virtues. It would tell us to keep our promises, but not always, and to refrain from harming people, but not always; and so on. And it would probably tell us to stop living in such luxury while each year millions of children die of preventable diseases.

At any rate, there is some combination of virtues, motives, and methods of decision making that is best *for me*, given my circumstances, personality, and talents—"best" in the sense that it will optimize the chances of my having a good life, while at the same time optimizing the chances of other people having good lives. Call this optimum combination *my best plan*. The right thing for me to do is to act in accordance with my best plan.

My best plan may have a great deal in common with yours. Presumably, they will both include rules against lying, stealing, and killing, together with understandings about when to make exceptions to those rules and the grounds on which exceptions can be made. They will both include virtues such as patience, kindness, and self-control. They may both contain instructions for raising children, including what virtues to foster in them. And there will be much more that my best plan has in common with yours.

But our best plans need not be identical. People have different personalities and talents. One person may find fulfillment as a priest while another could never live like that. Thus their lives might include different sorts of personal relationships and they might need to cultivate different virtues. People also live in different circumstances and have access to different resources—some are rich; some are poor; some are privileged; some are oppressed and persecuted. Thus the optimum strategy for living might be different for them.

In each case, however, the identification of a plan as the best plan will be a matter of assessing the extent to which it promotes the interests of everyone alike. So the overall theory is utilitarian, even though it may frequently endorse people acting from motives that do not look utilitarian at all.

14.4. The Moral Community

As moral agents, we should be concerned with everyone whose welfare might be affected by what we do. This may seem a pious platitude, but in reality it can be a hard doctrine. In the year between the time I write this and the book is published, about a million children will die of measles. People in the affluent countries could easily prevent this, but they will not. People would no doubt feel a greater sense of obligation if it were children in their own neighborhoods, rather than strangers in foreign countries, who were dying. But on the theory we are considering, the location of the children makes no difference: Everyone is included in the community of moral concern. If the interests of all children were taken seriously, wherever they lived, it would make an enormous difference in our behavior.

If the moral community is not limited to people in one *place*, neither is it limited to people at any one *time*. Whether people will be affected by our actions now or in the distant future makes no difference. Our obligation is to consider all their interests equally. One consequence of this concerns weapons of mass destruction. With the development of nuclear weapons, we now have the capacity to alter the course of history in an especially dramatic way. If the welfare of future generations is given proper weight, it is difficult to imagine any circumstances in which the large-scale use of these weapons would be justified. The environment is another issue in which the interests of future generations figure prominently: We do not have to think that the environment is important "in itself" to see that its destruction is a moral horror; it is sufficient to consider what will become of people if the rain forests, sea algae, and ozone layer are ruined.

There is one other way in which our conception of the moral community must be expanded. Humans, as we have noted, are only one of the species that inhabit this planet. Like humans, the other animals also have interests that are affected by what we do. When we kill or torture them, they are harmed, just as humans are harmed when treated in those ways. Bentham and Mill were right to insist that the interests of nonhuman animals must be given weight in our moral calculations. As Bentham pointed out, excluding creatures from moral consideration because of their species is no more justified than excluding them because of race, nationality, or sex. Impartiality requires the expansion of the moral community not only across space and time but across the boundaries of species as well.

14.5. Justice and Fairness

Classical Utilitarianism was criticized for failing to account for the values of justice and fairness. Can the complications we have introduced help?

One criticism had to do with punishment. We can imagine cases in which it promotes the general welfare to frame an innocent person. This is blatantly unjust, yet taking the Principle of Utility as our ultimate standard, it is hard to explain why it is wrong. More generally, as Kant pointed out, the basic utilitarian "justification" of punishment is in terms of treating individuals as mere "means."

If a policy of treating people as they deserve is justified by the general utilitarian standard, this may permit a somewhat different view of punishment than utilitarians have customarily taken. (In fact, the resulting view of punishment will be close to Kant's.) In punishing someone, we are treating him differently from the way we treat others—punishment involves a failure of impartiality. But this is justified, on our account, by the person's own past deeds. It is a response to what he has done. That is why it is not right to frame an innocent person; the innocent person has not done anything to deserve being singled out for such treatment.

The theory of punishment, however, is only one part of the subject of justice. Questions of justice arise any time one person is treated differently from another. Suppose an employer must choose which of two employees to promote, when she can promote only one of them. The first candidate has worked hard for the company, taking on extra work when it was needed, giving up her vacation to help out, and so on. The second candidate, on the other hand, has always done only the minimum required of him. (And we will assume he has no excuse; he has simply chosen not to work very hard.) Obviously, the two employees will be treated very differently: One will get the promotion; the other will not. But this is all right, according to our theory, because the first employee deserves to be advanced over the second, considering the past performance of each. The first employee has earned the promotion; the second has not.

202 THE ELEMENTS OF MORAL PHILOSOPHY

Insofar as fairness is concerned, a person's voluntary actions can justify departures from the basic policy of "equal treatment," but nothing else can. This goes against a common view of the matter. Often, people think it is right for individuals to be rewarded for physical beauty, superior intelligence, or other native endowments. (In practice, people often get better jobs and a greater share of life's good things just because they were born with greater natural gifts.) But on reflection, this does not seem right. People do not deserve their native endowments; they have them only as a result of what John Rawls has called "the natural lottery." Suppose the first employee in our example was passed over for the promotion, despite her hard work, because the second employee had some native talent that was more useful in the new position. Even if the employer could justify this decision in terms of the company's needs, the first employee would rightly feel that there is something unfair going on. She has worked harder, yet he is now getting the promotion, and the benefits that go with it, because of something he did nothing to merit. That is not fair. A just society, according to our conception, would be one in which people may improve their positions through work (with the opportunity for work available to everyone), but they would not enjoy superior positions simply because they were born lucky.

14.6. Conclusion

What would a satisfactory moral theory be like? I have outlined the possibility that seems most plausible to me. However, it is instructive to remember that a great many thinkers have tried to devise such a theory, and history has judged them to have been only partially successful. This suggests that it would be wise not to make too grandiose a claim for one's own view, whatever it might be. But there is reason for optimism. As Derek Parfit has observed, the earth will remain habitable for another billion years, and civilization is now only a few thousand years old. If we do not destroy ourselves, moral philosophy, along with all the other human inquiries, may yet have a long way to go.

Suggestions for Further Reading

General Suggestions

This book introduces moral philosophy by examining the most important general theories of ethics. There are other ways to approach the subject. Alasdair MacIntyre's *A Short History of Ethics* (New York: Macmillan, 1966) is an accessible historical treatment. Peter Singer's *Practical Ethics,* 2nd ed. (Cambridge: Cambridge University Press, 1993), is recommended as an introduction centered on such practical issues as abortion, racism, and so forth. The fact that these books are "introductions" should not be taken to mean that they are boringly elementary; each contains material that will be of interest even to sophisticated readers. Two state-of-the-art philosophical encyclopedias also deserve notice: *The Routledge Encyclopedia of Philosophy,* ed. Edward Craig (London: Routledge, 1998), and *The Encyclopedia of Ethics,* ed. Lawrence C. Becker and Charlotte B. Becker, 2nd edition (New York: Garland Press, 2001).

Chapter 1: What Is Morality?

Classic Cases in Medical Ethics, by Gregory E. Pence, 3rd ed. (New York: McGraw-Hill, 1999), is a good source of information about cases and issues in medical ethics, including issues concerning handicapped infants.

The Definition of Morality, edited by G. Wallace and A.D.M. Walker (London: Methuen, 1970), is a useful collection of articles on the question of what morality is. For additional reflections on the place of reason in ethics and its limits, see James Rachels, *Can Ethics Provide Answers?* (Lanham, MD: Rowman and Littlefield, 1997). On the idea of impartiality, see Peter Singer, "Is Racism Arbitrary?" *Philosophia* 8 (1978), pp. 185–204.

Chapter 2: The Challenge of Cultural Relativism

Two classic defenses of Cultural Relativism by social scientists are Ruth Benedict, *Patterns of Culture* (New York: Pelican, 1946); and William Graham Sumner, *Folkways* (Boston: Ginn and Company, 1906).

Among contemporary philosophers, Gilbert Harman is the leading defender of ethical relativism; see his book *Explaining Value* (New York: Oxford University Press, 2000). Kai Nielsen's essay "Ethical Relativism and the Facts of Cultural Relativity," *Social Research* 33 (1966), pp. 531–51, is an excellent discussion of the significance, or lack of it, of anthropological data. *Ethical Relativism,* edited by John Ladd (Belmont, CA: Wadsworth, 1973), is a good collection of articles on Cultural Relativism. *Relativism: Cognitive and Moral,* edited by Jack W. Meiland and Michael Krausz (Notre Dame: University of Notre Dame Press, 1982), is another useful anthology. A very good recent book is Thomas Nagel's *The Last Word* (New York: Oxford University Press, 1997). *Moral Relativism and Moral Objectivity* by Gilbert Harman and Judith Jarvis Thomson (Oxford: Blackwell, 1996) is heavy going in places but rewarding.

Chapter 3: Subjectivism in Ethics

David Hume defended an important version of Ethical Subjectivism in Book III of his *A Treatise of Human Nature* (London, 1738; today available in numerous editions). But perhaps his clearest and most readable presentation of the theory is in Section I and Appendix I of his *An Inquiry Concerning the Principles of Morals* (London, 1752; also available now in various editions).

In Chapter 3 of his little book *Ethics* (London: Oxford University Press, 1912), G. E. Moore gives the classic critique of Simple Subjectivism. C. L. Stevenson discusses Moore's arguments and points out that they do not refute Emotivism in "Moore's Arguments Against Certain Forms of Ethical Naturalism," which is included in the volume of Stevenson's collected essays *Facts and Values* (New Haven: Yale University Press, 1963). Reading Stevenson's essays is easier than attempting his great work *Ethics and Language* (New Haven: Yale University Press, 1944).

An accessible critical discussion of emotivism is J. O. Urmson, *The Emotive Theory of Ethics* (London: Hutchinson, 1968). Chapter 3 of G. J. Warnock's *Contemporary Moral Philosophy* (London: Macmillan, 1967) is also recommended.

J. L. Mackie's *Ethics: Inventing Right and Wrong* (Harmondsworth, Middlesex: Penguin, 1977) is a vigorous defense of Subjectivism. For essays on both sides of the issue, see James Rachels, ed., *Ethical Theory 1: The Question of Objectivity* (Oxford: Oxford University Press, 1998).

Richard Mohr is the leading philosophical writer on gay issues. His books are *Gay Ideas* (Boston: Beacon Press, 1994), *Gays/Justice* (New York: Columbia University Press, 1990), and *A More Perfect*

Union (Boston: Beacon Press, 1995). For a conservative view, see Roger Scruton, *Sexual Desire* (London: Weidenfeld and Nicolson, 1985).

Chapter 4: Does Morality Depend on Religion?

Two anthologies contain a wealth of material on this subject: *Religion and Morality*, edited by Gene Outka and John P. Reeder, Jr. (Garden City, NY: Anchor, 1973); and *Divine Commands and Morality*, edited by Paul Helm (Oxford: Oxford University Press, 1981). Both include articles that defend the Divine Command Theory, such as Robert Merrihew Adams's "A Modified Divine Command Theory of Ethical Wrongness," as well as critical papers. Norman Kretzmann's "Abraham, Isaac, and Euthyphro: God and the Basis of Morality," in *Hamartia*, edited by Donald Stump (Lewiston, NY Mellen, 1983) is a splendid essay, although it may be difficult to find. Kai Nielsen's *Ethics Without God* (London: Pemberton, 1973) is also recommended. *A Companion to Ethics*, edited by Peter Singer (Oxford: Basil Blackwell, 1991), contains two useful articles: Jonathan Berg, "How Could Ethics Depend on Religion?" pp. 525–33; and Ronald Preston, "Christian Ethics," pp. 91–105.

Stephen Buckle's "Natural Law," in *A Companion to Ethics*, edited by Peter Singer (Oxford: Basil Blackwell, 1991), pp. 161–74, is a good account. *Aquinas and Natural Law* by D. J. O'Connor (London: Macmillan, 1968) is a clear, readable introduction to the subject.

The literature on abortion is, of course, vast. Perhaps the easiest way into the philosophical debate is through Chapter 6 of Peter Singer's *Practical Ethics*, 2nd ed. (Cambridge: Cambridge University Press, 1993). Mary Anne Warren's "Abortion" in *A Companion to Ethics*, edited by Peter Singer (Oxford: Basil Blackwell, 1991), pp. 303–14, would also be a good place to start. Some of the best philosophical articles are collected in *The Problem of Abortion*, edited by Joel Feinberg, 2nd ed. (Belmont, CA: Wadsworth, 1984). One of the most important, but also most difficult, philosophical studies of abortion is Michael Tooley, *Abortion and Infanticide* (Oxford: Clarendon Press, 1983). See, too, Barbara Baum Levenbook's and Joel Feinberg's essay "Abortion" in *Matters of Life and Death*, edited by Tom Regan, 3rd ed. (New York: McGraw-Hill, 1993).

Chapter 5: Psychological Egoism

Thomas Hobbes defends Psychological Egoism in certain passages in his *Leviathan* (London, 1651) and in *On Human Nature* (London, 1650). The former work is available today in various editions; the latter may be found in Thomas Hobbes, *Body, Man, and Citizen*, edited by

Richard S. Peters (New York: Collier, 1962). Hobbes's view of human nature provoked much criticism; Joseph Butler's demolition of Psychological Egoism in his *Fifteen Sermons Preached at Rolls Chapel* (Oxford, 1726) is especially noteworthy.

Among more recent writings, Joel Feinberg's essay "Psychological Egoism," in *Reason and Responsibility,* edited by Feinberg (Encino, CA: Dickenson, 1965), stands out as a model of exposition and argument. Feinberg rejects the theory. A defense is Michael Slote, "An Empirical Basis for Psychological Egoism," *Journal of Philosophy* 61 (1964), pp. 530–37.

But perhaps the most interesting recent work on this issue has been done by evolutionary biologists, who observe that altruistic behavior occurs throughout the animal world and who explain this as the result of natural selection. For a brief account, see James Rachels, *Created from Animals: The Moral Implications of Darwinism* (Oxford: Oxford University Press, 1990), pp. 73–79, 147–64.

Chapter 6: Ethical Egoism

Alasdair MacIntyre, "Egoism and Altruism," in *The Encyclopedia of Philosophy,* vol. 2, edited by Paul Edwards (New York: Macmillan and Free Press, 1967), pp. 462–66, is a nice survey article. So is Kurt Baier's "Egoism" in *A Companion to Ethics,* edited by Peter Singer (Oxford: Basil Blackwell, 1991), pp. 197–204.

Robert G. Olson's *The Morality of Self-Interest* (New York: Harcourt, 1965) is the best contemporary work by a philosopher sympathetic to Ethical Egoism. The following articles amount to a more or less continuous debate about the merits of the theory: Brian Medlin, "Ultimate Principles and Ethical Egoism," *Australasian Journal of Philosophy* 35 (1957), pp. 111–18; John Hospers, "Baier and Medlin on Ethical Egoism," *Philosophical Studies* 12 (1961), pp. 10–16; W. H. Baumer, "Indefensible Impersonal Egoism," *Philosophical Studies* 18 (1967), pp. 72–75; Jesse Kalin, "On Ethical Egoism," *American Philosophical Quarterly Monograph Series, No. 1: Studies in Moral Philosophy* (1968), pp. 26–41; and James Rachels, "Two Arguments Against Ethical Egoism," *Philosophia* 4 (1974), pp. 297–314.

Peter Singer's *How Are We to Live?* (Amherst, MA: Prometheus Books, 1995), which defends the ethical life against the life of self-interest, is a wonderful book.

On our duty to contribute for famine relief, see Chapter 8 of Singer's *Practical Ethics,* 2nd. ed. (Cambridge: Cambridge University Press, 1993); William Aiken and Hugh LaFollette, eds., *World Hunger and Moral Obligation* (Englewood Cliffs, NJ: Prentice-Hall, 1977); and Onora O'Neill, "The Moral Perplexities of Famine Relief," in *Matters of Life and Death,* edited by Tom Regan, 2nd ed. (New York: Random House, 1985). Peter Unger's *Living High and Letting Die* (New York: Oxford University Press, 1996) is an important recent book.

Chapter 7: The Utilitarian Approach

The indispensable classic work is John Stuart Mill's *Utilitarianism* (London, 1861). It is available in many editions, including the collection *Mill's Ethical Writings,* edited by J. B. Schneewind (New York: Collier, 1965), which also contains Mill's important essay on Bentham. Henry Sidgwick's *The Methods of Ethics* (London: Macmillan, 1874), another 19th-century classic, is rewarding but less accessible. In the 20th century, R. M. Hare is a leading utilitarian thinker; see his *Moral Thinking* (Oxford: Oxford University Press, 1981) and *Essays in Ethical Theory* (Oxford: Oxford University Press, 1989).

For more about euthanasia, see James Rachels, *The End of Life* (Oxford: Oxford University Press, 1986). Also see Peter Singer, *Rethinking Life and Death* (New York: St. Martin's Press, 1996).

Singer's *Animal Liberation* (New York: New York Review Books, 1975; 2nd ed. 1990) is the book that made the question of animal welfare a topic of serious discussion among contemporary philosophers. It is lively, nontechnical, and easy to read. Also accessible is Singer's "Animals and the Value of Life" in *Matters of Life and Death,* edited by Tom Regan, 3rd ed. (New York: McGraw-Hill, 1993). See *Animal Rights and Human Obligations,* edited by Tom Regan and Peter Singer, 2nd ed. (Englewood Cliffs, NJ: Prentice-Hall, 1989), for a collection of readings representing diverse points of view. Tom Regan's *The Case for Animal Rights* (Berkeley: University of California Press, 1983) is the most thorough defense of a rights-based approach; and R. G. Frey's *Rights, Killing, and Suffering: Moral Vegetarianism and Applied Ethics* (Oxford: Blackwell, 1983) is the best presentation of the case on the other side.

Chapter 8: The Debate over Utilitarianism

In two books, the English philosopher W. D. Ross presented an uncompromising attack on Utilitarianism: *The Right and the Good* (Oxford: Oxford University Press, 1930) and *Foundations of Ethics* (Oxford: Oxford University Press, 1939). After Ross, much of the contemporary debate was carried on in the academic journals. An enormous number of articles debate the merits of the theory. Two useful collections contain some of the most important ones: Samuel Gorovitz, ed., *Mill: Utilitarianism—Text and Critical Essays* (Indianapolis: Bobbs-Merrill,

1971); and Michael D. Bayles, ed., *Contemporary Utilitarianism* (Garden City, NY: Anchor, 1968). Robert M. Adams, "Motive Utilitarianism," *The Journal of Philosophy* 78 (1976), pp. 467–81, is an important paper. Amartya Sen and Bernard Williams, eds., *Utilitarianism and Beyond* (Cambridge: Cambridge University Press, 1982) is a good collection; but also see Samuel Scheffler, *Consequentialism and Its Critics* (New York: Oxford University Press, 1988).

Also recommended are J. J. C. Smart and Bernard Williams, *Utilitarianism: For and Against* (Cambridge: Cambridge University Press, 1973); and two books by Richard B. Brandt, *A Theory of the Good and the Right* (Oxford: Clarendon, 1979), and *Morality, Utilitarianism, and Rights* (New York: Cambridge University Press, 1992).

David Lyons, "Utilitarianism," in the *Encyclopedia of Ethics*, vol. II, edited by Lawrence C. Becker and Charlotte B. Becker (New York: Garland Press, 1992), pp. 1261–68, is recommended for a recent overview of the subject.

Chapter 9: Are There Absolute Moral Rules?

A debate about absolute moral rules may be traced through the following articles: G. E. M. Anscombe, "Modern Moral Philosophy," *Philosophy* 33 (1958); Jonathan Bennett, "Whatever the Consequences," *Analysis* 26 (1966); P. T. Geach, *God and the Soul* (London: Routledge and Kegan Paul, 1969), Chapter 9; James Cargile, "On Consequentialism," *Analysis* 29 (1969); and James Rachels, "On Moral Absolutism," *Australasian Journal of Philosophy* 48 (1970). A book edited by Joram G. Haber, *Absolutism and Its Consequentialist Critics* (Lanham, MD: Rowman and Littlefield, 1994), contains some of these articles plus other useful ones.

The best translations of Kant's major ethical writings are *Foundations of the Metaphysics of Morals*, translated by Lewis White Beck (Indianapolis: Bobbs-Merrill, 1959); *Critique of Practical Reason*, translated by Lewis White Beck (Indianapolis: Bobbs-Merrill, 1956); *The Metaphysical Principles of Virtue*, translated by James Ellington (Indianapolis: Bobbs-Merrill, 1964); *The Metaphysical Elements of Justice*, translated by John Ladd (Indianapolis: Bobbs-Merrill, 1965); and *Lectures on Ethics*, translated by Louis Infield (New York: Harper, 1963).

Two good short introductions to Kant are Christine M. Korsgaard, "Kant" in the *Encyclopedia of Ethics*, vol. 1, edited by Lawrence C. Becker and Charlotte B. Becker (New York: Garland Press, 1992), pp. 664–74; and Onora O'Neill, "Kantian Ethics" in *A Companion to Ethics*, edited by Peter Singer (Oxford: Basil Blackwell, 1991), pp. 175–85. For longer discussions see Barbara Herman, *The Practice of Moral Judgment* (Cambridge, MA: Harvard University Press, 1993), and Onora O'Neill, *Constructions of Reason: Explorations of Kant's Practical Philosophy* (New York: Cambridge University Press, 1989).

Chapter 10: Kant and Respect for Persons

The best translations of Kant's writings are listed above. R. S. Downie and Elizabeth Teller, *Respect for Persons* (London: Allen and Unwin, 1969) is a useful treatment of this concept. Herbert Morris's essay "Persons and Punishment," *The Monist* 52 (1968), pp. 475–501, is a splendid introduction to the notion of Kantian respect. Even though Morris does not specifically set out to explain Kant, his argument is so clear and so Kantian that understanding Morris's point is an excellent way of coming to understand what Kant had in mind.

Thomas E. Hill, Jr., and Christine Korsgaard have both written superb essays in Kantian moral philosophy. Hill's essays are collected in his books *Autonomy and Self-Respect* (New York: Cambridge University Press, 1991) and *Dignity and Practical Reason* (Ithaca: Cornell University Press, 1992). Korsgaard's essays are brought together in her book *Creating the Kingdom of Ends* (Cambridge: Cambridge University Press, 1996).

The philosophical debate about the nature and justification of punishment is chronicled in two useful anthologies: *Philosophical Perspectives on Punishment,* edited by Gertrude Ezorsky (Albany: State University of New York Press, 1972); and *The Philosophy of Punishment,* edited by H. B. Acton (London: Macmillan, 1969). On capital punishment, see Hugo A. Bedau, *The Death Penalty in America: Current Controversies* (New York: Oxford University Press, 1998) and "Capital Punishment," in *Matters of Life and Death,* edited by Tom Regan, 3rd ed. (New York: McGraw-Hill, 1993). On the idea of "rehabilitation," see the landmark work prepared by the American Friends Service Committee, *Struggle for Justice* (New York: Hill and Wang, 1971).

Chapter 11: The Idea of a Social Contract

The classic works are Thomas Hobbes, *Leviathan* (1651); John Locke, *The Second Treatise of Government* (1690); and Jean-Jacques Rousseau, *The Social Contract* (1762). All are available today in various editions. David P. Gauthier, *The Logic of Leviathan: The Moral and Political Theory of Thomas Hobbes* (Oxford: Clarendon, 1969), is an excellent secondary discussion.

Interest in the Social Contract Theory was revived among contemporary philosophers largely through the work of the Harvard philosopher John Rawls. Rawls's *A Theory of Justice* (Cambridge, MA:

Harvard University Press, 1971), which argues for a kind of contractarian theory, was the most acclaimed work of moral philosophy in the past three decades. Critical assessments of Rawls may be found in Brian Barry, *The Liberal Theory of Justice* (Oxford: Oxford University Press, 1973); Robert Paul Wolff, *Understanding Rawls* (Princeton: Princeton University Press, 1977); and Norman Daniels, ed., *Reading Rawls* (New York: Basic Books, n.d.).

David Gauthier's *Morals by Agreement* (Oxford: Oxford University Press, 1986) is a major contribution to Social Contract Theory. Gauthier's essay "Why Contractarianism?" in Peter Vallentyne, ed., *Contractarianism and Rational Choice* (New York: Cambridge University Press, 1991), pp. 15–30, is especially recommended. Another important paper is T. M. Scanlon, "Contractualism and Utilitarianism," in Amartya Sen and Bernard Williams, eds., *Utilitarianism and Beyond* (Cambridge: Cambridge University Press, 1982), pp. 103–28.

Two good introductory pieces are Will Kymlicka, "The Social Contract Tradition," in *A Companion to Ethics,* edited by Peter Singer (Oxford: Basil Blackwell, 1991), pp. 186–96; and Lawrence C. Becker, "Social Contract," in the *Encyclopedia of Ethics,* vol. 11, edited by Lawrence C. Becker and Charlotte B. Becker (New York: Garland Press, 1992), pp. 1170–77.

On civil disobedience, see the essays collected in *Civil Disobedience: Theory and Practice,* edited by Hugo Adam Bedau (New York: Pegasus Books, 1969).

Chapter 12: Feminism and the Ethics of Care

Carol Gilligan's *In A Different Voice: Psychological Theory and Women's Development* (Cambridge: Harvard University Press, 1982) is the book that started the contemporary discussion of "caring" as a distinctively feminine ethic. Nel Noddings, *Caring: A Feminine Approach to Ethics and Moral Education* (Berkeley: University of California Press, 1984) is the most detailed account of such an ethic. For an excellent collection of articles discussing Gilligan's work, see Mary Jeanne Larrabee, ed., *An Ethic of Care: Feminist and Interdisciplinary Perspectives* (New York: Routledge, 1993).

Among the many general treatments of the subject, three are especially recommended: Jean Grimshaw, "The Idea of a Female Ethic," in Peter Singer, ed., *A Companion to Ethics* (Oxford: Blackwell, 1991), pp. 491–99; Alison M. Jaggar, "Feminist Ethics," in the *Encyclopedia of Ethics,* vol. 1, edited by Lawrence C. Becker and Charlotte B. Becker (New York: Garland Press, 1992), pp. 361–70; and Virginia Held, "Feminist Transformations of Moral Theory," *Philosophy and Phenomenological Research* 50 (1990), pp. 321–44. Eva Kittay and Diana Meyers, eds., *Women and Moral Theory* (Lanham, MD: Rowman and Littlefield, 1987) contains a number of worthwhile papers.

Annette Baier's *Moral Prejudices* (Cambridge: Harvard University Press, 1994) is a collection of her papers, including "What Do Women Want in a Moral Theory?" and "Ethics in Many Different Voices." Sara Ruddick's *Maternal Thinking* (Boston: Beacon Press, 1989) develops a moral view based on the distinctive concerns and insights of mothers.

Feminist writers have also addressed particular moral issues such as pornography, militarism, and the environment. For a good selection of articles, see Alison M. Jaggar, ed., *Living with Contradictions: Controversies in Feminist Social Ethics* (Boulder: Westview Press, 1994).

Alison M. Jaggar and Iris Young, eds., *A Companion to Feminist Philosophy* (Oxford: Blackwell, 1998) is a useful general reference work.

Chapter 13: The Ethics of Virtue

The classic work with which to begin is Aristotle's *Nicomachean Ethics*. Martin Ostwald's translation (Indianapolis: Bobbs-Merrill, 1962) is one of many available. Some of the most important recent books are Philippa Foot, *Virtues and Vices and Other Essays in Moral Philosophy* (Berkeley: University of California Press, 1978); James D. Wallace, *Virtues and Vices* (Ithaca: Cornell University Press, 1978); Edmund L. Pincoffs, *Quandaries and Virtues: Against Reductivism in Ethics* (Lawrence: University of Kansas Press, 1986); and Michael Slote, *From Morality to Virtue* (New York: Oxford University Press, 1992).

Alasdair MacIntyre's *After Virtue* (Notre Dame: University of Notre Dame Press, 1981) is a seminal work; it is probably the most discussed current treatment of the subject. MacIntyre's later volume *Whose Justice? Which Rationality?* (Notre Dame: University of Notre Dame Press, 1988) is a sequel. MacIntyre also wrote the article on "Virtue Ethics" in the *Encyclopedia of Ethics*, vol. 11, edited by Lawrence C. Becker and Charlotte B. Becker (New York: Garland Press, 1992), pp. 1276–82.

The following articles are also recommended: Jonathan Bennett, "The Conscience of Huckleberry Finn," *Philosophy* 49 (1974), pp. 123–34; Michael Stocker, "The Schizophrenia of Modern Ethical Theories," *Journal of Philosophy* 73 (1976), pp. 453–66; Susan Wolf, "Moral Saints," *Journal of Philosophy* 79 (1982), pp. 419–39; and Robert Louden, "Some Vices of Virtue Ethics," *American Philosophical Quarterly* 21 (1984), pp. 227–36.

Gregory E. Pence, "Recent Work on the Virtues," *American Philosophical Quarterly* 21 (1984), pp. 281–97, is a helpful guide to work through 1984. Pence is also the author of the article on "Virtue Theory" in *A Companion to Ethics*, edited by Peter Singer (Oxford: Basil Blackwell, 1991), pp. 249–58.

An excellent collection of articles by various writers is *Midwest Studies in Philosophy, Vol. XII. Ethical Theory: Character and Virtue,* edited by Peter A. French, Theodore E. Uehling, Jr., and Howard K. Wettstein (Notre Dame: University of Notre Dame Press, 1988). Martha C. Nussbaum's "Non-Relative Virtues: An Aristotelian Approach," in this volume, is especially recommended. Another good collection is *Identity, Character, and Morality,* edited by Owen Flanagan and Amelie Oksenberg Rorty (Cambridge, MA: Bradford Books, 1990). But *Virtue Ethics,* edited by Michael Slote and Roger Crisp (Oxford: Oxford University Press, 1997), is probably the best single volume on the subject.

Chapter 14: What Would a Satisfactory Moral Theory Be Like?

On the need for a more modest conception of the moral "importance" of humankind, see James Rachels, *Created from Animals: The Moral Implications of Darwinism* (Oxford: Oxford University Press, 1990).

For more on desert, see James Rachels, "What People Deserve," in *Can Ethics Provide Answers?* (Lanham, MD: Rowman and Littlefield, 1997), pp. 175–98.

Notes on Sources

Chapter 1: What is Morality?

The ethicists' comments about Baby Theresa are from an Associated Press report by David Briggs, "Baby Theresa Case Raises Ethics Questions," *The Champaign-Urbana News-Gazette*, March 31, 1992, p. A-6. The poll about separating conjoined twins is from the *Ladies Home Journal*, March 2001. The judges' comments about Jodie and Mary are from *Daily Telegraph*, September 23, 2000. The quotation from the doctor about medical record-keeping in the U.S. is from the *Birmingham News*, July 27, 2001.

Information about the Tracy Latimer case is from the *New York Times*, December 1, 1997, National Edition, p. A-3. The Tracy Walters quotation is from the Canadian Broadcasting Corporation, January 19, 2001.

Chapter 2: The Challenge of Cultural Relativism

The story of the Greeks and the Callatians is from Herodotus, *The Histories*, translated by Aubrey de Selincourt, revised by A. R. Burn (Harmondsworth, Middlesex: Penguin Books, 1972), pp. 219–20. The quotation from Herodotus toward the end of the chapter is from the same source.

Information about the Eskimos was taken from Peter Freuchen, *Book of the Eskimos* (New York: Fawcett, 1961); and E. Adamson Hoebel, *The Law of Primitive Man* (Cambridge: Harvard University Press, 1954), Chapter 5. The estimate of how female infanticide affects the male/female ratio in the adult Eskimo population is from Hoebel's work.

The William Graham Sumner quotation is from his *Folkways* (Boston: Ginn and Company, 1906), p. 28.

The *New York Times* series on female genital mutilation included articles (mainly by Celia W. Dugger) published in 1996 on April 15, April 25, May 2, May 3, July 8, September 11, October 5, October 12, and December 28.

Chapter 3: Subjectivism in Ethics

The quotation from Matt Foreman is from the *New York Times*, June 25, 2001.

The Gallup Poll information was taken from the Gallup Organization's internet site, www.gallup.com.

The Catholic view about homosexuality is quoted from *Catechism of the Catholic Church* (Mahwah, NJ: Paulist Press, 1994), p. 566.

The C. L. Stevenson quotation is from his *Ethics and Language* (New Haven: Yale University Press, 1944), p. 114.

Chapter 4: Does Morality Depend on Religion?

The information about Governor Cuomo's ethics panel and the quotation from the governor are from the *New York Times*, October 4, 1984, p. 1.

On surveys about religious belief, see George Bishop, "What Americans Really Believe," *Free Inquiry*, vol. 19, No. 3, pp. 8–42.

The Bertrand Russell quotation is from his essay "A Free Man's Worship," *Mysticism and Logic* (Garden City, NY: Doubleday, Anchor Books, n.d.), pp. 45–46.

Antony Flew makes the remark about philosophical talent in his *God and Philosophy* (New York: Dell, 1966), p. 109.

The Leibniz quotation is from his *Discourse on Metaphysics* (1686), which may be found in G. W. von Leibniz, *Philosophical Papers and Letters*, edited and translated by Leroy E. Loemker (Chicago: University of Chicago Press, 1956), vol. 1, pp. 465–66.

The quotations from Aristotle are from *The Basic Works of Aristotle*, ed. Richard McKeon (New York: Random House, 1941), p. 249, and *The Politics*, translated by T. A. Sinclair (Harmondsworth, Middlesex: Penguin, 1962), p. 40.

The quotation from St. Thomas Aquinas is from the *Summa Theologica*, III *Quodlibet*, 27, translated by Thomas Gilby in *St. Thomas Aquinas: Philosophical Texts* (New York: Oxford University Press, 1960).

Chapter 5: Psychological Egoism

For information about Raoul Wallenberg, see John Bierman, *The Righteous Gentile* (New York: Viking Press, 1981).

The quotation about David Allsop is from Peter Singer, *How Are We to Live?* (Amherst, NY: Prometheus, 1995), p. 163. I am indebted to Singer, who also discusses the Wallenberg case as an example of heroic altruism.

Hobbes's definitions of *charity* and *pity* are from *On Human Nature*, Chapter 9, parts 9 and 17, contained in vol. IV of the Molesworth edition of *The English Works of Thomas Hobbes* (London, 1845).

The story about Abraham Lincoln is from the Springfield (Ill.) *Monitor*, quoted by Frank Sharp in his *Ethics* (New York: Appleton Century, 1928), p. 75.

For information about the Rosenham study, see David L. Rosenham, "On Being Sane in Insane Places," in *Labeling Madness,* edited by Thomas J. Scheff (Englewood Cliffs, NJ: Prentice-Hall, 1975), pp. 54–74.

Chapter 6: Ethical Egoism

The quotations from Ayn Rand are from her book *The Virtue of Selfishness* (New York: Signet, 1964), pp. 27, 32, 80, and 81.

The newspaper reports are from the *Baltimore Sun,* August 28, 2001; the *Miami Herald,* June 2, 1989, August 28, 1993, and October 6, 1994; and the *Miami News,* September 8, 1976.

The quotations from Kurt Baier are from his book *The Moral Point of View* (Ithaca, NY: Cornell University Press, 1958), pp. 189–90.

Chapter 7: The Utilitarian Approach

The opening quotation from Bentham is from his *Principles of Morals and Legislation* (New York: Hafner, 1948), p. 2. The quotation concerning animals is from the same work, p. 311.

The quotations from Mill are from his *Utilitarianism* (Indianapolis: Bobbs-Merrill, 1957), p. 16; and *On Liberty* (Indianapolis: Bobbs-Merrill, 1956), p. 13.

The case of Matthew Donnelly is taken from Robert M. Veatch, *Case Studies in Medical Ethics* (Cambridge: Harvard University Press, 1977), p. 328.

The NIH study of terminally ill patients was reported by the Associated Press in the *Birmingham News,* November 15, 2000, p. 1.

The quotations from Aquinas about animals are from *Summa Theologica,* 11, 11, Q. 64, Art. 6; and *Summa Contra Gentiles,* 111, 11, 12. See *Basic Writings of Saint Thomas Aquinas,* edited by Anton C. Pegis, 2 vols. (New York: Random House, 1945).

Singer describes the experiment with the 40 dogs in *Animal Liberation* (New York: New York Review Books, 1975), p. 38. His discussion of the treatment of farm animals is in the same book, Chapter 3.

Chapter 8: The Debate over Utilitarianism

The quotation from Mill about impartiality is from *Utilitarianism* (Indianapolis: Bobbs-Merrill, 1957), p. 22.

McCloskey's example of the utilitarian tempted to bear false witness is from his paper "A Non-Utilitarian Approach to Punishment," *Inquiry* 8 (1965), pp. 239–55.

The quotation from John Cottingham is from his article "Partialism, Favouritism and Morality," *Philosophical Quarterly* 36 (1986), p. 357.

The Brandt quotation is from Richard B. Brandt, *A Theory of the Right and the Good* (Oxford: Clarendon Press, 1979), p. 194.

The J. J. C. Smart quotation is from J. J. C. Smart and Bernard Williams, *Utilitarianism: For and Against* (Cambridge: Cambridge University Press, 1973), p. 68.

Chapter 9: Are There Absolute Moral Rules?

The quotation from Franklin Roosevelt is from his communication, *The President of the United States to the Governments of France, Germany, Italy, Poland and His Britannic Majesty,* September 1, 1939.

Miss Anscombe's 1939 pamphlet "The Justice of the Present War Examined," as well as her 1956 pamphlet "Mr. Truman's Degree," can be found in G. E. M. Anscombe, *Ethics, Religion and Politics: Collected Philosophical Papers, vol. III* (Minneapolis: University of Minnesota Press, 1981). The quotations are from pp. 34, 64, and 65.

The excerpts from Harry Truman's diary are from Robert H. Ferrell, *Off the Record: The Private Papers of Harry S. Truman* (New York: Harper & Row, 1980), pp. 55–56.

Kant's statement of the Categorical Imperative is from his *Foundations of the Metaphysics of Morals,* translated by Lewis White Beck (Indianapolis: Bobbs-Merrill, 1959), p. 39.

Anscombe's criticism of Kant is from "Modern Moral Philosophy," *Philosophy* 33 (1958), p. 3; reprinted in *Ethics, Religion and Politics: The Collected Philosophical Papers of G. E. M. Anscombe, vol. III* (Minneapolis: University of Minnesota Press, 1981).

Kant's "On a Supposed Right to Lie from Altruistic Motives" can be found in *Critique of Practical Reason and Other Writings in Moral Philosophy,* translated by Lewis White Beck (Chicago: University of Chicago Press, 1949). The quotation is from p. 348.

The P. T. Geach quotation is from his *God and the Soul* (London: Routledge and Kegan Paul, 1969), p. 128.

MacIntyre's remark is from the opening of the chapter on Kant in his *A Short History of Ethics* (New York: Macmillan, 1966).

Chapter 10: Kant and Respect for Persons

Kant's remarks on animals are from his *Lectures on Ethics,* translated by Louis Infield (New York: Harper & Row, 1963), pp. 239–40.

The second formulation of the Categorical Imperative, in terms of treating persons as ends, is in *Foundations of the Metaphysics of Morals,* translated by Lewis White Beck (Indianapolis: Bobbs-Merrill, 1959), p. 47. The remarks about "dignity" and "price" are on p. 53.

Bentham's statement "All punishment is mischief" is from *The Principles of Morals and Legislation* (New York: Hafner, 1948), p. 170.

The quotations from Kant on punishment are from *The Metaphysical Elements of Justice,* translated by John Ladd (Indianapolis: Bobbs-Merrill, 1965), pp. 99–107, except for the quotation about the "right good beating," which is from *Critique of Practical Reason,* translated by Lewis White Beck (Chicago: University of Chicago Press, 1949), p. 170.

Karl Menninger's views are quoted from his article, "Therapy, Not Punishment," *Harper's Magazine* (August 1959), pp. 63–64.

Chapter 11: The Idea of a Social Contract

Hobbes's estimate of the state of nature is from his *Leviathan,* Oakeshott edition (Oxford: Blackwell, 1960), Chapter 13. The quotation is from p. 82.

The Rousseau quotation is from *The Social Contract and Discourses,* translated by G. D. H. Cole (New York: Dutton, 1959), pp. 18–19.

The quotations from King and Waldman may be found in *Civil Disobedience: Theory and Practice,* edited by Hugo Adam Bedau (New York: Pegasus Books, 1967), pp. 76–77, 78, 106, and 107.

The passage from Fontaine's memoirs is quoted in Peter Singer, *Animal Liberation* (New York: New York Review Books, 1975), p. 220.

Chapter 12: Feminism and the Ethics of Care

Heinz's Dilemma is explained in Lawrence Kohlberg, *Essays on Moral Development, volume 1: The Philosophy of Moral Development* (New York: Harper & Row, 1981), p. 12. For the six stages of moral development, see the same work, pp. 409–12.

Amy and Jake are quoted by Carol Gilligan in her *In a Different Voice: Psychological Theory and Women's Development* (Cambridge: Harvard University Press, 1982), pp. 26, 28. The other quotations from Gilligan are from pp. 16–17, 31.

The Virginia Held quotation is from her "Feminist Transformations of Moral Theory," *Philosophy and Phenomenological Research* 50 (1990), p. 344.

" 'Care' is the new buzzword" is from Annette Baier, *Moral Prejudices* (Cambridge: Harvard University Press, 1994), p. 19. The other quotations from Baier are from pp. 4 ("connect their ethics of love") and 2 ("honorary women").

The quotations from Nel Noddings are all from her book *Caring: A Feminine Approach to Ethics and Moral Education* (Berkeley: University of California Press, 1984), pp. 149–55.

Chapter 13: The Ethics of Virtue

The quotations from Aristotle are from Book II of the *Nicomachean Ethics*, translated by Martin Ostwald (Indianapolis: Bobbs-Merrill, 1962), except for the quotation about friendship, which is from Book VIII, and the quotation about visiting foreign lands, which is Martha C. Nussbaum's translation, given in her article "Non-Relative Virtues: An Aristotelian Approach," in *Midwest Studies in Philosophy, vol. XII. Ethical Theory: Character and Virtue*, edited by Peter A. French, Theodore E. Uehling, Jr., and Howard K. Wettstein (Notre Dame: University of Notre Dame Press, 1988), pp. 32–53.

Peter Geach's remarks concerning courage are from his book *The Virtues* (Cambridge: Cambridge University Press, 1977), pp. xxix, xxx. The story about St. Athanasius appears on p. 114.

Plato's *Euthyphro* is available in several translations; a useful one is Hugh Tredennick's in Plato, *The Last Days of Socrates* (Harmondsworth, Middlesex: Penguin Books, revised edition 1959).

Pincoffs's suggestion about the nature of virtue appears in his book *Quandaries and Virtues: Against Reductivism in Ethics* (Lawrence: University of Kansas Press, 1986), p. 78.

The Nietzsche quotation is from *Twilight of the Idols*, "Morality as Anti-Nature," part 6.

Michael Stocker's example is from his article "The Schizophrenia of Modern Ethical Theories," *Journal of Philosophy* 73 (1976), pp. 453–66.

The quotation from Mill is from *Utilitarianism* (Indianapolis: Bobbs-Merrill, 1957), p. 22.

Anscombe's proposal that the notion of "morally right" be jettisoned is made in her influential article "Modern Moral Philosophy," first published in *Philosophy* 33 (1958) and conveniently reprinted in *Ethics, Religion and Politics: The Collected Philosophical Papers of G. E. M. Anscombe, vol. III* (Minneapolis: University of Minnesota Press, 1981).

Chapter 14: What Would a Satisfactory Moral Theory Be Like?

Hume's statement about the universe not caring for us is from his essay "Of Suicide," which is conveniently reprinted in *Hume's Ethical Writings*, edited by Alasdair MacIntyre (New York: Collier, 1965), pp. 297–306. The quotation is from p. 301.

The quotation from Henry Sidgwick is from his book *The Methods of Ethics*, 7th ed. (London: Macmillan, 1907), p. 413.

Index